ANARCHIST DEVELOPMENT IN CULTURAL STUDIES

2013.2: Ontological Anarché

Beyond Materialism and Idealism

Duane Rousselle and Jason Adams, Editors

Anarchist Developments in Cultural Studies (ADCS) is an international peer-reviewed and open-access journal devoted to the study of new and emerging perspectives in anarchist thought. ADCS is an attempt to bring anarchist thought into contact with innumerable points of connection. We publish articles, reviews/debates, announcements, and unique contributions that: (1) adopt an anarchist perspective with regards to analyses of language, discourse, culture, and power; (2) investigate various facets of anarchist thought and practice from a non-anarchist standpoint, and; (3) investigate or incorporate elements of non-anarchist thought and practice from the standpoint of traditional anarchist thought.

Published + Distributed, 2013, by punctum books
Brooklyn, New York – United States
Email. punctumbooks@gmail.com
Web. http://punctumbooks.com

All content, including exclusive web content, is freely available at
www.Anarchist-Developments.org

General Contact: Duane Rousselle, Duane.Rousselle@egs.edu
Book Design: Eileen A. Joy
Typesetting & Copy-Editing: Andrew C. Doty
Other Technical Services: Angry Nerds (Aragorn!)
www.AngryNerds.com

ADCS is part of the Cultural Studies working group of the North American Anarchist Studies Network (www.naasn.org)

ISSN: 1923-5615

ANARCHIST DEVELOPMENTS IN CULTURAL STUDIES

2013: Issue 2: Ontological Anarché: Beyond Materialism and Idealism
ISBN#: 978-0615947686
Issue Editors: Duane Rousselle and Jason Adams

TABLE OF CONTENTS

Anarchist Developments in Cultural Studies
ISSN: 1923-5615
2013.2: Ontological Anarché: Beyond Materialism and Idealism

Editors' Introduction

Anarchism's *Other Scene*
Materializing the Ideal and Idealizing the Material

Duane Rousselle & Jason Adams

While more will be said about this below, we begin this issue in the simplest fashion: by recalling a few of the basic questions according to which the interventions here were initially assembled:

- Is it the case, as Marx famously held in *The German Ideology* and *The Poverty of Philosophy*, that anarchism has failed to account for the full complexity of the ontological?
- Has there been a lack of concern within anarchism (historically speaking) with the actual circumstances that would make social transformation possible?
- Has anarchism been a theory for which materiality was, as Marx put it, "distorted in the imagination of the egoist," producing a subject "for whom everything occurs in the imagination?"
- Should "Sancho" (Max Stirner), for example, have "descended from the realm of speculation into the realm of reality"?
- Is the opposition of materialism and idealism itself a barrier to a higher, more powerful convergence, as recent anarchist/anarchistic thinkers from Hakim Bey to Reiner Schürmann (and beyond) have argued?

Certainly, we would not reduce these questions purely down to a simplistic confrontation between "Marxist materialism" and "anarchist idealism"—and, particularly not today, when, in the wake of numerous post-anarchist and post-Marxist interventions, "anarchist materialists" and "Marxist idealists" alike are at least as common as their inversions were in the past. The case of Hakim Bey is perhaps one of the best examples of such reversals, in the anarchist camp.

The first lines of his 1994 book *Immediatism*, for instance, asserted the seemingly post-Kantian point that "all experience is mediated—by the mechanisms of sense perception, mentation, language, etc.—& certainly all art consists of some further mediation of experience."

But the central argument from this point forward in his book is the reverse: Bey essentially quantifies mediation as a matter of degree, championing the "least mediated." And yet, is it not the case that all experience is simultaneously an experience of mediacy and immediacy, of both conscious experience and unconscious experience, at once?

Today in particular, the experience of mediacy has been rendered in the form of immediacy as never before. By which we mean to say that what is experienced as immediacy is in fact mediated by a technoculture of digitally-networked social media and digitally-augmented broadcast media, as well as by perception and recollection, language and discourse, economics and politics. The "everyday" experience of the world as "unmediated" today—the sense that in the age of social media, we've finally overcome the tyranny of the editor—is an effect of a particular mode of perception, as it appears for a particular person, or a particular people, at a particular place, a particular time.

Today, ironically enough, the reigning hegemonic formation is not that of the mediate, but much to the contrary, precisely that of Bey's "immediatism." It is interesting then, that the term serves as a critique of mediation, an advocacy of returning, as much as possible, to direct, embodied, sensory experience—the very mode within which we are most thoroughly controlled, precisely because we fail to comprehend the mediation of the immediate that we imagine as truly immediate.

For abolitionists in the 19th century, the term immediatism referenced a rather different kind of critique: a temporal one. Immediatism referred at that time to a rejection of gradualism and an advocacy of abolishing the "peculiar institution" of slavery—right here, right now ("immediately"). The more radical abolitionists at least, recognized that all experience, including the experience of labor, is mediated, at a minimum, by the mode of production within which we necessarily live.

Immediatism in Bey's sense, as the reigning mode of perception, ignores precisely this: that registerable differences internal to mediacy/immediacy are actually differences of kind, not differences of degree. Tasting food and smelling flowers are in no way "less" mediated than reading newspapers or surfing the web; live media such as theater or musical performance are not necessarily any "more" immediate than more delayed mediums, like DVDs or CDs; and in terms of the demand for imagination championed by Bey two decades ago, film and television (as numerous "broadcast literature" examples attest to today), can require at least as much as print and radio, live theater, or live music.

Capitalism in its digital form—or authority more broadly, as it exists for us all today—relies not upon the logic of mediatization but that of *immediatization*: the invisibilization of the conditions of possibility for immediacy, which produces profound consequences for everyone. Immediatization rerenders everything from art to philosophy, science to religion, and politics to love, so that they all reappear as the capitalized instantaneity, interactivity, and ubiquity that characterize experience in our network-centric media environment.

The attendant commodification, however, is no more reducible to exchange-value in our time than it was in previous modes of perception. Because it also requires the allure of use-value, exchange-value never wholly sums up the process of commodification. The twin tendencies of digital technoculture and digital capitalism alike are such that production and consumption fall into indistinction: from Google to Facebook and YouTube to Twitter, consuming today means producing just as producing today means consuming.

Today, the Spectacle is no longer opposed to the Spectator: the Spectator now participates in producing not *the* Spectacle, but one's own, personal spectacle, networked with literally millions of other Spectator-Producers who are all engaged in the same activity—instantly, interactively, and ubiquitously. The greatest danger to aesthetics today (contra Bey) is not alienation from sensation by way of the mass media, but the sensation of disalienation by way of social media.

The very person who formally introduced the term "postanarchism," then, was himself caught up within ontologies which we still wrestle with today—and which form the core of this issue of *Anarchist Developments in Cultural Studies* (*ADCS*). In 2010,

Lewis Call announced, in the inaugural issue of *ADCS*, that post-anarchism was finally here to stay.

Post-anarchism, it appeared, was finally *on the scene*. The 2011 publication of *Post-Anarchism: A Reader* and *The Politics of Post-Anarchism* seemed to validate Call's claim. Post-anarchism was definitely *on the scene*, but *which* scene was it on? The question had long been asked: was post-anarchism a form of anarchism or was it something else entirely (such as post-structuralism)? Wasn't this a variation of the topological question: is post-anarchism inside (the tradition) or is it outside?

Here then, we assert that post-anarchism was (and is) *the other scene* of anarchism. Friends of the Freudian field will immediately note the distinction here: *the other scene,* for Freud, was one that was paradoxically *outside* the human animal but only to the extent that it was intimately *within* the human animal. For Freud, as for Lacan, *the other scene* was the hidden realm that has the privileged designation, namely, the unconscious. Thus, post-anarchism is the examination of anarchism's unconscious suppositions, those which remain imperceptible to "immediate," "everyday" experience.

We would be remiss if we did not add that post-anarchism is also the movement toward an articulation of anarchism's unconscious truth. There is thus, without a doubt, a negative as well as positive aspect to post-anarchist thinking. In any case, post-anarchism opened up a space within anarchist studies—and this continues to be the privileged function of post-anarchism—through which anarchism's own latent epistemological and ontological assumptions are questioned.

This, then, is our first point: *post-anarchism is a space that opens up anarchism to its own unconscious productions.*

Our second point deals with the consequences of the opening up of the privileged space of post-anarchism: post-anarchism was an answer to a demand that things must be different. Post-anarchism emerged as a response to a demand that anarchist studies and anarchism itself must be different. It is because anarchist studies must be different that it must also be more (and not less) true. Post-anarchism is a consequence of a demand made in the direction of a more true understanding of our political and philosophical tradition. If, therefore, the first point was that post-anarchism opened up a space for the analysis of anarchism's *other scene*, then the second was that post-anarchism was an answer to a demand that things be different and therefore more true.

All of this leads to our third, and much more relevant, point:

ADCS was inaugurated through a risk made by answering this demand for something different and therefore more true. The sum of these three points lead to the statement: *ADCS* was born so that anarchists (and those attracted to anarchist ideas) might not be overtaken by the representation of events as "immediate."

This was the sole aim for this journal: we must make ourselves worthy, as Deleuze and Guattari famously put it, of the full complexity and dynamism of the event. It was not without purpose, then, that Call wrote the following in his introduction to the first issue of *ADCS* on post-anarchism:

> Indeed, I feel that we *must* do this, or risk being overtaken by events. Post-anarchism waits for no one. When I speak of post-anarchism today, I also imply that there was post-anarchism *yesterday*. (Call, 2010: 9)

ADCS was born so that anarchists might not be overtaken by the reductive representation of events by which we are surrounded: so that they might not be overtaken by the immediatization of the mediate. Our journal is the answer that we give to the endless revolutionary imperative that dawns upon us.

Since its inception, our journal has always been a little bit different.

We answered the demand of post-anarchism early and today we find post-anarchist thinking all around the world. We shall continue to answer the demand because it is our sole aim to become worthy of the event (of the virtual event), to become worthy of that which is always a noumenon, always beyond reductive representation. So, the question that we are asking today is one that we feel we *must* ask. It is a question that demands to be asked if anarchism is not to be overtaken by the last decade: rather than reifying the event, we must counter-effectuate the event, or restore to it the dynamism and complexity that consciousness—collective and individual alike—evacuates.

Lewis Call, then, was right: *post-anarchism waits for no one.* The question that we are asking today, then, is different from the question that we were asking *yesterday*. Today's question is: how do anarchists respond to the demand made upon them for a truly radical ontology, and not just one that asks us to return to the individual, sensory body?

Is it possible for anarchism to think *with* the new ontologies and new materialisms, and is it possible to build a deeper anarchist philosophy which does not reduce the world to what it is for human animals within that world? Is it possible to think the question of a non-essentialist ontology?

Radical theory has always been beset by the question of ontology, albeit to varying degrees and under differing conditions. In recent years, in particular, political metaphysics has returned with force: the rise of Deleuze-influenced "new materialism," along with post-/non-Deleuzian speculative realism and object-oriented ontology, all bear testament to this. In this same period, anarchism has returned as a major influence on social movements and critical scholarship alike. What, then, are some of the potential resonances between these currents, particularly given that anarchism has so often been understood/ misunderstood as a fundamentally idealist philosophy?

This special issue of *ADCS* considers these questions in dialogue with new materialism, speculative realism, and object-oriented ontology, in order to seek new points of departure. It is in this sense that our journal strives to become worthy of recent discussions in the wider political, cultural, and philosophical milieu.

The special issue is split into two major sections: "Ontological Anarché" and "Anarchist Ontology." If, on the one hand, there are ontologies that are radically *anarchistic*, then, on the other hand, there are anarchists that are striving to create new *ontologies*. In some sense, these two approaches are digging from opposite sides of the same mountain. It shall be our task to show that they jointly create a single passageway through the mountain. On one side of the mountain: the *ontological* anarchists seem to be more skeptical about the political implications of their work. On the other side of the mountain: the *anarchist* ontologists seem to be more skeptical about the ontological implications of their work.

We begin with an article from Levi Bryant. Many anarchists have suspected that the new ontologies harbor profoundly *anarchistic* orientations. However, very few of the pioneers of these new ontologies have described their work using the conceptual framework of anarchism. But Levi Bryant *has* used the conceptual framework of anarchism at times: Bryant has made use of post-anarchist philosophy (especially the work of Todd May). This is what makes Bryant such an important point of departure for thinking about the convergence of anarchism and new materialism. In Bryant's article for this issue of *ADCS*, he gives his readers a very concise introduction to his updated ontology. Readers familiar with his last (open-access) book, titled *The Democracy of Objects* (however, he often notes that the book should have been titled *The Anarchy of Objects*), will notice that some of his conceptual framework has changed. Bryant's new ontology is named: *Machine-Oriented Ontology* (MOO). Here we have a brilliant example of how we can think *with* rather than *against* Einstein's general theory of relativity. Einstein offers us a profoundly *anarchistic* way in which to think about the relations that objects have within the world, and Bryant's brilliant writing offers us a passageway toward understanding Einstein's often misinterpreted and misapplied physical theories.

John W. M. Krummel, a former student of Reiner Schürmann, argues, through the work of Schürmann and Cornelius Castoriadis, that every metaphysic involves an imaginary first principle which grounds it. There is thus a profound similarity between the two thinkers: both Schürmann and Castoriadis acknowledge that meaning and order are subjected to radical finitude. This implies that order is fleeting and temporary. A challenge is therefore posed to us: how is it possible to move from such an imaginary ontology toward a materialist inspired practical political philosophy? This, it would seem, is the crucial question that most contributors to our volume seem interested in exploring.

As I've claimed above, the new ontologies, inspired by the speculative turn, have raised profoundly new questions about the meaning of political practice and political philosophy. The crucial question is: is it possible to move from ontological thinking toward political philosophy (and *vice versa*)? Hilan Bensusan looks backwards to the Heraclitean tradition and the notion of *polemos* in order to develop a "fire ontology." Bensusan makes a very powerful claim that "fire ontology" spreads and doesn't ground. Fire, unlike ground, operates through contagion rather than foundation.

This is how ontology and politics "meet on fire." There is thus a re-negotiation that takes place between ontology and politics. Ben Woodard, a veteran of the speculative turn, claims in his article that we need to rethink the assumption that ontology by necessity implies a form of politics. Woodard offers an analysis of Schelling's *Naturphilosophie* as a form of ontological philosophy that is suited to thinking through ecological politics today. And so, in some sense, there is a secret solidarity between all of the contributors to this volume. Each, in his or her own way, seeks to undermine any *arché,* any foundational ontology, which claims that some beings are more important than others.

Jason Harman claims that the very notion of ontological *anarché* is bound up with some notion of an *arché.* The alternative, Harman claims, is to think through the co-originality of the two as a form of being-*with*. The work of Jean-Luc Nancy therefore provides us with a nice point of departure for this possibility. Harmon asks: is it possible, after the speculative turn, to think a new form of radical community? The second group of contributors are digging from the other side of the mountain. They seem more interested in the question of what the new ontologies are *for anarchism*. In this respect, we are honored to have an article from Salvo Vaccaro, and translated by Jesse Cohn. Vaccaro raises the question: is anarchism a philosophy? Moreover, is anarchism, as a philosophy, foundationalist? Once again we seem to be dealing with an ontology which is multiple in its becomings rather than singular, statist, or essentialist. Jared McGeough explores a similar theme in his article. McGeough discusses the tension that occurred between Mikhail Bakunin's and Schelling's philosophies. For example, Bakunin dismissed Schelling's ontology as idealist, and then found him to be a conservative stooge for the Prussian government. McGeough asks us to consider an alternative reading of the significance of Schelling's philosophy for anarchists: Schelling's philosophy is "unconditioned," it is a "system of freedom," and it "destroys origins."

In a curious article from Christian Greer post-anarchists are asked to question their indebtedness to Hakim Bey's post-anarchism anarchy. Post-anarchists, Greer argues, must return to their place of origin in Hakim Bey's ontological anarchism. His claim is that no post-anarchist commentator has sufficiently analyzed the occult aspect of Hakim Bey's work. Greer highlights the various esoteric overtones of Hakim Bey's ontological and post-anarchisms and encourages post-anarchists to begin to think through the relationship between esoteric philosophy (such as Chaos Magick) and anarchist political philosophy.

Tom Marling, in "Anarchism and the Question of Practice: Ontology in the Chinese Anarchist Movement, 1919–1927," provides us with a very rich discussion of the place of ontology in the philosophies of the Chinese anarchist movement during the early part of the twentieth century. The claim is that post-anarchist and post-left anarchist ideas can be unearthed from the historical record. There was a shift in anarchist theory that took place within Chinese culture during these years toward a more subjective and localized theory which was epitomized in the debate between two anarchist factions: the old guard of leftist classicalists and the younger group of quasi-iconoclasts. The iconoclasts focused on pragmatism, locatedness, and de-centered analyses of power and revolution. What can we learn from this rich historical account?

Finally, Gregory Kalyniuk develops a Deleuzian inspired presentation of micropolitics in Leopold von Sacher-Masoch's novels. His belief is that these themes allow us to rethink anarchist political philosophy in a way which seems very faithful to Daniel Colson's post-anarchist neo-monadology. It is possible, Kalyniuk claims, to subvert the law through a humourous proliferation of successive contracts.

This issue of *ADCS* also includes a review of Mohammed A. Bamyeh's popular book *Anarchy as Order: The History and Future of Civic Humanity* by Shannon Brincat, as well as a sharp response to Brincat from Bamyeh himself.

Anthony T. Fiscella reviews Alexandre Christoyannopoulos's *Christian Anarchism: A Political Commentary on the Gospel.*

We've also included an interview that was conducted with Levi Bryant by the post-anarchist Christos Stergiou.

REFERENCES

Call, Lewis. 2010. "Editorial — Post-anarchism Today." *Anarchist Developments in Cultural Studies* 2010.1: http://www.anarchist-developments.org/index.php/adcs/article/view/20/1.

Anarchist Developments in Cultural Studies
ISSN: 1923-5615
2013.2: Ontological Anarché: Beyond Materialism and Idealism

The Gravity of Things
An Introduction to Onto-Cartography

Levi R. Bryant

ABSTRACT

Bryant's machine-oriented ontology has been increasingly seductive for
anarchist philosophers because of its ability to think through the autonomous dimension of objects and the way in which things influence social
and political relations. In this article, Bryant explores the way in which
semiotic and physical objects contribute to the form social relations take,
playing a key role in the movement and becoming of humans and collectives. Through analogy to Einstein's theory of relativity, Bryant proposes
the concept of "gravity"—roughly equivalent to the concept of power in
sociology—to denote how semiotic and material entities influence the
becoming and movement of subjects and collectives in time and space.
As a consequence, political questions of emancipation and resistance are
argued to be intimately related to questions of social time and space, and
the question of the political becomes that of how we might achieve
speeds required for attaining escape velocity with respect to oppressive
gravitational fields or social assemblages

KEYWORDS
Einstein, cartography, ontology, machines

In the year of 1916, Einstein proposed his general theory of relativity. The general theory of relativity was put forward to explain
the phenomenon of gravity. In *Principia Mathematica*, Newton
had discovered much about how gravity *functions*, yet the *mechanism* of gravity remained entirely mysterious. Indeed, within the
Newtonian framework we weren't to ask questions about *how*
gravity functions at all. It was enough that Newtonian theory

could make accurate predictions about the movement of planets, comets, moons, etc. It was enough that it allowed us to get our cannon balls where we wanted them. How gravity was able to affect objects in this way was set aside as a question in the euphoria of the new predictability occasioned by these simple equations, these few letters and symbols, which now allowed us to predict the movement of objects.

The problem was simple. Naturalistic and materialist thought has always argued that in order for a causal interaction to occur between two entities, there must be a *direct* interaction. One entity must touch the other to affect in it any way. In a masterpiece that was nearly destroyed by the Roman elite and Christian church,[1] the great Roman poet-philosopher Lucretius gives voice to this principle: "Our starting-point shall be this principle: *Nothing at all is ever born from nothing.*"[2] Lucretius's thesis was that in order for one entity to affect another there has to be a real material interaction between the two beings. With this axiom he challenged all superstition and broached the possibility of a rigorous science of causes. If Lucretius's first axiom was so anathema to all superstition, then this is because it undermined the idea of magic or action at a distance. For example, within a Lucretian framework a spell or curse cast against another person in the absence of that person could have no effect because there is no material interaction between the enunciation of the hex and the person. You cannot step on a crack and break your mother's back.

It is on the basis of a thesis such as Lucretius's first axiom that Newton's theory of gravity was so disturbing. For, like absurd beliefs such as the idea that you can step on a crack and break your mother's back, Newton's gravity appeared *occult*. How is Newton's thesis that the moon and sun are responsible for the tides any different than the idea that somehow a prayer at a distance can heal a person? How is it possible for one entity to affect another without the two touching in some way or another? Newtonians appealed to the concept of force to account for gravity, but it was difficult to see how force could be anything but an occult or magical agency insofar as no one could see how one thing

---

[1] For a discussion of the ill-fated history of Lucretius's *De Rerum Natura* and its amazing rediscovery, see Stephen Greenblatt, *The Swerve: How the World Became Modern* (New York: W.W. Norton, 2011).
[2] Lucretius, *The Way Things Are: The De Rerum Natura of Titus Lucretius Carus*, trans. Rolfe Humphries (Bloomington: Indiana University Press, 1969), 24.

could exercise force on another from a distance. How can one entity act on another without touching that entity?

It was in the context of questions such as these that Einstein's general theory of relativity constituted such a revolutionary leap forward. While Einstein, like Newton, did not yet provide a mechanism for gravity—we are only now beginning to unlock the mechanism of gravity through the discovery of the Higgs boson— he did go a long way towards demystifying the phenomenon of gravity by freeing it from the concept of force. Indeed, what Einstein showed is that gravity is not a force at all, but is rather a curvature of space-time produced by the mass of objects. Within the Einsteinian framework, gravity is not a force that *attracts* and *repels* other objects, but rather is an *effect* of how the mass of objects curves space-time. The moon orbits around the earth not because it is simultaneously attracted and repelled from the earth, but rather because the mass of the earth curves space-time, creating a *path* that the moon follows in its movement along a straight line; a line that is straight along the surface of a curve. To visualize this, imagine a bed sheet upon which a cantaloupe has been placed. The cantaloupe curves the surface of the sheet in such a way that if an orange is placed in the field of that curvature it will follow that path as it rolls along the sheet. Gravity is not a force, but is rather a field or a topology that other objects follow in their movement.

Within the framework of Machine-Oriented Ontology (MOO), Einstein's theory of gravity is of the greatest importance for two reasons. First, Einstein shows that space-time is not an indifferent milieu that is a given container in which entities are housed. In other words, space-time is not something in which entities are contained. Rather, space-time *arises* from the mass of objects or machines. Space-time doesn't pre-exist things, but rather arises from things. Second, Einstein shows that space-time is not homogeneous. The flow of time and the metric of space is not the same in all places. Rather, space-time has all sorts of lumps, contractions, dilations, and curvatures that differ from region to region. There are even space-times that are so powerfully curved that nothing can escape from them (for example, black holes), thus effectively rendering them self-contained space-times detached from other space-times. Einstein's thesis is that there isn't space-time, but rather *space-times*. Gravity is not a force of attraction and repulsion, but consists rather of space-time paths. As we will see, paths are both paths of becoming and paths of movement. Paths are those vectors that objects must follow in their move-

ment from one place to another and in their development or becoming.

I begin with Einstein's general theory of relativity and theory
of gravity because it provides us with a helpful analogy for understanding the basic theoretical claims of onto-cartography. Onto-cartography is both a theory of the space-time of objects as
they interact and a method for mapping these interactions. To be
sure, "gravity," as I am using the term here is a metaphor—or,
more optimistically, a philosophical concept in Deleuze's sense of
the word[3]—chosen to draw attention to how things and signs
structure spatio-temporal relations or paths along which entities
move and become. In terms more familiar within currently existing theory, we could refer to "gravity" as "force" or "power." If,
however, I have chosen to speak of gravity rather than power,
then this is because the concept of power within the world of
philosophy and theory has come to be too anthropocentric, immediately drawing attention to sovereigns exercising power, class
power, symbolic power, and things such as micro-power and biopower. While I have no wish to abandon forms of analysis such
as those found in Marx, Foucault, and Bourdieu, the manner in
which these anthropological connotations have become sedi-
mented within the institutions that house the humanities, both at
the level of training and scholarship—itself a form of gravity—
have rendered it difficult to imagine nonhuman things exercising
power as anything more than blank screens upon which humans
project their intentions and meanings. As Stacy Alaimo has written, "[m]atter, the vast stuff of the world and of ourselves, has
been subdivided into manageable 'bits' or flattened into a 'blank
slate' for human inscription."[4] By far, the dominant tendency of
contemporary critical theory or social and political theory is to
see nonhuman entities as but blank slates upon which humans
project meanings. Things are reduced to mere carriers or vehicles
of human power and meaning, without any serious attention devoted to the differences that nonhumans contribute to social assemblages. While I have no desire to abandon more traditional
semiotically driven forms of critical analysis insofar as I believe
they have made tremendous contributions to our understanding
of why our social worlds are organized as they are, it is my hope

---

[3] See Gilles Deleuze and Felix Guattari, *What is Philosophy?*, trans. Hugh
Tomlinson and Graham Burchell (New York: Columbia University Press,
1994).
[4] Stacy Alaimo, *Bodily Natures: Science, Environment, and the Material
Self* (Bloomington: Indiana University Press, 2010), 1.

that the term "gravity" will be foreign enough to break old, familiar habits of thought, to overcome a certain blindness at the heart of much contemporary theory, providing us with a far richer understanding of why social relations take the form they take, thereby expanding the possibilities of our political interventions.

The "onto" of "onto-cartography" refers to the word "ontic," from the Greek ὄντος, denoting materially existing entities, substances, or objects. "Cartography," of course, is the practice of constructing or drawing maps. An onto-cartography would thus be a map or diagram of things—and more precisely things and signs—that exist within a field, situation, or world. By "situation" or "world" I mean an ordered set of entities and signs that interact with one another. A world or situation is not something other than the externally related entities and signs within it, but is identical to these entities and signs. Onto-cartography is thus not a map of space or geography—though we can refer to a "space of things and signs" in a given situation or field and it does help to underline the profound relevance of geography to this project insofar as onto-cartographies are always geographically situated —but is rather a map of things or what I call machines. In particular, an onto-cartography is a map of the spatio-temporal gravitational fields produced by things and signs and how these fields constrain and afford possibilities of movement and becoming.

But towards what end? When we do an onto-cartography are we merely making a *list* of things and signs that exist? A list is an inventory of entities that exist within a situation, but is not yet a map or cartography. Rather, in order for something to count as a cartography, it must show how things are distributed and related to one another rather than merely enumerating or listing them. In particular, a central thesis of onto-cartography is that space-time arises from things and signs. Onto-cartography is thus the practice of mapping the spatio-temporal paths, the gravitational fields, that arise from interactions among things. Central to this project is the recognition that things and signs produce gravity that influences the movement and becoming of other entities. This gravity is not, of course, the gravity of the physicists— though it would include that sort of gravity as well—but is a far broader type of gravity that influences the movements and becomings of all entities. With Einstein, onto-cartography argues that the gravities of things and signs produce spatio-temporal paths along which entities are both afforded certain possibilities of movement and becoming and where their possibilities of movement and becoming are constrained. Further, with Einstein, onto-cartography rejects the notion that there is one space-time that contains all entities, instead arguing that there are a variety of space-times arising from the gravity exercised by entities in a milieu or situation.

While the term "onto-cartography" is perhaps new, bits and pieces of onto-cartographical theory and investigation have been around for quite some time. When Latour writes "Where are the Missing Masses" and argues that we must refer to nonhumans such as hinges on doors and speed bumps to account for many of the regularities we find in society, he is proposing what we would call an onto-cartographical analysis of the world.[5] There Latour shows us how the nonhumans of the world in the form of various technologies encourage us to behave in certain ways or follow certain paths that we would not ordinarily follow in their absence. He shows, in short, how these nonhumans exercise a certain gravity over us, leading us to follow certain paths of movement and becoming.

In the first volume of *Civilization & Capitalism*, the historian Braudel proposes to draw up "an inventory of the possible"[6] defined by both the inherited habits of a particular group of people at a particular point in time and the material conditions of that time. As Braudel writes,

> Can it not be said that there is a limit, a ceiling which restricts all human life, containing it within a frontier of varying outline, one which is hard to reach and harder still to cross? This is the border which in every age, even our own, separates the possible from the impossible, what can be done with a little effort from what cannot be done at all. In the past, the borderline was imposed by inadequate food supplies, a population that was too big or too small for its resources, low productivity of labour, and the as yet slow progress of controlling nature.[7]

The inventory of the possible that Braudel here refers to is not

---

[5] Bruno Latour, "Where are the Missing Masses? The Sociology of a Few Mundane Artifacts," in *Shaping Technology/Building Society: Studies in Sociotechnical Change*, ed. Wiebe E. Bijker and John Law (Cambridge: MIT Press, 1992).

[6] Fernand Braudel, *The Structure of Everyday Life: Civilization & Capitalism, 15th–18th Century, Volume I*, trans. Sian Reynolds (New York: Harper & Row, 1981), 28.

[7] Braudel, *The Structure of Everyday Life*, 27.

that of logical or formal possibility where we wonder after the manner of Quine, for example, how many possible people might be standing in an empty doorway or whether pigs can fly; but is that of *material* possibility. Material possibility consists of what is *really* possible within a particular milieu or situation, given the material structuration of that milieu in terms of resources available, existing technologies, properties of things that populate the milieu, etc. What, Braudel wishes to know, is materially possible within a particular historical milieu or situation?

To understand these structures of material possibility, take the example of the city of Cologne as it existed in the 15th century. Braudel notes that with a population of 20,000 people, Cologne was one of the largest cities in all of Europe. But why was this city, at this time, unable to expand beyond this size? As Braudel notes, in order to sustain this population,

> [i]t needed every available flock of sheep from the Balkans to support it, rice, beans and corn from Egypt, corn and wood from the Black Sea; and oxen, camels and horses from Asia Minor. It also required every available man from the Empire to renew its population in addition to the slaves brought back from Russia after Tartar raids or from the Mediterranean coasts by Turkish fleets.[8]

A city is not merely an entity, a thing that sits there, but is rather a machine or organism that faces the problem of how to produce and maintain the elements that belong to it (citizens, occupations, social order, buildings, goods, etc.) and to produce the things that also grow out of it through the processes or activities that take place within it. To be precise, a city is a "dissipative structure" that is only able to maintain its organization or structure through flows of energy passing through it.[9] In order for the Cologne of the 15th century to maintain its existence and stave off entropy or dissolution, it required flows of energy in the form of wood for building and fuel, food of all sorts to sustain its population (every human body, occupation, and social grouping re-

---

[8] Braudel, *The Structure of Everyday Life*, 52.
[9] For a discussion of dissipative, compare with Ilya Priogogine and Isabelle Stengers, *Order Out of Chaos: Man's New Dialogue With Nature* (New York: Bantam Books, 1984), sec. 5.3. For an excellent discussion of far-from-equilibrium systems, cf. Jeffrey A. Bell, *Philosophy at the Edge of Chaos: Gilles Deleuze and the Philosophy of Difference* (Toronto: University of Toronto Press, 2006), chap. 6.

quires a certain number of calories to be possible), labor to carry out the various functions of the city, and so on. These things, in their turn, were dependent on currently existing agricultural technologies, the presence or absence of roads between regions of the countryside and other cities that would allow food and other goods to be transported, existing maritime technologies and how much ships could carry, existing storage techniques allowing food to be preserved, medical and sewage technologies preventing disease and epidemics, possibilities of communication between regions remote from one another, population densities in the surrounding region providing sources of labor, and a host of other things. We can refer to all of these required elements as "infrastructure." While not the sole cause of the form that the city of Cologne took during the 15th century, this historically specific infrastructure did afford and constrain the possibilities of the city in all sorts of ways.

The infrastructure in which the Cologne of the 15th century was embedded formed a massive gravitational field defining spatio-temporal paths along which becoming and movement was structured. Let us take a few examples to illustrate this point. Currently existing storage and preservation techniques placed limits on how much food could be stored to provide for the population of the city, what sorts of foods could be stored, as well as what it was possible to ship to the city over land or water to the city. At the level of the temporal, this had a tremendous impact on what size the city could reach as well as the health and development of the people of the city. On the one hand, the city could only reach a certain population density or size because it only had so much food to go around. The countryside could only produce so much food to feed its citizens and itself required a requisitely large labor force to produce that food. The properties of food along with then-existing storage and food preservation technologies, as well as existing agricultural technologies in the form of cultivation and pesticides and existing transportation technologies, insured that food sources could only be transported from particular distances, and even then only foods of particular sorts, lest the food spoil and become useless. Today, for example, we scarcely recognize what a luxury oranges in the winter are. Temporally, of course, this entailed that the development of human bodies was seasonally dependent on what was available, and that it was highly susceptible to the ravages of drought and pestilence because food could not be shipped in from elsewhere under these circumstances. This could not help but have an impact on the health of bodies, how they develop, the longevity of lives, etc.; that is, these things affect all those things that pertain to the becoming of bodies or their qualitative properties. We are often struck when we look at the uniforms of French and American revolutionary soldiers in museums, noting just how diminutive these people were. Have humans evolved to become tall giants? Not at all. What has changed is not the genes of humans but the availability of nutrients in abundance throughout the year, such as greens, milk, proteins, and so on. These changes have been made possible as a result of transformations in agricultural technologies, transportation technologies, storage and preservation technologies, and even communication technologies. If communications technologies prove so pivotal, then this is because different regions of the world must communicate to signal to each other what foodstuffs are required by one region or the other. The shift from communications carried on horseback by a courier over regions of the world lacking roads to communications by satellite technologies is not a difference in degree but a difference in kind, fundamentally transforming social relations and what is possible for a group of people. It is not simply—as is oft noted—that now ideas can circulate much more quickly and pervasively, but also that simple things like signaling the need for particular foods across vast distances between different climatological zones is now possible. Nor do these variations in food availability simply affect the physical body. As anyone knows who goes a day or two without food or only eating food of a particular sort, what we eat and whether we eat has a profound impact on our cognition, our ability to think at all, as well as our emotions. Famine does not simply destroy bodily health, but generates emotional states and social relations of a particular sort that can be catastrophic to any social order.

All of these things are differences contributed not by signs, not by signifying differences, but by the properties of things themselves: the properties of cultivation techniques and the tools used, the properties of water, the properties of grains and animals, the properties of communication techniques, the properties of waste and microbes, the properties of boats and horses, etc. Once we begin to discern this power of things, the way in which they bend or curve time and space, we can discern contributions to onto-cartographical theory all over the place. We see it in Marshall McLuhan's thesis that media are an extension of humans.[10]

---

[10] Marshall and Eric McLuhan, *Laws of Media: The New Science* (Toronto: University of Toronto Press, 1992).

Indeed, we could say that onto-cartography is a media theory in the tradition of McLuhan. We see it in Andy Clark's extended mind hypothesis, where it is argued that mind is not something inside the head, but is instead a relation between body, brain, and, above all, the tools we use when navigating the world.[11] We see elements of a theory of onto-cartography in Friedrich Kittler's analysis of how various communications technologies affect and transform social relations.[12]

We see other elements in Walter Ong's analysis of how writing transformed the nature of cognition, rendering things such as mathematics and "universal" law possible.[13] We see it in DeLanda's assemblage theory of society and materialist accounts of world history.[14] We see it in Marx's analysis of the impact of the factory and rigid machines on working life and the bodies and minds of workers. We see it in Sartre's analysis of how the "practico-inert" takes on a life of its own structuring the lives of people.[15] We see it in Stacy Alaimo's account of trans-corporeality or how bodies are enmeshed in one another.[16] We see it in Lacan's analysis of Poe's "The Purloined Letter," where a letter determines the position of an agent within a social network irregardless of that agent's intentions, meanings, beliefs, or thoughts. Here too there is gravity, a gravity exercised by signs and texts. Similarly, we see it in David Graeber's analysis of debt, another semiotic entity, and how it structures lives and social relations.[17] We also see elements of such a theory in Judith Butler's *Gender Trouble*, where it is argued that gender is not an intrinsic feature of human bodies but rather results from the performance of human bodies based on discourses.[18] What we lack is not elements

---

[11] Andy Clark, *Supersizing the Mind: Embodiment, Action, and Cognitive Extension* (Oxford: Oxford University Press, 2010).

[12] Friedrich A. Kittler, *Gramophone, Film, Typewriter*, trans. Geoffrey Winthrop-Young and Michael Wutz (Stanford: Stanford University Press, 1999).

[13] Walter J. Ong, *Orality & Literacy* (New York: Routledge, 2002).

[14] Manuel DeLanda, *A Thousand Years of Nonlinear History* (New York: The MIT Press, 2000).

[15] Jean-Paul Sartre, *Critique of Dialectical Reason: Volume 1*, trans. Alan Sheridan-Smith, (New York: Verso, 2004).

[16] Stacy Alaimo, *Bodily Natures: Science, Environment, and the Material Self* (Bloomington: Indiana University Press, 2010).

[17] David Graeber, *Debt: The First 5,000 Years* (Brooklyn: Melville House, 2011).

[18] Judith Butler, *Gender Trouble: Feminism and the Subversion of Identity* (New York: Routledge, 2006).

of a theory, but a unified theory that's able to pull all of this to-gether. Instead we get competing camps that situate these discov-eries as oppositions, as conflicts of interpretation, rather than as contributions to a generalized theory.

There is both a theory and an empirical practice of onto-cartography. The practice of onto-cartography is simply the anal-ysis or mapping of spatio-temporal gravitational paths produced by various things and signs in a given situation or world. If this practice must be empirical, then this is because nothing allows us to decide in advance what entities and semiotic beings inhabit a situation, how they interact, what paths they produce, how they behave in this particular context or environment, and so on. The project of onto-cartography is massive and likely not to be the work of any one person because it is profoundly multi-disci-plinary, requiring knowledge of the natures of the things that inhabit the situation, their specific properties, literature, mythol-ogy, semiotics, political theory, history, various sciences, technol-ogies, etc. The difficulty of this practice is further exacerbated by the fact that many things crucial to understanding the gravita-tional field of a situation never make it into texts or the archive; at least, the archive that people in the humanities tend to be fa-miliar with. How people prepare and cultivate food, sanitation structures, the details of power grids, the technologies available, disease epidemiologies, the distribution of texts throughout the world, the layout of roads, etc., are not things that we normally attend to in our analyses of why societies take the form that they take, nor are they things that tend to appear in the texts or ar-chive we tend to consult to capture traces of the social world. As a consequence, they tend to become invisible even though they exercise crucial gravitational forces on people and play a central role in explaining why certain forms of oppressive social organi-zation persist. As Latour notes throughout his work, this system-atically leads to the impression that societies are held together merely by beliefs, laws, norms, signifying systems, discourses. It is not that these things are not necessary components of certain types of societies—and here I follow Whitehead in treating a soci-ety as any assemblage of entities, regardless of whether humans or living beings are involved[19]—but that societies also take the form they take because of vast networks of nonhuman entities and the gravity they exercise over other entities within that mi-lieu. This dimension of social relations often goes unrecognized

---

[19] See Alfred North Whitehead, *Process and Reality* (New York: The Free Press, 1978), 83–109.

because, on the one hand, it tends to function well (thereby becoming invisible), while on the other hand, it goes unremarked in much of the archive we tend to consult in our critical social and political investigations. It is not until there is a massive power outage such as the one discussed by Bennett in *Vibrant Matter*, or something like Hurricane Katrina comes along shutting down entire cities that we become aware of just how central a role nonhumans have in maintaining certain types of social relations.[20]

A theory of onto-cartography, by contrast, lays out the basic concepts of onto-cartography and how they interrelate. Without being exhaustive, these basic concepts are concepts such as object, gravity, path, becoming, movement, world, pluralistic spatiotemporality, relation, sign, etc. Additionally, onto-cartography outlines the constraints on interactions between entities. In particular, with Lucretius, onto-cartography endorses the thesis that "nothing can come from nothing." There is no action at a distance. For one entity to affect another, there must be a direct interaction between them. There must be some medium through which they come to be related to one another. There must be some material mediator or daimon that passes between the one entity and the other. If current physics is right—and so far it seems to be holding up—then it follows that no two entities can interact at rates that exceed the speed of light. This entails that wherever interactions at a distance take place, time will be a factor insofar as it takes time for the daimon, signal, or simulacrum to travel from one entity to another. Since the mediums through which most simulacra travel is far slower than the speed of light, these temporal rates will exercise profound gravity on a variety of different entities. Think, for example, of all the ways in which communication about vital matters with a government bureaucracy can affect our lives. Time and speed play a crucial role in the forms that social relations take.

This emphasis on the materiality of transmissions or messages between entities, along with the time it takes for these simulacra to travel, leads us to think about signs, texts, and representations differently. Our tendency is to focus on the *aboutness* of signs, texts, representations, and messages, forgetting that these simulacra are not simply about something, they *are* something. As a consequence, the material reality of signs becomes invisible or forgotten. The situation with signs is similar to what Heidegger

---

[20] See Jane Bennett, *Vibrant Matter: A Political Ecology of Things* (Durham: Duke University Press, 2010), chap. 2.

discusses with respect to Dasein's experience of spatiality and a pair of spectacles. As Heidegger writes,

> [w]hen . . . a man wears a pair of spectacles which are so close to him distantially that they are 'sitting on his nose', they are environmentally more remote from him than the picture on the opposite wall.[21]

As Heidegger observes, in our comportment towards the picture, our glasses become invisible, withdrawing from presence, insofar as we are directed towards the painting. Heidegger wishes to argue that this demonstrates that there is a more fundamental spatiality than that of Euclidean or Newtonian space, where proximity is defined not by metric closeness, but rather by our concernful dealings with the world around us. In these concernful dealings, we look *through* our glasses. What is close in lived experience is not the glasses, but rather the picture we are regarding in our concernful dealings. Yet if theorists such as Andy Clark are right with their extended mind hypothesis, a near-sighted person wouldn't even be able to comport towards the picture at all without his body entering into a coupling with the spectacles.

The situation is the same with signs, texts, and messages. Signs draw our thought beyond the vehicle that carries them—the signifier through which they are transported—to whatever signified they might be about. What we forget in our dealings with signs—and what Heidegger forgets when he talks about the spectacles—is that in order for signs to refer to something beyond themselves in the first place, it is necessary for signs to themselves be material entities that are present. In other words, like any other entity, signs must be material entities that travel through time and space and that are limited by time and space. Signs always require some medium in which to exist. This medium can be the air through which they travel, for sounds cannot travel through a void. They can be inscribed on paper, in computer data banks, in brains, in smoke signals, flags, skywriting, etc. They can be inscribed in a variety of different forms of writing ranging from computer code to cuneiform. However, even if the sense of a sign is itself incorporeal as Deleuze and Guattari argue,[22] signs are nonetheless always attached to what Peirce called

---

[21] Martin Heidegger, *Being and Time*, trans. John Macquarrie and Edward Robinson (San Francisco: Harper San Francisco, 1962), 141.
[22] Gilles Deleuze and Felix Guattari, "Postulates of Linguistics," in *A Thousand Plateaus: Capitalism and Schizophrenia*, trans. Brian Massumi

a "sign-vehicle" or some sort of material medium that transports them. This might appear to be a minor, obvious point, but I believe it has tremendous implications. What we need is a sort of inverted transcendental ἐποχή, that for the moment suspends any focus on the sense of signifying entities, instead attending solely to their material or embodied being. This would entail that like the distribution of a virus or microbe in a particular environment, signs also have an epidemiological distribution in the world, a geography of where they are located in the world. Because every text requires a material embodiment in order to travel throughout the world, they will be located in particular times and places. To see why this is important take projects such as critiques of ideology. Critiques of ideology tend to focus on the incorporeal dimension of cultural artifacts and practices—their meaning or sense—ignoring the material distribution of ideologies. While I do not doubt the veracity of many of these critiques, the problem is that in focusing on the incorporeal dimension of ideological texts, their sense or meaning, these critiques behave as if these ideologies exist everywhere. Yet different places have different ideologies because ideologies, like anything else, are spatio-temporally situated entities. Just as we wouldn't want to spray a pesticide for West Nile Virus in an area where West Nile Virus doesn't exist, it is a waste of time and effort to critique an ideology when it doesn't exist in this particular place. We need means of identifying *where* the signifying constellations are and of discerning ways of intervening in those particular signifying constellations.

Attentiveness to signifying entities always raises questions about just who ideological interventions are for. While I don't share a number of his meta-theoretical claims, I think many of Žižek's ideological critiques are on target. Aping Žižek's style, the question to ask, however, is that of precisely *who* these critiques are for. We would imagine that Žižek's critiques are directed at those who labor under these ideologies. After all, it wouldn't make much sense to critique an ideology if it wasn't directed at changing those who labor under that ideology. Yet when we reflect on Žižek's critiques, we notice that they require a high degree of theoretical background to be understood, requiring acquaintance with Lacan, Hegel, and a host of other theorists. Every entity requires a sort of "program" to receive and decipher messages of a particular sort from another entity. Reading Žižek's work requires a particular sort of training if the recipient is to

(Minneapolis: University of Minnesota Press, 1987).

decipher it. When we evaluate Žižek's work by this criteria and critique him immanently—clearly he endorses the Marxist project of not simply representing the world but of changing it—we can ask, on *material* grounds, about the adequacy of his project. Such a critique is not a critique of the accuracy of his critiques, but rather of the adequacy of his practice. It is a question that only comes into relief when we evaluate the material properties of texts, the entities to which they're addressed, and the adequacy of how these texts are composed. When judged by these criteria, we might conclude that such critiques are not addressed at those laboring under such ideologies at all, but rather at others that possess the requisite programs to decipher these sendings. We might thereby conclude that such a practice is actually a mechanism that reproduces these sorts of social relations rather than transforming them as it leaves the ideology itself untouched while simultaneously giving the ideological critic the impression that he's intervening in some way. Note, this critique has nothing to do with the accuracy and truth of these critiques—in many instances, they're quite true—but with how they materially function. Such an analysis would then not dismiss these ideological critiques, but would instead ask what additional operations must be engaged in to insure that the critiques reach their proper destination and produce effects within those networks.

Temporarily suspending our focus on meaning or content, an attentiveness to sign-vehicles would lead us to approach semiotic entities in much the same way as we approach disease epidemiology or population growth and diffusion. Here there are obvious cross-overs between how onto-cartography approaches the materiality of semiotic entities and meme theory.[23] Such an analysis would be particularly attentive to how various mediums of transmission or carriers of sign-vehicles (air, written text, internet, etc.) influence meaning and social relations, how various forms of inscription influence messages, and how sign-vehicles affect people, etc. Here, for example, we might think of Benedict Anderson's analysis of the role that newspapers played in forming national identities.[24] While the content of these newspapers, their *aboutness*, certainly played a crucial role in the formation of national identities, the sheer materiality of the newspaper as a

---

[23] For a discussion of memes, see Daniel C. Dennett, *Darwin's Dangerous Idea: Evolution and the Meanings of Life* (New York: Simon and Schuster, 1995), chap. 12.
[24] Benedict Anderson, *Imagined Communities: Reflections on the Origin and Spread of Nationalism* (New York: Verso, 2006).

medium played a central role. If this is the case, then it is because the newspaper allowed particular messages or forms of expression to circulate broadly, providing a platform to engage in shared identifications despite the fact that these people had no direct contact or communication with one another due to being at vast distances from one another. As McLuhan liked to say, the medium, in its sheer materiality, is the message.

The project of onto-cartography arises from issues arising out of my concept of regimes of attraction. In *The Democracy of Objects* I introduced the concept of "regimes of attraction" to account for why objects are individuated as they are.[25] There I argued that objects, which I now call machines, are split between a virtual dimension that I refer to as "virtual proper being" and another dimension I refer to as "local manifestation."[26] Drawing on Deleuze and Guattari as well as autopoietic theory, I thematize a machine as an entity through which flows of matter or energy pass, reworking and being reworked by that matter as it operates upon it, producing some sort of output. The central feature of a machine is that it operates or functions, producing either its own parts or some sort of product through its operations. Machines are always internally heterogeneous, being composed of a variety of parts or smaller machines that are coupled with one another, and perpetually face the threat of entropy or dissolution over the course of their existence. Machines are not so much brute clods that sit there, but rather are processes or activities. Take the example of a machine such as a tree. A tree is a machine through which flows of matter such as sunlight, water, nutrients in the soil, carbon dioxide, etc., pass. Indeed, in order for a tree to continue to exist rather than dissolve or fall apart (die and rot), it must continuously draw on these flows. In drawing on these flows, the tree reworks them, producing its parts out of sunlight, soil nutrients, carbon dioxide, water and forming these matters into various types of cells, but also the fruit that will fall from the tree, oxygen, and other outputs. As Deleuze poetically puts it,

> What we call wheat is a contraction of the earth and humidity, and this contraction is both a contemplation and

---

[25] Levi R. Bryant, *The Democracy of Objects* (Ann Arbor: Open Humanities Press, 2011), chap. 5.

[26] For a discussion of machines, see Levi R. Bryant, "Machine-Oriented Ontology: Towards a Pan-Mechanism" at *Larval Subjects*, June 21, 2012: http://larvalsubjects.wordpress.com/2012/06/21/machine-oriented-ontology-towards-a-pan-mechanism.

the auto-satisfaction of that contemplation. By its existence alone, the lily of the field sings the glory of the heavens, the goddesses and gods—in other words, the elements
that it contemplates in contracting. What organism is not
made of elements and cases of repetition, of contemplated
and contracted water, nitrogen, carbon, chlorides and sul-
phates, thereby intertwining all the habits of which it is
composed?[27]

Not only does a tree draw on other unique machines, but it is
itself composed of other tiny machines—a cell is a little machine,
itself drawing on all sorts of flows from other cells—and producing other machines such as fruit, odors, oxygen, etc. A focus on
entities as machines rather than objects draws our attention to
how entities function, what they do, how they couple with other
entities, and what they produce in these operations, rather than
what qualities or properties entities might have.

However, it would be a mistake to conclude that the relationship between machines and the matters that flow through them is
a relation between the active (machine) and the passive (matter),
or unformed matter and formative machine. As Stacy Alaimo
suggests with her concept of trans-corporeality, machines are as
much modified by the matters that flow through them as they
modify the matters that pass through them.[28] The tree will grow
differently depending on that chemical composition of the water
that it draws on, the nutrients available, the temperatures in
which it grows, the nature of the air about it; even the altitude at
which it grows and the wind it encounters will modify the nature
of the tree. For example, near my house I have a tree that tilts in a
particular direction. I suspect that this tree grew in that way because the area of Texas I live in is often quite blustery. The
growth of the tree was a sort of compromise, a synthesis, of the
tendency of the tree to grow upwards and the commonly present
force of fierce wind. This tree, as it were, is petrified wind; wind
that has been inscribed in the flesh of wood.

Here we have a beautiful example of gravity as conceived by
onto-cartography. The trans-corporeality of machines entails that
machines are *plastic* or *malleable*. Their qualities are not fixed,
but rather can change as a result of their encounters with other

---

[27] Gilles Deleuze, *Difference and Repetition*, trans. Paul Patton (Columbia:
Columbia University Press, 1994), 75.
[28] Stacy Alaimo, *Bodily Natures: Science, Environment, and the Material
Self* (Bloomington: Indiana University Press, 2010).

machines in a regime of attraction or spatio-temporal gravitational field. It is this that necessitates the distinction between virtual proper being and local manifestation. If it is true that a machine can undergo qualitative variations while remaining that machine, it becomes clear that a machine can no longer be defined by its qualities. Rather, qualities must not be conceived as *properties* of a thing, as something a thing *has*, but rather as *activities* or events on the part of a thing. Qualities are *doings*. The color of a ball, for example, varies depending on the lighting conditions in which the ball currently exists. It is now bright red, now rust colored, now deep red, and now black or colorless depending on changes in the type of light the ball interacts with. If we had an ontologically accurate language, we would not say that the ball *is* red, because the ball is many colors depending on changing circumstances, but rather would say that the ball *reds* under particular lighting conditions. If we cannot individuate a machine by its qualities, then it follows that the being of machines must be individuated by something else. I argue that this something else consists of powers, capacities, and the operations of which the machine is capable. Here it should be noted that the powers and operations of a machine can fluctuate and change as a result of the trans-corporeal encounters it undergoes. For example, my power of cognition is temporally diminished—and perhaps permanently so—as a result of encounters with alcohol. These powers and operations are the virtual proper being of a machine. The important thing here is that the domain of a machine's powers is always broader than whatever qualities it happens to embody at a particular time and place. As Spinoza said, "we do not know what a body can do."[29]

Every body, every machine, is always capable of more than it happens to actualize at any given time. By contrast, the local manifestation of a machine refers to its actualized properties or qualities at a particular point in time and space. Local manifestations are manifestations because they are actualizations of a particular property or act. For example, the red of the ball. They are local, because they are actualizations of this property under particular local conditions. Given other local conditions, very different qualities and acts would manifest themselves. The ball would actualize the color of rust rather than bright red. Thus, for example, two grains of wheat with identical genomes might display very different properties when grown at different altitudes. The

---

[29] Benedict de Spinoza, *Ethics*, in *Spinoza: Complete Works*, trans. Michael L. Morgan (Indianapolis: Hackett Publishing Company, 2002), 280–281.

distinction between virtual proper being and local manifestation
allows us to mark the excess of potentiality harbored within any
being over any of its actualized features. As such, I here follow
Deleuze's prescription to not trace the transcendental from the
empirical.[30] The virtual proper being of a machine never resembles its actualized qualities. It is the power to produce these qualities, but that power always harbors within itself the power to
produce other, different qualities.

The locality of local manifestation is what I refer to as a "regime of attraction." Regimes of attraction are the relations a machine shares to other machines playing a role in the manifestations or actualizations that take place in the machine. A regime of
attraction attracts in the sense that the flows that pass through
the machine from other machines "draw out", as it were, various
manifestations or actualization in the machine. They are the contextual or environmental perturbations that lead the machine to
actualize particular qualities. In short, regimes of attraction are
the spatio-temporal gravitational fields that play a key role in
both the becoming and movement of entities. We already saw an
example of the role played by these fields in becoming with respect to our tree as petrified wind. There the tree grew as it did, it
became as it did, as a result of how it integrated wind with the
development of its cells. It was this integration in time and space
that led the tree to actualize this particular bent shape.

Yet these gravitational fields or regimes of attraction also play
a key role in the movement of entities. From the standpoint of
onto-cartography, space and time are not the same everywhere,
and movement is not materially possible in all directions. In
short, onto-cartography proposes a network conception of space
and time. The way in which roads are laid out in a city play a role
in what is related to what, how one entity has to move in order to
reach another place, as well as the time it takes to get from one
place to another. In Euclidean space, two locations might be quite
proximal to one another, but because of the presence of fences
and how the walls are laid out, it can become quite difficult to
reach a particular location. The walls and roads exercise a certain
gravity on movement that affects social relations. While, in Euclidean space, I am metrically much closer to the president of my
college than to Eileen Joy, who resides in Ohio, she is spatially
and temporally much closer to me than the president in onto-
cartographical space and time because I can contact her more
directly, whereas with the president I must pass through all sorts

---

[30] Deleuze, *Difference and Repetition*, 135.

of levels of administration to interact with him. The bureaucracy of the college functions as a spatio-temporal gravitational field, distending time in a variety of ways, impacting my ability to influence the president of my college. Additionally, entities are only selectively open to influences from their environment. Rocks are not responsive to speech. Bones cannot be healed through talk therapy. In *The Trial* and *The Castle*, Joseph K. discovers that bureaucracies speak entirely different languages that we cannot understand and that do not understand our language. I cannot be perturbed by light in the ultra-violet spectrum of light, yet mantis shrimp can.

It is these complicated dynamics of becoming and movement characteristic of regimes of attraction that onto-cartography seeks to theorize. Where *The Democracy of Objects* sought to theorize the structure of machines and their dynamics, onto-cartography strives to theorize relations between machines and how they create spatio-temporal vectors and paths of becoming and movement. This project is not merely one of intellectual interest—I hope—but also generates a practice that I refer to as "terrarism," denoting a practice in and of the earth.[31] The practice of terrarism has three dimensions: cartography, deconstruction, and terraformation. Cartography consists in the mapping of fields of material and semiotic machines so as to discern the spatio-temporal gravitational fields they produce or the paths and vectors of movement and becoming they generate. Deconstruction refers to the severing of relations that inhibit the becoming and movement of entities we're partial to within a regime of attraction. Sometimes deconstruction will consist in classic modes of semiotic critique and analysis such as we find in cultural studies (deconstruction, psychoanalytic critique, ideology critique, cultural Marxist critique, cultural feminist critique, queer critique, genealogical critique, etc.). At yet other times, deconstruction will consist in literally striving to remove certain entities from a regime of attraction so that they no longer inhibit the becoming and movement of entities. For example, environmental work that strives to reduce greenhouse gas emissions because of their impact on living beings is an example of material deconstruction. Similarly, recognizing that malaria has a profound impact on people culturally and economically, preventing them from pursuing other ends, might lead us to strive for ways to remove malari-

---

[31] For a discussion of terrarism, see Levi R. Bryant, "Terraism," *Larval Subjects*, October 4, 2011: http://larvalsubjects.wordpress.com/2011/10/04/terraism.

al microorganisms from particular environments. Finally, ter-raformation consists in the attempt to construct regimes of attraction or spatio-temporal networks at the level of semiotic and material machines that allow for better becomings and forms of movement. The point that we must always remember, however, is that every machine harbors hidden potentials at the level of its virtual proper being, forever haunting us with the possibility that it will behave in destructive ways when subtracted from existing regimes of attraction or when placed in new spatio-temporal fields. Terrarism must always be practiced with caution and humility, premised on an understanding that we do not fully know what any machine can do and that no machine can be fully mastered.

Levi R. Bryant is a former psychoanalyst and professor of philosophy at Collin College outside of Dallas, Texas. He is the author of *The Democracy of Objects* (Open Humanities Press, 2011), *Difference and Givenness: Deleuze's Transcendental Empiricism and the Ontology of Immanence* (Northwestern University Press, 2008) and co-editor, along with Nick Srnicek and Graham Harman of *The Speculative Turn: Continental Materialism and Realism* (re.press, 2011). He has written numerous articles on Deleuze, Badiou, Lacan, and Žižek, and has written widely on social and political thought, cultural theory, and media theory at his blog *Larval Subjects*.

Anarchist Developments in Cultural Studies
ISSN: 1923-5615
2013.2: Ontological Anarché: Beyond Materialism and Idealism

Reiner Schürmann and Cornelius Castoriadis Between Ontology and Praxis

John W.M. Krummel

ABSTRACT
Every metaphysic, according to Reiner Schürmann, involves the positing of a first principle for thinking and doing whereby the world becomes intelligible and masterable. What happens when such rules or norms no longer have the power they previously had? According to Cornelius Castoriadis, the world makes sense through institutions of imaginary significations. What happens when we discover that these significations and institutions truly are imaginary, without ground? Both thinkers begin their ontologies by acknowledging a radical finitude that threatens to destroy meaning or order. For Schürmann it is the ontological anarchy revealed between epochs when principles governing modes of thinking and doing are foundering but new principles to take their place have not yet emerged. For Castoriadis it is chaos that names the indetermination-determination that governs the unfolding of the socio-historical with contingency and unpredictability. And yet for both thinkers their respective ontologies have political or ethical implications. On the basis of the anarchy of being, Schürmann unfolds an anarchic praxis or *ethos* of "living without why." And on the basis of his notion of being as chaos, Castoriadis develops his political *praxis* of autonomy. The challenge for both is this move from ontology to practical philosophy, how to bridge theory and practice. The key for both seems to be a certain ontologically derived sense of freedom. In this paper, I analyze and compare their respective thoughts, and pursue the question of how anarchy or chaos and the implied sense of an ontological freedom might be made viable and sensible for human praxis, how radical finitude in the face of ontological groundlessness might nevertheless serve to situate a viable political praxis.

KEYWORDS

Schürmann, Castoriadis, ontology, praxis, ontological anarchy, chaos, autonomy, letting, the open, world

Every metaphysic, according to Reiner Schürmann, involves the positing of a First—a principle or principles for thinking and doing—whereby the world becomes intelligible and masterable. Hence the question: What happens when such rules or norms for thinking and doing no longer have the power they had over our convictions, when they wither away and relax their hold? According to Cornelius Castoriadis, the world makes sense through institutions of imaginary significations. So what happens when we discover that these significations and institutions truly are imaginary, without any transcendent ground to legitimate them?

One knowledge from which we can never escape, "even if the natural metaphysician in each of us closes his eyes to it," as Reiner Schürmann puts it, is the knowledge of our natality and mortality, that we are born and we die (Schürmann, 2003: 345). Pulled between these two ultimates, we seemingly have no choice but to live our lives by realizing—discovering?, constructing?, inventing?, imposing?—some sort of meaning or value in our existence. Yet even as we try to construct meaningful lives, death as "a marginal situation" is always there looming beyond the horizon, threatening with *anomy* the meaningful reality we construct.[1] As a collective we set up institutions to deal with such marginals that occasionally invade with a-meaning our otherwise meaningful lives. Inserted and torn between the double bind of natality and mortality, we live our lives filled with contingencies, beginning with the ultimate contingency of birth and ending with that of death. Schürmann described such events of contingency as singulars in that they defy subsumption to some meaning-giving universal representation. One of the central points of his ontology is that being is a multiplicity and flux of singulars that defy the metaphysical attempt to unify and fix them steady. That is to say that singulars unfold their singularity both diachronically and synchronically, through their mutability and their manifold. If principles are what steadies and unifies that flux of multiplicity, preceding the emergence or positing of the

---

[1] For death as *anomy* radically puts into question our taken-for-granted, "business-as-usual," attitude in regard to everyday existence. See Peter L. Berger, *The Sacred Canopy* (New York: Random House, 1990), 23, 43–44. Peter Berger opposes *anomy* to *nomos* throughout this book.

principle or *arché* (ἀρχή), being is an-archic. Schürmann called this "ontological anarchy" (Schürmann, 1978a: 220; 1990: 10; 2010: 252). And to see being as such would be "tragic sobriety" (Schürmann, 1989: 15ff).

Roughly a contemporary of Schürmann, Cornelius Castoriadis noticed in the ancient Greeks a similar recognition of the blind necessity of birth and death, genesis and corruption, revealed in tragedy. The ancient Greeks, such as Hesiod in his *Theogony*, ontologically conceived of this unfathomable necessity in terms of *chaos* (χάος). According to Castoriadis chaos is indeed what reigns supreme at the root of this apparently orderly world (Castoriads, 1991: 103; 1997b: 273) and from out of which man creates—imagines—a meaningful and orderly world.

Both Schürmann and Castoriadis thus begin their ontologies by acknowledging a radical finitude that threatens to destroy meaning or order. And to make their case they look to history: Ontological anarchy for Schürmann becomes most apparent between *epochs* when principles that governed human modes of thinking and doing for a certain period are foundering, no longer tenable, but new principles to take their place have not yet emerged. For Castoriadis chaos is a name for the coupling of indetermination-determination that governs the unfolding of what he calls "the socio-historical" with irreducible contingency and unpredictability.

What are we to make of this—anarchy and chaos? Their onto-logies have political implications. Both thinkers are interested in deriving some sort of an *ethos* or *praxis* from out of their respective ontologies. On the basis of the anarchy of being, Schürmann unfolds an *ethos* of "living without why" (Schürmann, 1978a: 201; 1978b: 362; 1990: 287; 2001: 187) that he calls anarchic praxis. Castoriadis, on the other hand, uses the term *praxis* to designate his explicitly political project of autonomy, which he bases upon his understanding of being as chaos. The challenge for both thinkers is precisely how to make that move from ontology to practical philosophy, from thinking about being to a prescription for acting. One common though implicit link that bridges theory and practice, ontology and politics, for both, I think, is some sense of freedom with its ontological significance. How can ontological freedom, with the recognition of no stable ground—anarchy or chaos—be made viable and sensible for human praxis? This is the question I want to pursue in this paper. I intend, ultimately, to develop an understanding of that freedom in a spatial direction, as *opening*, that perhaps may hold relevance for us in today's shrinking globe that paradoxically expands the world. I will begin with explications of Schürmann's and Castoriadis' respective ontologies and then their respective thoughts on praxis. Through a comparative analysis I seek to arrive at some understanding of how radical finitude in the face of ontological groundlessness might nevertheless serve to situate a viable political praxis.

ONTOLOGICAL ANARCHY: THE PRINCIPLE OF NO PRINCIPLE

Reiner Schürmann's ontological starting point is the singular, which he distinguishes from the particular. Particulars are determined by concepts, that is, they are conceived through subsumption to universals. Singulars on the other hand are ireducible and cannot be thought in terms of concepts or universals. But metaphysics, arising from a natural drive towards generalization and the "need for an archaeo-teleocratic origin" (Schürmann, 1990: 204), the "want of a hold" (Schürmann, 1990: 252), attempts to conceal that which inevitably thrusts itself upon us in our finite encounters with finite beings, in our finite comprehension within a finite situation—the occurrence of singularity. The singular resists the "phantasm" that would subordinate that encounter to the rule of some overarching and hegemonic phenomenon—e.g., the One, God, Nature, Cogito, Reason, etc. According to Schürmann, if "'to think being' means to reflect disparate singulars" (Schürmann, 1989: 3), the path of traditional metaphysics that would subsume the many qua particulars under broader categories is not open. We can only mirror being in its plurality and difference. And yet we cannot so simply disintoxicate ourselves from that metaphysical temptation in utmost sobriety to think nothing but the singular (Schürmann, 1989: 15). We are caught in a conflict—Schürmann calls this a *différend*, borrowing the term from Lyotard—that can reach no settlement (Schürmann, 1989: 2–3). And this, according to Schürmann, is the "tragic condition" of humanity: to be driven to posit a grand narrative and yet to inevitably hear the demand of finitude.[2]

Taking this finitude as his phenomenological starting point, Schürmann understands being at its most originary root to be irreducibly finite, multiple, and in flux, escaping the rule of any principle or *arché*. Instead being—or the origin symbolized by

---

[2] Joeri Schrijvers, "Anarchistic Tendencies in Continental Philosophy: Reiner Schürmann and the Hubris of Philosophy," *Research in Phenomenology* 37.3 (2007), 417–439, 420–421.

being—is anarchic (Schürmann, 1978a: 212). It is the very multifarious emergence of phenomena around us—whereby finite constellations of truth assemble and disassemble themselves. Uprooting rational certainty diachronically and synchronically, perpetually slipping from a oneness that would claim universality or eternity, being emerges ever anew, always *other*. Being in its "radical multiplicity" (Schürmann, 1990: 148) is without destiny or reason. It plays itself out in "ever new topological multiplicities" (Schürmann, 1978a: 212). For Schürmann this means that the *archai* or principles that claim universality and eternity are not truly universal or permanent. Instead they come and go, exercising their rule within specific regions and specific epochs; they are epochally and regionally specific. Once the *arché* that has dominated a specific region for an epoch—providing the meaning, reason, and purpose for being—is no longer believable, being is laid bare in its *an-arché* as the "ceaseless arrangements and rearrangements in phenomenal interconnectedness" (Schürmann, 1990: 270). Anarchy—*an-arché*—as such is the indeterminate root of being that simultaneously establishes and destabilizes any determination of being.

Schürmann traces that ontological anarchy through a series of readings of a variety of authors[3] but he is most known for his reading of Martin Heidegger. For Schürmann, Heidegger proves exemplary in his "phenomenological destruction" (Schürmann, 1978a: 201; 1979: 122; 2010: 245) of the history of ontology that looks upon its past—the history of philosophy as the history of being—without reference to an ultimate standard for judgment and legitimation that would transcend that history. In Schürmann's view, the Heideggerian program of collapsing metaphysical posits comes at the end of an era when such posits have been exhausted, to make clear that being in its origin neither founds, nor explains, nor justifies. It simply grants beings without "why." On this basis the ontological difference thought metaphysically in terms of the relationship between beings (*Seiende*) and their beingness (*Seiendheit*)—the latter being their mode of presence universalized as principle—shifts with its phenomenological destruction to designate the relationship between beingness and be*ing* (*Sein*)—the latter now understood as the granting or releasing, the very *giving* to presence, or *presencing*, of beings and their beingness. Schürmann understands this move

---

[3] This includes Parmenides, Plotinus, Cicero, Augustine, Meister Eckhart, Immanuel Kant, Martin Luther, Friedrich Nietzsche, Martin Heidegger, and Michel Foucault.

to be a temporalization of the difference between what is present (*das Anwesende*) with its mode of presence (*Anwesenheit*) on the one hand and its presencing (*Anwesen* as a verb) on the other, in other words, the historical process or perdurance (*Austrag*) of unconcealing-concealing (*entbergend-bergende*)[4] (Schürmann, 1978a: 196–97), whereby the way things are present, their mode of presence (i.e., beingness), varies from epoch to epoch. The rise, sway, and decline of such a mode is its origin as *arché* and its foundation is its origin as *principium* (Schürmann, 2010: 246). Principles (as *arché* and as *principium*) thus have their uprise, reigning period, and ruin (Schürmann, 2010: 247). Schürmann (Schürmann, 2010: 254n9) refers to Heidegger's definition of *arché* as "...that from which something takes its origin and beginning; [and] what, *as* this origin and beginning, likewise keeps rein *over*, i.e., preserves and therefore dominates, the other thing that emerges from it. *Arché* means at one and the same time beginning and domination."[5] The principle as such opens up a field of intelligibility for the epoch or the region, putting it in order, providing cohesion, regulating its establishment, instituting its public sense, setting the standard for the possible, establishing a milieu for our dwelling (Schürmann, 2010: 247). The prime example in modernity for Schürmann is the principle of sufficient reason, that "nothing is without reason," or "nothing is without why" (Schürmann, 1978a: 204; 2010: 247).[6] But at the end of an epoch, such principles become questionable and indeed questioned. Schürmann thus paradoxically calls the "principle" of the Heideggerian enterprise, the "anarchy principle," a principle without principles (Schürmann 1990: 6).

If Heidegger understands *being* in terms of on-going un-concealment (*a-lētheia*; ἀλήθεια) to human thinking, *beingness*, according to Schürmann, names the order that articulates a particular aletheiological (or: aletheic) constellation for thought. It provides the epochal principle (*arché*, *principum*) for the way being appears—an "economy of presence" that reigns for a period of history. Seen from within the domain where they exercise their

---

[4] Martin Heidegger, *Identity and Difference*, bilingual edition, trans. Joan Stambaugh (Chicago: University of Chicago Press, 1969), 65, 133.

[5] Martin Heidegger, *Wegmarken* (*Gesamtausgabe* Band 9) (Frankfurt: Vittorio Klostermann, 2004), 247; *Pathmarks*, ed. William McNeill (New York: Cambridge University Press, 1998), 189.

[6] Martin Heidegger, *Der Satz vom Grund* (Frankfurt: Vittorio Klostermann, 1997), 73; *The Principle of Reason*, trans. Reginald Lilly (Bloomington: Indiana University Press, 1991), 49.

hegemony, principles appear to be eternal and universal when in fact they are contingent upon the event of their presencing (*Anwesen*). Beingness (the mode of presence) as such must tacitly refer to that event. But being as that event of presencing escapes reduction to—refuses explication in terms of—those principles that rule the epochal mode of presence. In that sense it cannot refer to any ultimate reason beyond itself. The shifting motility of presencing-absencing, from which grounds, reasons, and principles spring-forth, is "only play" and "without why" (Schürmann, 1990: 179). Being in its true origin—simple presencing—is unpredictable, incalculable, singular, unprincipled, anarchic.[7] Once we thus shift our attention to *origin* in this sense of what Heidegger called *Ursprung* rather than as *arché* or principle, we find that the principles and *archai* that previously appeared to found being are confined to specific fields, epochs, as they rise and fall without warning (Schürmann, 2010: 247, 248). In the interim between epochs when constellations of presence are being dismantled and reconfigured, we cannot help but shift our attention to that ungrounding origin, anarchy. In our present period then "at the threshold dividing one era from the next, ontological anarchism appears, the absence of an ultimate reason in the succession of the numerous principles which have run their course" (Schürmann, 2010: 249). Yet anarchy as such is also what has been operative *throughout* history, whereby finite constellations assemble and disassemble in ever-changing arrangements, establishing and destabilizing epochs. It is not only what appears at the end of modernity when we no longer find sufficient reasons for action. The process of presencing-absencing that brings entities into presence under the reign of specific principles, is itself without principle, anarchic.

Schürmann reminds us that traditional philosophies of action, or practical philosophy, have always been supported by a philosophy of being, an ontology (Schürmann, 1978a: 195). Traditional theories of action answer the question of "what should I do?" by reference to some allegedly ultimate norm. Metaphysics was the attempt to determine a referent for that question by discovering a principle—be it God, Reason, Nature, Progress, Order, Cogito, or anything else—to which "words,

---

[7] Making use of the Schürmannian motif of anarchy, Jean-Luc Nancy states that the *es gibt* of being in Heidegger is of the "each time" of an existing, singular occurrence that is an-archic. See Jean-Luc Nancy, *The Inoperative Community*, ed. Peter Connor (Minneapolis: University of Minnesota Press, 1991), 105.

things, and deeds can be related" (Schürmann, 1990: 6), a principle that functions simultaneously as foundation, beginning, and commandment. The *arché* imparts to action meaning and *telos* (Schürmann, 1990: 5). If the realm of politics derives legitimacy of conduct from principles belonging to ontology, Heidegger's inquiry into being deprives practical philosophy of its metaphysical ground (Schürmann, 1979: 100). If metaphysics has indeed exhausted itself, the rule that would impart intelligibility and control upon the world loses its hold and practical philosophy can no longer be derived from a first philosophy and praxis can no longer be founded upon theory. The end of metaphysics and the crisis of foundations put the grounding of practice into question. We are deprived of any ground or reason for legitimating action. As the "severalness of being" uproots rational security, its "peregrine essence" uproots practical security. In other words, being in its manifold and mutability—or, in Castoriadis' terms, alterity and alteration—ungrounds. The question thus looms: when practical philosophy, including political thought, can no longer refer to a First as its norm or standard and instead faces an abyss in the lack of legitimating ground, what are we to do, how ought we act? But the suggestion is that precisely *this*—when anarchy is laid bare—is when one truly *is*. Schürmann quotes (Schürmann, 1978a: 204; 1978b, 362; 1990: 10) Heidegger's reference to Meister Eckhart via Angelus Silesius: "Man, in the most hidden ground of his being, truly is only when in his own way he is like the rose—without why."[8] The above question leads Schürmann to a novel vision of anarchic praxis.

CHAOS: THE ONTOLOGY OF MAGMA

Cornelius Castoriadis' ontology of chaos in some ways runs parallel to Schürmann's ontology of anarchy in its recognition of a primal indeterminacy and fluidity. It recognizes an indeterminacy preceding determinate constellations that make being intelligible while concealing, at least for some time, their own historical contingency. History for Castoriadis is the creation of "total forms of human life," the self-creation of society in its self-alteration (Castoriadis, 1991: 84; 1997b: 269; 2007: 223). The creator is the instituting society, and in instituting itself it creates the human world (Castoriadis, 1991: 84; 1997b: 269). Every society involves history in this sense as its temporal alteration. But history as such can neither be explained nor predicted, whether

---

[8] Heidegger, *Der Satz vom Grund*, 57–58; *The Principle of Reason*, 38.

on the basis of mechanical causality or identifiable patterns, because—even as it determines—Castoriadis contends, it is not determined by natural or historical laws (Castoriadis, 1991: 84; 1997b: 269). The socio-historical as this complex of history and society in a perpetual flux of self-alteration (Castoriadis, 1998: 204) is thus irreducible, whether in terms of mechanical causality or in terms of function or purpose. Both society and history, according to Castoriadis, contain a non-causal element consisting of unpredictable as well as genuinely creative behavior that posits new modes of acting, institutes new social rules, or invents new objects or forms, the emergence of which cannot be deduced from previous situations (Castoriadis, 1998: 44).

On the basis of this notion of the socio-historical Castoriadis develops an ontology of human creation that refuses to reduce being to determinacy.[9] History instead resides in "the emergence of radical otherness, immanent creation, non-trivial novelty" (Castoriadis, 1998: 184). More broadly, Castoriadis explains time itself to be the emergence of *other* figures, given by *otherness*, and by the appearance of the *other* (Castoriadis, 1998: 193). Time as such is the "otherness-alteration of figures"—figures that are *other* in that they shatter determinacy and cannot themselves be determined (Castoriadis, 1998: 193). In *The Imaginary Institution of Society* he characterizes such time as the bursting, emerging, explosion or rupture of what is, "the surging forth of ontological genesis," of which the socio-historical provides a prime exemplar (Castoriadis, 1998: 201). Broadening his view of history, by the late 1990s, he more explicitly ontologizes the claim to state that *being itself* is *creation and destruction*, and that by creation he means discontinuity or the emergence of the radically new (Castoriadis, 2007: 190). Castoriadis thus attempts to construct an ontology that would acknowledge novelty as intrinsic to being itself. The social institution on the other hand, while born in, through, and as the rupture of time—a manifestation of the self-alteration of instituting society—exists only by positing itself as *outside* time, in self-denial of its temporality, concealing its socio-historicity, including its creative self-institution (Castoriadis, 1998: 214).

Being, regardless of what the social institution may claim, nevertheless harbors within itself an indeterminacy that permits for its own creation and destruction. It is "neither a determinable

---

[9] See Suzi Adams, *Castoriadis's Ontology: Being and Creation* (New York: Fordham University Press, 2011), 5.

ensemble nor a set of well-defined elements."[10] Castoriadis
metaphorically designates this aspect of the socio-historical that
is not—and can never be exhaustively covered by—a well-ordered
hierarchy of sets or what he calls "ensidic" or "ensemblist"
organization, *magma* (Castoriadis, 1997b: 379; 1998: 182, 343;
2007: 186–87). *Magma* characterizes the flux that becomes
meaning or signification, the organization of which belongs to
"non-ensemblist diversity" as exemplified by the socio-historical,
the imaginary, or the unconscious (Castoriadis, 1997b: 211–212;
1998: 182). We are told that some flows of magma are denser than
others, some serve as nodal points, and that there are clearer or
darker areas and condensations into "bits of rock" (Castoriadis,
1998: 243–244). From out of its flow an indefinite number of what
he calls "set-theoretic (ensemblist)" structures or organizations
can be extracted (Castoriadis, 2007: 251–252). But the shape it
takes is never complete or permanent, and the magma continues
to move, to "liquefy the solid and solidify the liquid," constantly
reconfiguring itself into new ontological forms (Castoriadis, 1998:
244).[11] Rather than being a well-defined unity of plurality, the
social is then a *magma of magmas* (Castoriadis, 1997b 211; 1998:
182).[12]

Despite his characterization of magma as neither a set of
definite and distinct elements nor pure and simple chaos (Castoriadis, 1998: 321), Castoriadis will go on to use the characterization
of *chaos*, especially in his later works, to underscore the indeterminacy of our creative nature. He defines this chaos as the
irreducible inexhaustibility of being. *Chaos* designates being in its
bottomless depth, the abyss behind everything that exists
(Castoriadis, 2007: 240). As such, "being is chaos" (Castoriadis,

---

[10] Adams, *Castoriadis's Ontology*, 39.

[11] Also see Adams, *Castoriadis's Ontology*, 222.

[12] According to Suzi Adams, Castoriadis initially used the term *magma* to
characterize the mode of being of the psyche as radical imagination—its
representational flux—but in the course of writing *Imaginary Institution
of Society* broadens its significance to characterize the being of the socio-
historical with its collective social imaginary. And by the final chapters
of the book he broadens it further beyond the human realm and into
being in general as involving the interplay of indetermination-determination (or: *chaos-cosmos, apeiron-peras*). He also extends its meaning
specifically into nature to rethink the ontological significance of the
creativity of nature itself—a rethinking which he will later in the 1980s
extend further with his focus on the Greek notion of *physis* in terms of
creative emergence. See Adams, *Castoriadis's Ontology*, 102, 103, 137, 147,
205.

1991: 117; 1997b: 284). And the entire cosmos is a part of that chaos and begot out of it while continuing to be rooted in its abysmal depths. At the roots of the world, beyond the familiar, chaos always reigns supreme with its blind necessity of genesis and corruption, birth and death (Castoriadis, 1991: 103; 1997b: 273).

In elucidating his notion of chaos Castoriadis refers to its ancient Greek meaning as a sort of fecund void or nothingness— *nihil*—from out of which the world emerges *ex nihilo* minus the theological connotations. He refers to Hesiod's use of the term in the *Theogony* that takes *chaos* as the primal chasm from out of which emerge earth and heaven as well as other divinities.[13] But Castoriadis contends that *chaos* in addition to being the empty chasm also had the sense of disorder from which order, *cosmos*, emerges (Castoriadis, 1991: 103; 1997b: 273). For him this signifies an a priori ontological indeterminacy (Castoriadis, 2007: 240) that would account for novelty. *Nihilo* or *chaos*, one may then say, is an indeterminable complex that exceeds rational comprehension. Being at bottom is chaos in that sense as the absence of order *for man*, or an order that in itself is "meaningless" (Castoriadis, 1991: 117; 1997b: 284). It's a-meaning, the social world's *other*, is always there presenting a risk, threatening to lacerate the web of significations that society erects against it (Castoriadis, 1991: 152). In the same sense that an-archy for Schürmann accounts for the singularity of events in history, chaos for Castoriadis thus accounts for the unpredictability and novelty of events in history.

Castoriadis emphasizes however that indetermination here is not simple privation of determination, but as creation involves the emergence of *new and other* determinations. The indetermination here means that there can be no absolute determination that is once and for all for the totality of what is so as to preclude, exclude, or render impossible the emergence of the new and the *other* (Castoriadis, 1997b: 308, 369). Chaos as a *vis formandi* causes the upsurge of forms. In this creativity, being is thus *autopoiesis*, self-creating.[14] And that self-creating "poietic" (creative) element within man drives him/her to superimpose social imaginary significations upon chaos to give shape to the world. Through poietic organization humanity thus gives form to chaos—the chaos that both surrounds (as nature) and is within (as psyche). And

---

[13] See Hesiod, *Theogony and Works and Days*, trans. M.L. West (New York: Oxford University Press, 2008), 6–7, and also see the translator's note, 64n116.

[14] See Adams, *Castoriadis's Ontology*, 149.

chaos qua *vis formandi* is *itself* operative in this formation as the radical imagination in both the psyche of the individual and in the social collective as the instituting social imaginary (Castoriadis 1997b: 322). In other words, chaos forms itself and individual human beings as well as societies are fragments of that chaos, agencies of that *vis formandi* or ontological creativity (Castoriadis, 2007: 171). If radical creation in this sense of determining the indeterminate appertains to the human, it is because it is an aspect of being itself as a whole (Castoriadis, 1997b: 404). As we stated above Castoriadis' ontology of chaos was to account for novelty as intrinsic to being itself. But by this he means more specificially the inexhaustibility of being and its creativity, its *vis formandi* (Castoriadis, 2007: 240).

Each and every society creates within its own "closure of meaning"—its social imaginary significations—its own *world* (Castoriadis, 2007: 226). That world emerges from out of the chaos as a relative solidification of the magmatic flow. The world as we know it then is a world—to borrow a phenomenological term—"horizoned" by the constructions instituted by that particular society: "the particular complex of rules, laws, meanings, values, tools, motivations, etc.," an institution that is "the socially sanctioned . . . magma of social imaginary significations" (Castoriadis 1991: 85; 1997b: 269). The creative imagination, *Einbildung*, transforms the natural environment into an "order-bearing configuration of meaning"[15]—a *cosmos*—woven into the chaos (Castoriadis, 1998: 46). This formation—*Bildung*—is culture, and the form is meaning or signification, which together constitute a world, a *cosmos* (Castoriadis, 1997b: 342–43). But beyond that forming, there is no ultimate ground for the meaningfulness of the world. Prior to the construction of the socially meaningful world and always at its root, there is chaos.

Now if the creation of the world, the institution of the network of imaginary significations, as self-creation or creation *ex nihilo,* can claim no "extrasocial standard of society, a norm of norms, law of laws"—whether it be God, Nature, or Reason—that would ground or legitimate political truths, we arrive at the same *aporia* Schürmann noticed. According to Castoriadis, the recognition that no such ground exists opens up the questions of just law, justice, or the proper institution of society as genuinely interminable questions (Castoriadis, 1991: 114; 1997b: 282). The question looms if nature both outside and within us—*chaos*—is always something *other* and something more than the construc-

---

[15] See Adams, *Castoriadis's Ontology,* 219.

tions of consciousness (Castoriadis, 1998: 56): To what extent can we intentionally or consciously realize our autonomy? How does the alterity and alteration of being (chaos, magma, indetermination) affect Castoriadis's project of autonomy? How do we realize our freedom with the knowledge that being is chaos?

ANARCHIC PRAXIS: BEING WITHOUT WHY

How are we to assess the political implications of these ontologies of anarchy and chaos? Both Schürmann and Castoriadis understood their own respective ontologies as having a practical, indeed political, significance. How does one derive a viable political praxis when standards for meaningful action, whether as institutions or as *archai*, are shown to be contingent upon the groundless flow of time?

The Heideggerian program Schürmann inherits excludes reference to any ultimate standard for judgment and legitimation. The on-going unconcealing-concealing of truth qua *aletheia* provides no stable, unquestionable, ground from which political conduct can borrow its credentials.[16] There is no ground or reason (*Grund*) to which we can refer action for legitimacy. Instead— Schürmann tells us—being as "groundless ground" calls upon existence, a subversive reversal or "overthrow . . . from the foundations" (Schürmann, 1978a: 201). The consequence Schürmann surmises is that human action, notably political practice, becomes thinkable *differently* in this absence of ground (Schürmann, 2010: 249).

The praxis ontological anarchy calls for however is distinct from classical forms of anarchist political philosophy. Schürmann contends classical political anarchism still remains caught within the field of metaphysics in deriving action from the referent of reason or rationality, which it substitutes for the principle of authority (Schürmann, 1990: 6). In choosing a new criterion of legitimacy anarchism maintains the traditional procedure of legitimation. With the Heideggerian destruction of metaphysics, however, any metaphysical grounding, even its rational production, becomes impossible. This breaking-down of the metaphysical sche-

---

[16] Schürmann (Schürmann, 2010: 245, 250–51, 253n2) thus cites Werner Marx's comment concerning "the extremely perilous character of Heidegger's concept of truth," a comment that suggests Heidegger's work may be harmful for public life by depriving political action of its ground. See Werner Marx, *Heidegger and the Tradition*, trans. Theodore Kisiel and Murray Greene (Evanston, IL: Northwestern University Press, 1971), 251.

ma, as Miguel Abensour puts it in his reading of Schürmann, liberates action from all submission to principles to give birth to an action devoid of any *arché*, anarchic action.[17] In this way Schürmann derives from ontological anarchy, or "the anarchy principle," a mode of action he calls *anarchic praxis*. Ontological anarchy calls for a recognition of the loosening of the grip of principles, metaphysical posits, to leave behind attachment to them, and instead to embark on a path of detachment that Schürmann, using Heideggerian-Eckhartian terminology, designnates "releasement." Releasement (*Gelassenheit*) is taken to be the Heideggerian candidate for anarchic praxis that responds to the withering away of metaphysical principles. It is an "acting other than 'being effective' and a thinking other than strategical rationality" to instead be attuned to the presencing of phenolmenal interdependence (of actions, words, things) (Schürmann, 1990: 84). Schürmann takes this to express what medieval mystic Meister Eckhart himself implied in his "life without why" (Schürmann 1990, 10). He quotes more than once (Schürmann, 1978a: 204; 1978b: 362; 1990: 10) Heidegger's appropriation in *Der Satz vom Grund* of Eckhart (*via* Angelus Silesius): "Man, in the most hidden ground of his being, truly is only when in his way he is like the rose—without why."[18] Tying this in with Heidegger's historical concerns, Schürmann asks: When is it that man can be like the rose? And he answers: It is when the "why" withers. He is referring to the withering of metaphysics at the end of modernity (Schürmann, 1990: 38).

This raises the issue of the relationship between theory and practice. Schürmann asks: What happens to their opposition once "thinking" means no longer "securing some rational foundation" for knowing and once "acting" no longer means "conforming one's enterprises . . . to the foundation so secured" (Schürmann, 1990: 1)? With the Heideggerian deconstruction of metaphysics, action itself loses its foundation (*arché*) and end (*telos*): "in its essence, action proves to be an-archic" (Schürmann, 1990: 4). This also means that thinking is no longer in contrast to action as mere theory. Instead a thinking that is *other* than mere theory proves receptive to the anarchy of presencing-absencing. Refraining from imposing conceptual schemes upon phenomena as they enter into "interdependence unattached to principles" (Schürmann, 1990: 85, 269), such non-representational thinking—what

---

[17] Miguel Abensour, "'Savage Democracy' and 'Principle of Anarchy,'" *Philosophy and Social Criticism* 28.6 (2002), 703–726, 715.

[18] Heidegger, *Der Satz vom Grund*, 57–58; *The Principle of Reason*, 38.

Schürmann here calls "essential thinking"—complies with that flux of presencing-absencing (Schürmann, 1990: 269, 289). More specifically this entails the attitude and itinerary of "without why," whereby we see things in their presencing without reference to whence or why, and whereby being itself appears as letting beings be "without why" (Schürmann, 1979: 114). In response to the purposeless flow of presencing—ontological releasement—man is called-forth to let be, to "live without why." Thinking as such does what being does, it is releasement, it lets beings be: "[T]o think being as letting-phenomena-be, one must oneself 'let all things be'" (Schürmann, 1990: 287). To think being is to follow the event (*Ereignis*) of being (Schürmann, 1990: 289). And to follow that play of why-less presencing, one must oneself "live without why" (Schürmann, 1990: 287). The mode of thinking here is made dependent on the mode of living (Schürmann, 1990: 237): to think anarchic presencing requires anarchic existence. Under the practical a priori of anarchic acting that *lets* rather than *wills*, thinking arrives at the event-like presencing that is be*ing*. For this we must relinquish the willful quest for a founding ultimate. This means be*ing* without fettering oneself to a fixed or static way of being.[19] And this may also imply, Schürmann surmises, "the deliberate negation of *archai* and principles in the public domain" (Schürmann, 2010: 252). The *theoria* and the *praxis* of anarchy are thus inextricably linked in Schürmann's thinking in the non-duality of "essential thinking" and "un-attached acting" (Schürmann, 1990: 269) that simultaneously reveal and respond to the principle of anarchy.

There are three ways, according to Schürmann, in which ontological difference manifests. The turn to anarchic praxis is the consequence of the third. The first is the metaphysical difference between beings or present entities and their beingness or mode of presence universalized and eternalized as *arché*. The second is the phenomenological or temporal difference between beingness and be*ing*. Here be*ing* as a verb means the presencing-absencing of beingness. And that presencing-absencing proves to be anarchic. This revelation of ontological anarchy puts into question institutionalized authority. The third is what Schürmann in his early works of the late 1970s called the symbolic difference

---

[19] In his reading of Michel Foucault from the mid-1980s, Schürmann accordingly develops his idea of a practical "anarchistic subject" who responds to that phenomenal flux that constitutes and destroys temporal networks of order, fluidly shifting into and out of their shifting fields (see CA 302).

between what *being* might signify in its intellectual comprehension and what *being* means as existentially lived. It entails the
active response to the practical summons to exist without why
(Schürmann, 1978a: 207). The ontological anarchy that is revealed
in the phenomenological difference becomes directly known in
the symbolic difference through a particular mode of existing,
anarchic praxis (Schürmann, 1978a: 220; 1979: 103). But since the
destruction of metaphysics reveals being not as a self-same
universal or a self-subsisting oneness but as multifarious—a many
and in flux as an ever-new event—the praxis called for by being's
symbolic difference would be "irreducibly polymorphous" (Schürmann, 1978a: 199). Existence without why, without *arché* or *telos*,
is existence "appropriated by ever new constellations," the
polymorphousness, of truth (Schürmann, 1978a: 200). Anarchic
praxis as such is a "polymorphous doing" that co-responds to the
field of "polymorphous presencing" (Schürmann, 1990: 279).
Schürmann states that in Nietzschean terms "it gives birth to the
Dionysian child" (Schürmann, 1978a: 206). In more concrete terms
it means "the practical abolition of *arché* and *telos* in action, the
transvaluation of responsibility and destiny, and the protest
against a world reduced to functioning within the coordinates of
causality" (Schürmann, 1978a: 216). Ultimately it means the
anarchic essence of being, thinking, and doing altogether.[20]
Symbolic difference, Schürmann contends, thus "allows for the
elaboration of an alternative type of political thinking" in regard
to a society that "refuses to restrict itself to the pragmatics of
public administration as well as to the romantic escapes from it"
(Schürmann, 1978a: 221).[21] And that accomplishment where

---

[20] Schürmann unpacks the five practical consequences of the symbolic
difference in greater detail in some key essays from the late 1970s,
including "Political Thinking in Heidegger" and "The Ontological Dif-
erence and Political Philosophy" as well as "Questioning the Foundations
of Practical Philosophy": 1) the abolition of the primacy of teleology in
action; 2) the abolition of the primacy of responsibility in the legitimation of action; 3) action as protest against the administered world; 4) a
certain disinterest in the future of mankind due to a shift in the
understanding of destiny; and 5) anarchy as the essence of what can be
remembered in thought ("origin") and of what can be done in action
("originary practice") (Schürmann, 1978a: 201; 1979: 122n29; and see in
general 1978b).
[21] On the other hand, if we are to reserve the term "political philosophy"
for theories of "collective functioning and organization," Schürmann
agrees that we ought then to abandon this title for the practical

REINER SCHÜRMANN AND CORNELIUS CASTORIADIS | 47

thinking, acting, and being (presencing-absencing), loosened from the fetters of principles, work together in mutual appropriation (or: "enownment," *Ereignis*), Schürmann calls "anarchic economy" (Schürmann, 1990: 243, 273): On the basis of "actions—assimilating to that economy, *turning* into a groundless play without why," essential thinking "receives, hears, reads, gathers, unfolds . . . the anarchic economy" (Schürmann, 1990: 242–43).

Anarchic existence is also authentic existence. Schürmann reads an ateleology behind Heidegger's notion of authentic resoluteness (*eigentliche Entschlossenheit*) from *Sein und Zeit* (*Being and Time*) in the anticipation of one's own not-being—death as one's nonrelational ownmost possibility that throws one back upon one's ownmost potentiality-of-being[22]—and takes this also to be anarchic in that it escapes delimitation by both *arché* and *telos* (Schürmann, 1978a: 218). That is to say that authentic existence is without why, it exists in the face of death for its own sake, with no extrinsic reasons or goals. One wonders then, in light of our ensuing discussion of Castoriadis' project of autonomy, whether authentic existence qua anarchic existence is also *autonomous* existence, an existence that has discarded the need for heteronomous references. Understood from out of the "anarchic essence of potentiality," Schürmann suggests that the play of "ever new social constellations" becomes an end in itself. Its essence is boundless interplay without any direction imposed by an authority (Schürmann, 1978a: 219).[23] With the deprivation of

---

consequences of thinking the symbolic difference (Schürmann, 1979: 122).

[22] See Martin Heidegger, *Sein und Zeit* (Tübingen: Max Niemeyer Verlag, 1993), 250; *Being and Time*, trans. Joan Stambaugh (New York: SUNY Press, 1996), 232).

[23] One is reminded here of an example for non-authoritarian association often used by political anarchists, the spontaneous collective play of the dinner party, without any need for externally imposed rules or calculations, where people get together and enjoy company "without why." See Stephen Pearl Andrews, *The Science of Society* (Weston, MA: M&S Press, 1970); Hakim Bey, *T.A.Z.: The Temporary Autonomous Zone, Ontological Anarchy, Poetic Terrorism* (New York: Autonomedia, 1991, 1985), 140–141. Also see the talk given by Banu Bargu, "The Politics of Commensality," delivered at a conference on The Anarchist Turn held at the New School for Social Research in 2011 and included in the online special virtual issue of *Anarchist Developments in Cultural Studies* (2011) at http://www.anarchist-developments.org/index.php/adcs/article/view/ 29/24. Here any *nomos* of a collective would be engendered spontaneously—autonomously—and not imposed from any extrinsic source.

ground or reason (*Grund*) the paradigm of action here becomes *play* (Schürmann, 1979: 102). For Schürmann this opens "an alternative way of thinking of life in society" (Schürmann, 1978a: 220). Instead of rule-by-one or a *telos*-oriented pragmatics then, we have practices, multiple and mutable: "The groundwork for an alternative to organizational political philosophy will have to be so multifarious as to allow for an ever new response to the calling advent by which being destabilizes familiar patterns of thinking and acting" (Schürmann, 1979: 115). The political consequence is "radical mutability in accordance with an understanding of being as irreducibly manifold" (Schürmann, 1978a: 221). Can we concretize this further in Castoriadian terms as an opening to alterity and alteration—what Schürmann calls manifold and mutability— that might approach Castoradis' project of autonomy?

Surprisingly Schürmann, at one point, invokes "direct democracy" as what the critique of metaphysics sustaining "contract theories . . . government contracts and the mechanisms of representative democracy" moves towards (Schürmann, 1984: 392). Yet undeniably one gets the impression from his overall project that his primary concern is an existential-ontological hermeneutic of anarchy as a way of life, "life without why," that is, a mode of existence broadly construed. This certainly has political and revolutionary implications as he suggests himself but he never elaborates on this or develops this into an explicitly political program.[24] Miguel Abensour, nevertheless, interestingly suggests a proximity between Schürmann's principle of anarchy and Claude Lefort's notion of "savage democracy" or the "savage essence" of democracy[25] that evokes the spontaneous emergence of democratic forms, independent of any principle or authority

---

Taking anarchy as autonomy in this sense of such self-engendered spontaneity might also resonate with the Chinese sense of "nature," *zhiran* (自然), which has the literal sense of "self-so" or "self-engendering."

[24] Could this be out of fear that such an elaboration might fall into the trap of a metaphysic that yet again posits norms and principles claiming universality?

[25] Both phrases express a paradox: "anarchy destroys the idea of principle, the savage overthrows the idea of essence" (Abensour, "'Savage Democracy' and 'Principle of Anarchy,'" 717). One might also bring into the mix Jean-Luc Nancy's designation of the an-archy and singularity of being that refuses subsumption to any essence, as its "in-essence" that "delivers itself as its own essence." See Jean-Luc Nancy, *The Experience of Freedom*, trans. Bridget McDonald (Stanford: Stanford University Press, 1993), 16.

and refusing to submit to established order, whereby democracy "inaugurates a history in which people experience a fundamental indeterminacy as to the foundations of power, law, and knowledge, and . . . of . . . relations . . . at every level of social life"—an experience of the *loss of foundation* which is also an experience of the *opening of being*.[26] Abensour states that Schürmann's thesis of the "principle of anarchy" curiously connects to the question of democracy.[27] For the decline of the scheme of reference obliges us to formulate the question of politics otherwise than in terms of principles and their derivations. Lefort's "savage democracy" thus has something in common with anarchy in that it manifests an "action without why."[28]

Schürmann's point appears to be that the contingency and finitude revealed in tragic sobriety is at the same time liberating. It liberates us from dead gods and ineffective idols. The deconstruction of foundations and the refusal of the metaphysical project is the liberation from ideals or norms projected as heteronomous authorities. This clears the way for an origin that no longer dominates and commands action as *arché* but which, as manifold and mutability, *liberates action*.[29] Schürmann's contemporary, Jean-Luc Nancy, has taken such ontological anarchy to thus mean freedom: "The fact of freedom is this deliverance of existence from every law and from itself as law."[30] According to Nancy, Schürmann, without really analyzing freedom, supposes or implies freedom throughout his book on Heidegger.[31] And

---

[26] Claude Lefort, *Democracy and Political Theory*, trans. David Macey (Minneapolis: University of Minnesota Press, 1988), 19. And also see Abensour, "'Savage Democracy' and 'Principle of Anarchy,'" 707, 708, 710.

[27] Abensour, "'Savage Democracy' and 'Principle of Anarchy,'" 711.

[28] Abensour thus asks whether its "savage essence" makes democracy a special form of the political that is distinct from traditional political systems and, if so, what relationship it might have to the principle of anarchy. See Abensour, "'Savage Democracy' and 'Principle of Anarchy,'" 714. Needless to say, he has in mind Schürmann's thesis that the Heideggerian destruction of metaphysics opens an alternative way of thinking the political.

[29] See Abensour, "'Savage Democracy' and 'Principle of Anarchy,'" 715, 716.

[30] Nancy, *The Experience of Freedom*, 30, and also see 13. Jean-Luc Nancy has expressed sympathy towards Schürmann's philosophy of anarchy on many occasions.

[31] Nancy, *The Experience of Freedom*, 187n3.

another contemporary, Frank Schalow, reads Schürmann to mean that the deconstruction of epochal and normative principles, shifting our attention to the vacillation of truth between its arrival and withdrawal, opens up a new spacing for divergence.[32] By enduring the interplay of unconcealment-concealment, presencing-absencing, the zone of their strife becomes for us a creative nexus that can engender new meanings and reconfigure a political space for alternatives in thought and action. This permits a reciprocal mosaic of human forms of dwelling in the experience of freedom as "letting-be" (or releasement). The suggestion is that the ontology of freedom—anarchy—as letting-be provides an a-principial guidance for co-being within the larger expanse wherein we may cultivate our place of dwelling. Schalow thus wonders whether anarchic praxis might enable the rescue of the diversity of human origins from domination under the contemporary rule of technology.[33] In our attempt to conceive of the relevance of ontological anarchy in our globalized existence today we might thus focus on its aspect of *freeing* that opens a space for alterity and alteration, manifold and mutability.

PRAXIS: THE PROJECT OF AUTONOMY

Castoriadis' ontology of creation is intimately linked with his project of autonomy. Castoriadis calls this activity which aims at autonomy *praxis* (Castoriadis, 1991: 76). And *politics* for Castoriadis is "the activity that aims at the transformation of society's institutions to make them conform to the autonomy of the collectivity . . . to permit the *explicit*, reflective, and deliberate self-institution and self-governance of this collectivity" (Castoriadis, 1991: 76). This political project, while there are differences, in certain aspects resonates with Schürmann's protest against the technologically administered world accompanied by calculative (*telos*-oriented) thinking. For a similar sort of target in Castoriadis's project is the "empty phantasm of mastery" that accompanies the accumulation of gadgetry that together mask our essential mortality, making us forget that we are "improbable

---

[32] Frank Schalow, "Revisiting Anarchy: Toward a Critical Appropriation of Reiner Schürmann's Thought," *Philosophy Today* 41.4: 554–562, 555–556. Schalow takes this more concretely to mean a letting-be that enables human beings "to cultivate their place on earth and respond to the welfare of others" (555). Such cultivation of a place for dwelling is certainly never made so explicit in Schürmann himself.

[33] Schalow, "Revisiting Anarchy," 560.

beneficiaries of an improbable and very narrow range of material conditions making life possible on an exceptional planet we are in the process of destroying" (Castoriadis, 1997a: 149). For Castoriadis this phantasm is a manifestation of what he calls "ensemblistic-identitary logic-ontology," and his political project is to break its hold to make possible the realization of an autonomous society: the point is that we make our laws and hence we are also responsible for them (Castoriadis, 1997b: 312).[34] We can be genuinely autonomous only by facing our finitude and taking responsibility for our lives in the face of contingency.

So how exactly does Castoriadis' political project of autonomy relate to his ontology of chaos? Just as his ontology was inspired by the ancient Greek notion of chaos, Castoriadis looks to the ancient Greek *polis* as an inspiration for his project of autonomy.[35] The Greek vision that the world is not fully ordered and that *cosmos* emerges from *chaos*—a vision of disorder at the bottom of the world, whereby chaos reigns supreme with its blind necessity of birth and death, genesis and corruption—allowed the Greeks, Castoriadis claims (Castoriadis, 1997b: 273–274), to create and practice both philosophy and politics. If the world were sheer chaos, there would be no possibility of thinking, but if the world were fully ordered, there would be no room for political thinking and action. Instead it was the belief in the interplay of chaos with cosmos that proved favorable for the emergence of democracy and autonomy in ancient Greece.

To explain autonomy, Castoriadis contrasts it with heteronomy. All societies make their own imaginaries (institutions, laws, traditions, beliefs, behaviors, *nomoi*). But in heteronomous

---

[34] The sense of responsibility we find here in Castoriadis is obviously distinct from the sense of responsibility Schürmann attacks in his explication of the symbolic difference. For Castoriadis, in refusing to posit a heteronomous *nomos* for our laws we take responsibility for our laws through the explicit recognition that "we" (society) creates them. The "responsibility" that Schürmann targets is really the claim of a grounding in a principle that would legitimate action, which in Castoriadian terms would be a projected *hetero-nomos*.

[35] In light of our earlier reference to Jean-Luc Nancy as a contemporary philosopher who makes use of Schürmann's notion of anarchy, it may be interesting to note here that Nancy points to the Greek city as *autoteleological* in the sense that it refers to no signification external to its *own* institution. Its identity is nothing other than the space of its citizens' co-being with no extrinsic (extra-social) grounding for its collective identity. See Jean-Luc Nancy, *The Sense of the World*, trans. Jeffrey S. Librett (Minneapolis: University of Minnesota Press, 1997), 104.

societies, members attribute their imaginaries to some extra-
social authority (i.e., God, ancestors, historical necessity, etc.). In
autonomous societies, by contrast, members are aware of this
fact—the socio-historical creation of their imaginaries—to participate in the explicit self-institution of society. Autonomy as such
is the capacity of human beings, individually or socially, to act
deliberately and explicitly in order to modify their laws or form
of life, *nomos* or *nomoi* (Castoriadis, 1997a: 340). *Auto* (αὐτο)
means "oneself" and *nomos* (νόμος) means "law." *Auto-nomos*
(αὐτόνομος) is thus to give oneself one's laws, "to make one's
own laws, knowing that one is doing so" (Castoriadis, 1991: 164).
Autonomy must be of both individuals and of society in that
while an autonomous society can only be formed by autonomous
individuals, autonomous individuals can exist only in and
through an autonomous society (Castoriadis, 2007: 196). One
cannot want it without wanting it for everyone (Castoriadis, 1998:
107). *Nomos*, law is necessary for society, and human beings
cannot exist without it. For society, autonomy then entails
acceptance that it creates its own institutions without reference
to any extra-social basis or extrinsic norm for its social norms
(Castoriadis, 2007: 94). An autonomous society sets up its own
laws without resorting to an illusory nonsocial source or
foundation or standard of legitimation. This means that it is also
"capable of explicitly, lucidly challenging its own institutions"
(Castoriadis, 2007: 49). The legitimation of its own existence will
be through its own accomplishments evaluated by itself, through
its own instituted imaginary significations (Castoriadis, 2007: 49).

Castoriadis asserts that it is the *ekklēsia* (ἐκκλησία), the
democratic assembly ("people's assembly"), that "guarantees and
promotes the largest possible sphere of autonomous activity on
the part of individuals and of the groups these individuals form..."
(Castoriadis, 1997b: 411). Social autonomy as such implies
democracy, meaning that the people make the laws of society.
The democratic movement, he states, is this "movement of
explicit self-institution," i.e., autonomy (Castoriadis, 1997b: 275).[36]

---

[36] As periodic and transient realizations of social autonomy, in addition
to the ancient Greek *ekklēsia*, Castoriadis points to the town meetings
during the American Revolution, *sections* during the French Revolution
and the Paris Commune, and the workers' councils or *soviets* in their
original form—all of which have been repeatedly stressed by Hannah
Arendt herself (see Castoriadis, 1991: 107). We might mention that
Schürmann mentions these as well in his discussion of Arendt. To the list
Schürmann adds the attempted revival of the Paris Commune in May

But the tragic dimension of democracy is that there is no extra-social benchmark for laws. Democratic creation abolishes all transcendent sources of signification—there are no gods to turn to—at least in the public domain. Castoriadis thus contends that democracy entails we accept that we create meaning *without ground*, that we give form to chaos through our thoughts, actions, works, etc., and that this signification has *no guarantee* beyond itself (Castoriadis, 1997b: 343–344). Yet this "tragic dimension of democracy" is also "the dimension of radical freedom: democracy is the regime of *self-limitation*" (Castoriadis, 2007: 95). As in Schürmann, tragedy and freedom belong together. Revolutionary praxis begins by accepting being in its profound determinations—that is, indeterminate determinations—and as such, Castoriadis argues, it is "realistic" (Castoriaids, 1998: 113). Autonomy then is not a given but rather emerges as the creation of a project—of lucid self-institution in the face of contingency, chaos (Castoriadis, 1997b: 404). Such sobriety means humility and a weary eye that looks out for the totalitarian impulse.

To what extent then can we be deliberate, intentional, lucid, in instituting our own laws when the very source of our creativity, our *vis formandi*, as *chaos* is never completely rationalizable or determinable? If significations and their institutions are imaginary creations of the instituting imaginary whose creativity is a *vis formandi ex nihilo* or out of chaos, a creativity irreducible to reason or determinable causes, we cannot exhaustively comprehend that creative process. In what sense can we be autonomous then in our self-institution? To what degree is the *nihil* of the *ex nihilo* one's *own* (*auto*) and not an *other* (*hetero*), constitutive of one's autonomy and not heteronomy? Castoriadis is aware of this issue. He suggests, for example, that the unconscious can never exhaustively be conquered, eliminated or absorbed, by consciousness (Castoriadis, 1997b: 379; 2007: 196). We can neither eliminate nor isolate the unconscious. He tells us that we can be free only by "establishing a reflective, deliberative subjectivity" in relation to the unconscious, whereby one knows, *as far as possible*, what goes on in it (Castoriadis, 2007: 196). The world as well, "with its chaotic, forever unmasterable dimension" is also something that we will never master (Castoriadis, 2007: 149). What Castoriadis means by autonomy then cannot be a

---

1968, the German *Räte* (councils) at the end of the First World War, and the latter's momentary revival in Budapest of 1956—all as exemplifying the absence of governance, anarchy (see Schürmann, 1989: 4). Can we add to this list the Occupy Wall Street movement of 2011?

completely rational endeavor, for it remains inextricably intertwined with the imagination in its creativity that springs *ex
nihilo*, from the unintelligible and unpredictable chaos within and
without. The lucidity of a creativity that is autonomous would
have to be the sort that is not necessarily explicable in terms of
rationality.[37] Castoriadis' reverses Freud's psychoanalytic maxim,
"Where id was . . . ego shall come to be" (*Wo Es war, soll Ich
werden*)[38] with: "Where the ego is, id must spring forth" (*Wo Ich
bin, soll Es auftauchen*) (Castoriadis, 1998: 104). He explains that
desires, drives, etc.—namely, the irrational elements that are not
always intelligible or determinable—are also a part of one's self
that need to be brought to expression. Autonomy does not mean
clarification without remainder nor the total elimination of the
unconscious (the discourse of the other). He tells us that it is the
establishment of a different kind of relationship to alterity, *within
and without*—an elaboration rather than its elimination (Castoriadis, 1997b: 180, 182; 1998: 104, 107). An autonomous discourse
then would be one that "by making clear both the origin and the
sense of this discourse, has negated it or affirmed it in awareness
of the state of affairs, by referring its sense to that which is
constituted as the subject's own truth" (Castoriadis, 1998: 103).[39]
Perhaps autonomy then requires a sense of authenticity, or
coming to terms, in regard to the source of one's situation—
opening rather than closing one's eyes to it. Only by accepting
mortality and finitude—chaos, including the uncon-scious—can
we start to live as autonomous beings and does an autonomous
society become possible (Castoriadis, 1997b: 316).

Autonomy as such designates for Castoriadis a new *eidos*, a
new form of life, which involves "unlimited self-questioning
about the law and its foundations as well as the capacity, in light
of this interrogation, *to make, to do*, and *to institute*" in an endless

---

[37] Would artistic creation provide a model for this sort of creativity,
where one acknowledges the power of that creative indeterminacy
sounding from an abyss?

[38] This is at the end of the thirty-first lecture, "The Dissection of the
Psychical Personality," in Sigmund Freud, *The Complete Introductory
Lectures on Psychoanalysis*, trans. James Strachey (New York: W.W.
Norton, 1966), 544.

[39] Nevertheless there is here a complex set of issues concerning self and
other, consciousness and the unconscious, rational and irrational, the
nature of their distinctions and relations, the nature of reason, the nature
of the self, the degree to which reason is the self or not, the degree to
which the irrational is the self or not, and what all of this means in terms
of autonomy vs. heteronomy.

process (Castoriadis, 1991: 164). Its requirement is that we learn to accept the limit to rationality and intelligibility and the fact that there is no supra-collective guarantee of meaning other than that created in and through the social context and its history, or the socio-historical. Once it is recognized that there is no extra-social standard or ground given once-and-for-all, not only the forms of social institution but their possible ground can be put into question *again and again*. And in this process of creating the good under "imperfectly known and uncertain conditions" (Castoriadis, 1997b: 400) self-institution is made more or less explicit, whereby we are responsible for our creations so that we cannot blame evil, for example, on Satan or on the original sin of the first man. As an ongoing open-ended project this means that "explicit and lucid self-institution could never be total and has no need to be" (Castoriadis, 1997b: 410). Autonomy is not the utopia of a completed, perfect, society. We cannot rid ourselves of the risks of collective *hubris*, folly, or suicide, nor the element of arbitrariness (Castoriadis, 1991: 106, 115; 1997b: 275, 282). The project of autonomy requires the recognition of contingency, ambivalence and uncertainty.

With this recognition, we are to look out for the hubristic drive. Can autonomy then be *willed* without hubristic self-delusion? Castoriadis states that the "will is the conscious dimension of what we are as beings defined by radical imagination, that is, . . . as potentially creative beings" (Castoriadis, 2007: 117). The suggestion is that willing is positing, creating. Should autonomy then be *willed*? If the source of creativity is not completely rational, hence not masterable, how are we to avoid the will's degeneration into a totalitarian drive that would institute heteronomy? The prevention of totalizing hubris seems to call for humility vis-à-vis finitude. One wonders then whether the Schürmannian attitude of *letting* vis-à-vis freedom might be the more appropriate mode of existential comportment than *willing* freedom? Castoriadis tells us that autonomy is really an ontological *opening* that goes beyond the "informational, cognitive, and organizational closure characteristic of self-constituting, but *heteronomous*, beings." To go beyond this closure means altering the existing system and constituting a new world and a new self according to new laws, the creation of a new *eidos* (Castoriadis, 1997b: 310). If willing as positing tends to closure, one might add that such opening then requires a *letting*, a letting-be of the manifold and mutability, opening a space for alterity and alteration.

WILLING OR LETTING: AUTONOMY AND RELEASEMENT AS OPENING

Both Schürmann and Castoriadis set their respective ontological
inquiries with a deconstructive critique of traditional metaphysical assumptions—assumptions of an absolute ground or
foundation of meaning and norms. The toppling of grounds
however, in both cases, is paradoxically freeing. It frees a space
for a new mode of being. In both the manifesting of an ontological indeterminacy is intrinsic to their political projects that
aim to undo obtrusive paradigms and structures and opens the
possibility of overcoming their historically perpetrated organizational schemes. For Schürmann ontological anarchy is the
source of man's tragic condition, and yet tragic sobriety vis-à-vis
this condition signals *release* from epochal constraints in anarchic
praxis. For Castoriadis, the recognition of chaos or the magmatic
flow behind the instituted order of the world as the source of
creativity makes possible an autonomous as opposed to a heteronomous mode of institution. Anarchy in Schürmann accounts for
the singularity of events in history that escape epochally established intelligibility; and chaos in Castoriadis accounts for novelty
in history that can neither be predetermined nor predicted. Both
then recognize in history an indeterminacy—anarchy, chaos—that
refuses reduction to, or subsumption under, grounds or reasons
or causes that ultimately are human-made intelligibles contingent
to that very process of history. Both thinkers thus call for an
authenticity vis-à-vis groundlessness and finitude in human
existence, including knowing and doing, due the fact that we are
imbedded within the unfolding play of historicity, time. And to
recognize and accept this fact in present times when epochal
principles have exhausted themselves, for Schürmann, opens up
the possibility of anarchic praxis as a life of releasement, "life
without why." In Castoriadis' case, the lucid awareness of the
contingency of heteronomous institutions that restrict our freedom, opens the possibility of the praxis of autonomy as a political
project. Castoriadis' project of autonomy by comparison with
Schürmann's anarchic praxis is explicitly and unabashedly
political. But even Castoriadian praxis is predicated upon the
recognition and acceptance of—or in Heideggerian terms authenticity in comportment towards—finitude vis-à-vis an ontological
excess irreducible to human rationality or institutions.

In Schürmann's case, however, such authenticity that is freeing is predicated upon the existential comportment of *letting*. It is
the relinquishing of voluntarism with its hubristic positing of

norms that accompanies the displacement of metaphysics and an opening to being in its singularity, multiplicity, and mutability. Freedom in the sense of Schürmannian anarchy then is not the freedom of the will, but the freedom of, or in, releasement. The suggestion here is that the activity of the will posits and reifies and thus tends toward metaphysical paradigms. From Schürmann's perspective, "if positing is no longer the paradigmatic process of ontology, there are neither speculative positions . . . for thinking to hold nor any political positions that may ensue" (Schürmann, 1979: 113–114). In that case *to will* freedom may undo its own project.

Can we reinterpret Castoriadian autonomy as a creative act of its *own nomos for itself—auto-nomos—*in light of anarchic praxis, and in terms of releasement, in its refusal to posit—*will*—a heteronomous *nomos* or *arché* to legitimate its origin? The imagination, just as it escapes reduction to reason, cannot be reduced to volition. The *vis formandi* behind the imagination's formation of the world and its institution of meaning exceeds the rational and the volitional. If willing means constructing heteronomous grounds for legitimation, autonomy vis-à-vis that free creativity, one might argue, entails released action, an atelic or ateleological praxis that is the spontaneity of play. I refer to the example popular among some anarchists of the dinner party[40] wherein norms spring spontaneously and immanently without reference to any transcendent and legitimating *nomoi* or *archai* or *teloi* or principles. Instead of willing the fun, it is *allowed* to happen. In enjoyment of its own being, the party as play simply *is* without why. And in opening the space for manifold and mutability, alterity and alteration, the play—one might say—is interplay. Furthermore the potential scope of that opening of/for interplay today is global.

VI. CONCLUSION: OPENING THE WORLD

The world continues to become complex as social imaginaries, or regions, each with its own "world," interact, collide, merge and intermix with one another. This is not irrelevant to our discussion of Schürmann and Castoriadis as the contemporary situation makes evident more than ever the contingency of—the chaos or anarchy behind—alleged absolutes previously taken to be universal and eternal. Under a globalized paradigm where consumption is the thin veneer of meaningfulness concealing its own empti-

---

[40] See note 25.

ness, the world globalized becomes one giant mall. Tragic
sobriety, on the other hand, that refuses to be enthused by its
jingles and ever new line of techno-gadgets for consumption, in
seeing its emptiness, might also see therein a freeing of space
with liberating potential.

Both Schürmann, inheriting Heideggerian terminology, and
Castoriadis himself repeatedly make use of the metaphor of
opening or openness. Both the praxis of autonomy and anarchic
praxis are *opening*. Taking their ontological premises, can we
conceive of that opening of anarchy and chaos, explicitly *spatially*, as the opening of the world? Schürmann for the most part
inherits Heidegger's focus on the event-character, *Ereignis*, of
ontological anarchy. But that verbal nature of be*ing*, even in
Heidegger, can also be found to be place-like, as in the spatial
motifs of clearing, open, region, etc., all of which have the sense
of a withdrawing that makes room.[41] Schürmann himself occasionally made use of spatial metaphors. For example, he makes
the point that when anarchy strikes the foundation stone of
action, "the principle of cohesion . . . is no longer anything more
than a blank space deprived of legislative, normative, power"
(Schürmann, 1990: 6–7). When freed from the constraint of
principles and posits, beyond the horizon of our willing projections, phenomena appear under the mode of letting, as released
within an *open expanse*, whereby they show themselves to be
"emerging mutably into their . . . mutable 'world'" (Schürmann,
1990: 280). He describes this freeing as a *translocation* "from a
place where entities stand constrained under an epochal principle
to one where they are restored to radical contingency" (Schürmann, 1990: 280). May we understand that *blank space* that is the
location of radical contingency as an opening for difference,
plurality, co-being without the hegemony of a normative or
normalizing oneness? Schürmann characterizes that open clearing or region as a "field of phenomenal interdependence" (Schürmann, 1990: 278).[42] The abyss is a gaping chasm that engulfs,
enfolds, and unfolds interdependent fields of interdependence.

---

[41] See my articles on this topic: "The Originary *Wherein*: Heidegger and
Nishida on 'the Sacred' and 'the Religious,'" *Research in Phenomenology*,
40.3 (2010), 378–407; and "Spatiality in the Later Heidegger: Turning—
Clearing—Letting," *Existentia: An International Journal of Philosophy*,
XVI.5–6 (2006): 425–404.

[42] This association of interdependence or interconnection, place or field,
being/nothingness, and mutability that we find throughout Schürmann's
works also occurs in East Asian Mahāyāna Buddhism. There was a

We already discussed Castoriadis' reference to Hesiod's *chaos* (χάος), but we ought to underscore here its spatial significance. For *chaos*, which in Hesiod means "chasm," derives from the verb *chainō* (χαίνω) for *opening*, with the root *cha-* (χα-) implying "yawning," "gaping," "opening," "hollow."[43] In Hesiod, the earth and the heavens emerge from out of the dark emptiness that is *chaos*, to in turn engender the *cosmos* of divine beings (Castoriadis, 2007: 239).[44] Although Castoriadis himself does not pursue the implied connection between primal spacing and primal undifferentiatedness even when he discusses *chōra*, we might pursue a reading of Castoriadian *chaos* from out of which the world of imaginary significations is articulated or defined in the spatial direction as that *wherein* the world is established. Everything happens in relation to everything else, near and far, in its contextual implacement. Things are predicated upon the space wherein they belong, their concrete place—the world that gives them significance. But those environing or contextualizing conditions continually recede the further we inquire after them, without ever revealing any absolute *reason* for the way things *are*. The clearing continually recedes into the darkness of in-definition, to reveal *chaos* as the chasm wherein *archai* and *nomoi* are established and toppled. The world in its naked immanence, with nothing beyond, no heteronomous model or extrinsic principle or end, we might say, is this origin as chaos from out of which being and meaning arises.

---

period in Schürmann's younger years, as a student studying in France, when he avidly practiced Zen meditation under Sōtō Zen Buddhist master Deshimaru Taisen. Schürmann discusses his Zen experience in Reiner Schürmann, "The Loss of the Origin in Soto Zen and Meister Eckhart," *The Thomist* 42.2 (1978): 281–312.

[43] See Max Jammer, *Concepts of Space* (Cambridge, MA: Harvard University Press, 1970), 9, and F.M. Cornford, *Principium Sapientiae* (New York: Harper & Row, 1965), 194n1. Also see Edward Casey, *Fate of Place* (Berkeley: University of California Press, 1997), 345n13.

[44] And see Hesiod, 6–7, and also see the translator's note, 64n116. One might mention here that *chaos* is also etymologically related to *chōra* that appears in Plato's *Timaeus* and which has similar connotations of a primal space that is indeterminate. It is interesting as well to notice similar connections made in East Asian thought between formlessness and space—e.g., in the Chinese word *kong* and the Japanese *kū* (空) which literally means sky or space but in the Mahāyāna Buddhist context means emptiness or non-substantiality; and the word *wu* (Jp. *mu*) (無) which means chaos as well as nothingness. In Chan (Jp. Zen) thought *kong* (*kū*) and *wu* (*mu*) become used interchangeably.

Similar to how the viability of metaphysical principles have become questionable with the revelation of their historical contingency, so also has globalization unveiled the spatial or regional contingency of socially instituted worlds. Despite the global expansion of techno-capitalism and the universalizing claims of the global mall, an alternative space is opened up in what Jean-Luc Nancy has called mondialization.[45] Along with the temporal difference between epochal constellations that Schürmann pointed to, we are in a position to attend to the spatial difference between "worlds" now placed in tense and dynamic proximity, juxtaposition, and overlap making explicit their co-relative contingency.[46]

Being in its origin in Schürmann's terms is anarchy that refuses legitimation or ground, and in Castoriadis's terms chaos behind the congealing of magmatic flow into institutions—in both, the indetermination accompanying determination. If that anarchy be conceived spatially as the *différend* revealed in global encounters of regions of normativity or social imaginaries, exceeding each imaginary as their empty clearing and toppling heteronomous or transcendent claims to legitimacy to reveal an abyss; *and* if that chaos is indeed the yawning or opening chasm of that abyss as its etymology suggests, we then have an abysmal space opened on a global scale that is a space of difference—presupposed by epochs and regions and socially instituted worlds —a space we *already* share with others and are called to acknowledge. Therein multiplicities abound. Such a space of difference is one of co-being, by necessity. To open ourselves to this clearing upon the earth is an opening to co-difference—temporally and spatially, alteration and alterity, mutability and manifold. Autonomy and liberation necessitates an appropriation or cultivation of this space—as the place of our co-being in difference—into an an-archic and autonomous *polis*, a site that is "the political," "the public conjunction of things, actions, speech" (Schürmann, 1990: 40), but where dissent may also be voiced and heard—as Abensour states, a place of *situating* "things, actions,

---

[45] See Jean-Luc Nancy, *The Creation of the World or Globalization*, trans. François Raffoul and David Pettigrew (Albany: SUNY Press, 2007).

[46] In fact Schürmann himself does occasionally speak of "region" or "regional" alongside "epoch" or "epochal" (e.g., Schürmann, 2010: 247) as if to acknowledge that in addition to epochal diachrony there is the spatial *différend* between synchronic regions or what I am here calling socially instituted "worlds."

and speech," rather than founding them.[47] Autonomy here might then also be construed in terms of the autonomy of the world itself reciprocally and co-constituted with its singular members as the empty space of their dwelling, the clearing they share as the world, the place of their co-existence or co-being and co-relations that give space to their mutual difference, and in opposition to the positing of any transcendent law (heteronomy) that would level them under its hegemony. We would need to heed the multiplicity of voices that sound within that space, and to refuse or resist closing it up. This necessitates an ongoing protest against hegemonizing and totalizing tendencies. The appropriate response to this anarchic world-space or world chaos would be to let it be *autonomous* rather than subjecting it to legitimating or grounding norms or principles. This seems to be the ethical implication of both Schürmannian anarchy and Castoriadian autonomy as praxis requiring artful navigation. In short we find two points of convergence between Schürmann and Castoriadis through: 1) a reinterpretation of autonomy as anarchic and ateleological play; and 2) a reinterpretation of both anarchy and chaos as entailing a space or openness for difference—alterity and alteration—in interplay.

APPENDIX: ANONTOLOGICAL SPACE

Before closing I would like to respond briefly to the issue of idealism vs. materialism concerning anarchism (as found originnally in the contention between Max Stirner and Karl Marx). The issue would be beside the point for both Schürmann's ontological anarchism and Castoriadis' chaos-ontology in the sense that such dichotomies are themselves products of epochs and institutions. Furthermore it is not only the question of whether being is mind or matter that is epochal and instituted but the more fundamental distinction of being and non-being itself that issues from the epoch or the institution. In deciding that being is mind rather than matter, one is determining what is being vis-à-vis non-being. In that sense ontological anarchy or chaos as prior to that distinction is truly a *triton genos*, an "it" that gives (as in the German *es gibt*) but tolerates no name, escaping not only the designations of mind and matter, ideal and material, but also being and non-being. Corresponding to neither term of opposites, it instead provides the clearing for such dichotomies and oppositions. Schürmann, taking off from Heideggerian premises, states

---

that being conceived in terms of beings can never be encountered among them and in that sense is *nothing* (Schürmann, 2001: 197). In recognizing the limits of language (and conceptual thought), Heidegger was often unsure about the very term "being" (*Sein*)[48] and, according to Schürmann, could no longer even hear the word "being" towards the end of his life (Schürmann, 1990: 3).[49] Heidegger struggles throughout his career to make this point: *being is no thing*, it has no opposite that can stand-opposed to it. As such, it surpasses even the being/non-being distinction that pertains properly to entities (beings). What escapes the duality then is a *nothing*. This is not the opposite of being but rather an excess preceding the very distinction between being and its negation. And if Schürmann's anarchy is *the nothing* from which principles emerge, Castoriadis' chaos is the *nihil* of what he calls *creatio ex nihilo*, the Hesiodian chaos as the void or empty opening (*chainō*) from which institutions of significations emerge. Schürmann at one point characterizes this originary nothingness of *an-arché* as *ontological* (Schürmann, 1990: 141). But if both principles or *archai* in Schürmann and imaginary institutions in Castoriadis govern the distinction between what is and what is not, being and non-being, along with the distinction between *nomos* and *anomy*, sense and nonsense, meaning and a-meaning, the source of their emergence and the space of their distinction can neither be said to be *ontological* nor *meontological*. Taking a clue from Heidegger's reluctance concerning the word "being" (*Sein*) and Schürmann's own warnings about stopping at a *merely ontological* (i.e., nominalized, hypostatized) notion of anarchy, we would have to take the anarchy that precedes *on* and *mēon*—being and non-being—as thus *neither* ontological *nor* meontological. Hence we might call it *anontological*. *An-on* here designates *an-arché* or *chaos* as prior to, and irreducible to, principles and institutions, *nomoi* and *archai*, including those that rule the very logic of opposition—e.g., between being and non-being, affirmation and negation, etc.

For Schürmann, the *nothing* in Heidegger *also* refers to the very absencing-*spacing* of the field that permits the presencing of

---

[48] In the 1930s he tried using the eighteenth-century spelling *Seyn*—which has been rendered into English variously as "be-ing," "beyng," and "beon" among others—to connote a different sense than the metaphysical sense of a supreme being. He also experiments by writing "being" with a cross over it.

[49] Instead he preferred "to speak of 'presencing' [*Anwesen*], of 'world' [*Welt*], or of 'event' [*Ereignis*]" (Schürmann, 1990: 3).

beings, a clearing, whereby *alētheia* "appears as the 'free space of the open'" (Schürmann, 1990: 173)—"the open" (*Offen*) that opens up to release being/s. Beyond the horizon of our willing projections, things are released or let-be in the open expanse, freed from the constraint of principles and posits, restored to their radical contingency. Therein they show themselves to be "emerging mutably into their . . . mutable 'world'" (Schürmann, 1990: 280). It is the space or opening that "grants being and thinking [and] their presencing to and for each other."[50] We might then say that the anarchy or chaos is the gaping abyss that spatially engulfs, enfolds and unfolds—clears the space for—presencing-absencing, coming-going, generation-extinction, *genesis-pthora*, birth-death, *Angang-Abgang, alētheia-lēthē, on-mēon*. Anarchy / chaos as such is the *anontological space* bearing the distinction between what is and is not because it bears the principles and institutions of thought and being, whereby we adjudicate or declare what is and what is not, what is meaningful and what is meaningless. That anontological space, as the clearing for such opposites, would be what makes the controversy between idealism and materialism even thinkable.[51]

John W.M. Krummel received his Ph.D. in Philosophy from the New School for Social Research in 1999 and his Ph.D. in Religion from Temple University in 2008. He studied under Reiner Schürmann from 1990 to 1993 prior to Schürmann's passing, and earned his MA in Philosophy under his guidance. His dissertation at The New School was on Heidegger and Kant. And his dissertation at Temple University was on the dialectic of Nishida. His writings on various topics (many on Heidegger, Nishida, Schürmann, and Buddhist philosophy but also on other topics) have been, or will be, published in *Auslegung, PoMo Magazine, Dao, International Philosophical Quarterly, Existentia, Philosophy Today, Vera Lex, Journal of Chinese Philosophy, Research in Phenomenology, Philosophy East and West, H-Net*, and *Diaphany*, as well as in several books as chapters. He is the co-translator of,

---

[50] Martin Heidegger, *Zur Sache des Denkens* (Tübingen: Max Niemeyer, 1988), 75; *On Time and Being*, trans. Joan Stambaugh (New York: Harper & Row, 1972), 68.
[51] For a more detailed reading of ontological anarchy in Schürmann as anontological nothing, see my "Being and Nothing: Towards an Anontology of Anarchy" in Vishwa Adluri and Alberto Martinengo, ed., *Hegemony and Singularity: The Philosophy of Reiner Schürmann* (Evanston: Northwestern University Press, forthcoming).

and author of the introduction for, *Place and Dialectic: Two Essays by Nishida Kitarō* (New York: Oxford University Press, 2011). His scholarly interests include continental philosophy, phenomenology, Heidegger, Schürmann, Kant, Nietzsche, Buddhism, Dōgen, Kūkai, Japanese and Kyoto school philosophy, Nishida, Nishitani, Dostoevsky, Mishima, comparative philosophy/ religion, nihilism, the social imaginary, the philosophy of religion, anarchism, and mysticism, among others. He was born and raised in Tokyo, Japan in a bilingual family. He is currently an Assistant Professor in the Department of Religious Studies at Hobart and William Smith Colleges in Geneva, New York and is also the Assistant Editor of *The Journal of Japanese Philosophy*, published by SUNY Press.

REFERENCES

Castoriadis, Cornelius (1991). *Philosophy, Politics, Autonomy: Essays in Political Philosophy* (Curtis, David Ames, ed.). New York: Oxford University Press.

Castoriadis, Cornelius (1997a). *World in Fragments: Writings on Politics, Society, Psychoanalysis, and the Imagination* (Curtis, David Ames, ed.). Stanford: Stanford University Press.

Castoriadis, Cornelius (1997b). *The Castoriadis Reader* (Curtis, David Ames, ed. & trans.). Oxford: Blackwell.

Castoriadis, Cornelius (1998). *The Imaginary Institution of Society* (Blamey, Kathleen, trans.). Cambridge: MIT Press.

Castoriadis, Cornelius (2007). *Figures of the Thinkable* (Arnold, Helen, trans.). Stanford: Stanford University Press.

Schürmann, Reiner (1978a). "Political Thinking in Heidegger," *Social Research: An International Quarterly of the Social Sciences* 45.1 (Spring): 191–221.

Schürmann, Reiner (1978b). "Questioning the Foundations of Practical Philosophy," *Human Studies: A Journal for Philosophy and the Social Sciences* 1.4: 357–368.

Schürmann, Reiner (1979). "The Ontological Difference in Practical Philosophy," *Philosophy and Phenomenological Research* 40.1 (September): 99–122.

Schürmann, Reiner (1984). "Legislation-Transgression: Strategies and Counter-strategies in the Transcendental Justification of Norms," *Man and World* 17: 361–398.

Schürmann, Reiner (1986). "On Constituting Oneself an Anarchistic Subject," *Praxis International* 6.3: 294–310.

Schürmann, Reiner (1989). "Introduction: On Judging and its Issues." In *The Public Realm: Essays on Discursive Types in Political Philosophy*, ed. Reiner Schürmann, 1–20. New York: SUNY Press.

Schürmann, Reiner (1990). *Heidegger on Being and Acting: From Principles to Anarchy.* Bloomington: Indiana University Press, 1987.

Schürmann, Reiner (2001). *Wandering Joy: Meister Eckhart's Mystical Philosophy.* Great Barrington: Lidisfarne Books, 1978.

Schürmann, Reiner (2003). *Broken Hegemonies.* Bloomington: Indiana University Press.

Schürmann, Reiner (2010). "Principles Precarious: On the Origin of the Political in Heidegger." In *Heidegger: The Man and the Thinker,* ed. Thomas Sheehan, 245–256. New Brunswick: Transaction Publishers.

Anarchist Developments in Cultural Studies
ISSN: 1923-5615
2013.2: Ontological Anarché: Beyond Materialism and Idealism

Polemos Doesn't Stop Anywhere Short of the World
On Anarcheology, Ontology, and Politics[1]

Hilan Bensusan

ABSTRACT

Current widespread renewal of interest in ontology—especially in the so-called Speculative Turn—has raised questions concerning the place of the political in the world. This work examines the connections between ontology and politics reintroducing the Heraclitean notion of the *polemos*. I start out looking at how a bedrock view of ontology has been prevalent and yet flawed. Then I introduce an alternative view of ontology and consider it under the lights shed by current tendencies in speculative realism. Finally I present some recent anarcheological work on Heraclitus that reintroduces the idea of the *polemos* in the debate.

KEYWORDS:
Polemos, anarcheology, ontology and politics, speculation

> *it depends whether our passions reach fever heat and influence our whole life or not. No one knows to what he may be driven by circumstances, pity, or indignation; he does not know the degree of his own inflammability*
>
> Nietzsche (2008)

---

[1] An earlier version of this essay was presented in Ontology and Politics Workshop at Mancept, University of Manchester, in early September of 2011. Part of the inspiration for some of its ideas came from the English riots of August, where fire was always present. The riots showed that politics deals in the inflammable material to be found everywhere. I would like to thank Simon Choat, Paul Rekret, the organizers, and everyone in the workshop for a fruitful discussion. I would also like to thank the ANARCHAI research group at the University of Brasilia for many invaluable insights.

The impact of ontology on politics is itself political. Ontology has been regarded as a measure of fixity surrounding the movement of politics. Often, ontology is thought in connection to the unchangeable and, as such, it provides a frame for any political endeavor. It is thought as the realm of underlying stability, of what exists by subsisting and, often, of the natural. Existence is therefore normally thought in terms of what persists or resists, what underlies all predication. The ontological is related to the substrata, to what ultimately lies underneath, the *hypokeimenon*. As such, ontology is thought as a domain of *archés*. When presented as such, ontology introduces order into politics by encircling it with something beyond any politics. An attitude of avoiding *archés* could then translate into a single-handed rejection of all ontological claims. This essay, in line with the contemporary resurgence of attention to ontology, reclaims the notion of *polemos* as a starting point for an ontology without *archés* and paving the ways for an an-*arché*-ist ontology.

It is often maintained that ontological questions are questions about grounds. Ontology has presented itself as first philosophy, as the realm of basic assumptions, and as stage setting for science, politics and to anything polemic. Ontology, according to this view, is the basis. It is associated to what is naturally so, to what persists *per se*, to what is not up for grabs. As such, it is presented as bedrock. Bedrock is not merely what grounds something else, but also something under which no further excavation is possible—no further archeology, no further search for *archés*, can take place. We could be wrong about what is the ultimate ground—ontological claims are revisable—but if we're not, they carry a sort of necessity in the sense that they go unaffected by anything else they allegedly ground. They are therefore immune to politics (and to anything else non-ontological, for that matter). Ontology is viewed as an enclosed domain and, as such, as unreachable by any political move.

This conception of ontology hasn't, however, gone unchallenged. Since before Aristotle took metaphysical claims to be about *arches aition* (the first causes or the ultimately governing principles)[2], philosophers have presented different images of the nature of claims about what there is. In fact, Aristotle defended the idea that to exist is to be substantial—what primarily exists are substances[3]—against a background of claims about what

---

[2] See, for example, Aristotle, *Metaphysics* (1924/1953), Alpha, 3.
[3] See, for example, Aristotle, *Metaphysics* (1924/1953), Lambda 6, 1071b.5, where he says: *ousiai protai ton onton*. This conception of existence as

flows, what changes and what persists from the philosophers of his time.[4] Other philosophers such as Hume, Nietzsche, Whitehead, and Deleuze have since put the association of metaphysics with what is impervious to other influences into question.[5] Their attempts have been to understand ontology not as an archeology and, as such, not as preceding or grounding politics. Criticism of metaphysics—and of the possibility of ontological claims—has also been fuelled by suspicions of this view of them as bedrock. This anti-foundational inspiration claims that if it is inextricably connected to *archés*, ontology should be exorcized.

My strategy, as it will become clearer in the next section, is to rather rethink the connection between *archés* and the political. Recent developments that place ontology and metaphysics again in central stage invite these attempts to reconsider their connection to anything political. An *ontological turn* (in the phrase of Heil & Martin [1999]) has been joined by a *speculative turn* (see Bryant, Srnicek, and Harman [2011]) where questions concerning what exists and how they exist are reclaimed as crucial to a philosophical endeavor. Many reasons can be presented for this current renaissance—including post-humanist takes on politics (see, for example, Serres [1990], Bryant [2011]), exhaustion with the linguistic turn and its variations (see, for example, Heil & Martin [1999], Williamson [2004], Harman [2009]), enthusiasm for modalities—typically through the work of Kripke (1972) and Lewis

---

(primarily) substantial, was influential in the way, for instance, realist debates were framed. An interesting alternative to the substantiality of reality can be found in Souriau's conception of different modes of existence (2009). It is however not straightforward to fully debunk this Aristotelian connection between subsistence and existence—or between reality and resistance. Latour, as influenced by Souriau as he is, writes in *Irréductions* (1984), 1.1.5: *Est reel ce qui résiste dans l'épreuves* ("It is real what resist the tests"). Latour, of course, doesn't commit to any fixed substance but he still thinks of the real as what resists.

[4] In particular, Empedocles and Heraclitus have hinted towards no privilege of the stable over the unstable. They seemed to have favored the idea that things are in interaction and there are no furniture of the universe unless its pieces all move on wheels.

[5] Hume, read as contemporary metaphysicians have done—Ellis (2002) or Mumford (2004), for instance, read him as defending the distinctness of all things unconnected by any modal tie, but also Harman 2009 who reads him as a sort of occasionalist -, Nietzsche as portrayed by Haar (1993) where metaphysics is not rejected but deemed at odds with any discourse as discourse presupposes the grammar of predication and Whitehead (1929) and Deleuze (1968) as defenders of the irreducible character of processes.

(1986)—and failures to demarcate metaphysics out of science and philosophy (see DeLanda [2002], Ellis [2002], Brassier [2007] or Protevi [2013]). Ontological concerns have been increasingly present in social science (see Latour, [2012], Viveiros de Castro, (2009)), in feminism (Alaimo & Hekman, [2008]), in sexuality studies (see, for example, Parisi [2004], Ahmed [2006]) and in cultural studies in general (see, for example, Shaviro [2009] and Bogost [2012]). The renewed interest in metaphysics, however, often seems to come with some distancing of political issues that could be a symptom that the bedrock view is tacitly accepted. It is my contention in this essay that this renewal of interest in metaphysics brings about interesting elements to rethink this view. In particular, it opens opportunities to readdress the issue of governing *archés*. I have recently explored the strategy of an *anarcheology*—as the study of the ungrounded, of the inauthentic and of the ungoverned simultaneously (see Bensusan et al. (2012)). In this essay I directly present an alternative view of how ontology relates to politics. They relate in a political way, but their connection is not drawn by *archés* of any sort.

It is important to distinguish grounds—and bedrock—from floors. Recent developments in geophilosophy (Negarestani, [2008], Woodard, [2012, 2013]) have attempted to replace the image of ground with a more geologically informed conception of interdependent strata. Hamilton Grant (2006) has developed a geology-oriented account of dependency, conditionality, and sufficient reason. A sufficient reason for something can only be conceived, in his account, by thinking within nature and the multiple layers left by past events. There is no ultimate ground but ontology is to be conceived as a many-speed process of grounding and ungrounding. Instead of ground, the geophilosophical emphasis is on floor—both constituted and supporting what takes place on it. A ground, but not a floor, is unaffected by what stands on it. But if ontology is a floor, politics can reshape it. If it is a ground, it is oblivious to anything political. The view I propose here is an alternative to bedrock ontology where grounds are the main characters. It does not, however, undermine geophilosophy. In fact, anarcheology and geophilosophy can join forces to free politics (and ontology) from any *arché*.

Ontology, Hauntology, and Bedrocks

This is the common image concerning ontology and politics: ontology grounds, politics comes later. Politics is what is up for

grabs, what can be affected by alliances, negotiations, governments, resistance movements, change of rule, revolutions and the
balance of forces. Where politics ends, we find a *bedrock*, something that is often predicated as natural, as beyond all political
swing. This is where ontology is. A *bedrock* that is never at
stake—it is simply present. A bedrock is immune to political fire.
The *bedrock view* is not about rolling stones but rather about fixed
rocks—those that can ground. It holds that any ontology is to
underlie all politics.

Now adopting the bedrock view is clearly a political stance.
To be sure, it depends on an architectural decision: here lies ontology; there lies whatever comes on top of it. This architectural
plan provides a landscape for orientation and as such it guides
political decisions. The bedrock view has ontology as something
that grounds, that is stable and fixed once and for all. It defers to
ontology what is deemed unchangeable for it is the domain of
what is structural, or of what is internally related to reality. Ontology could be no more than the rules of the game of reality—
and, surely, the Ur-rules for all the political games. If we adopt
such a position, we are left with two options: either there is
something like an ontology that precedes all politics or there is
no ontology at all.

The first option entails that politics has an outer boundary—
the border where things are already determined, where there is a
ready-made order or a set of rules for all games. This grounding
ontological bedrock can be solid and dense or made of quicksand
like some general logical principles (say, that the world satisfies
classical logic), but it is a realm of its own, under no jurisdiction
of any political agent and subject to its own laws. It means that
ontology is safe from any political fire—that it is made of non-
inflammable things. A law-like realm of nature, stable and structural, is a common candidate to give flesh to the idea of *a bedrock
ontology*. It is an example of a domain that is beyond any political
incendiary. Bedrock ontology can be an attractive idea for those
who want an end to political dispute—even if it is to be found
deep down inside a neutrino.

The second option provided no such closure for politics—it is
all-pervasive. However, it allows for the ghost of a bedrock to
haunt politics—there is a lack of ontology. This lack is the lack of
bedrock—no fire can replace the solid, well-shaped, enduring and
clear-edged stone. In this case we are left with a void of ontology,
a hauntology, to borrow a word from Derrida, where nothing can
be said about what there is because to be is still understood as to

be bedrock. Often, such *a bedrock hauntology* ends up placing politics in people's head and makes most of it depend on human election. Bedrock hauntology refrains from any ontological claims because they could not be anything but something fixed, stable and immune to the influence of anything else. It is therefore impossible to say anything about what there is, as nothing political can really look like bedrock. It is then interesting to consider variations of the move to make politics precede ontology. At least in the context of bedrock hauntology, the move would make it impossible to consider what ontology could follow from politics—as ontology is attached like Sisyphus to a rock.

If the bedrock view is abandoned, the bedrock dilemma—bedrock ontology versus bedrock hauntology—fades away. The common assumption behind both horns of the dilemma is that ontology is some sort of ground, immune to anything else and, in particular, alien to all political dispute. Ontology, if there is any, is bedrock underneath anything political. If this assumption is put aside, ontology needs no longer to be placed as something stable under the political busts; the quest for what exists is placed rather amid political endeavors and not grounding their feet. A different view would then reject the idea of a ground and therefore the friction between politics and ontology would no longer be a matter of priorities. A first possible alternative image is to take ontology and politics to be the same. If this is so, they can either have merely an identity of processes and mechanisms or also an identity of scope. So, for instance, when we talk about a politics of nature—or a natural contract (Serres [1990]), or democracy of objects (Bryant [2011])—we can understand it as describing a natural ontology or we can take it as being both ontology and politics. If we take them to have different scopes, the bedrock image can still find itself vindicated: the politics of nature could be taken as a ground for all other politics.

Instead of a view of ontology and politics being the same, I would like to propose and explore one where they interconnect heavily while nevertheless remaining distinct. The image is that of fire where the difference between what is in flames and what is inflammable is not a matter of substance but rather a matter of *position*. It is the position of the wood that determines where the flames will catch. Inflammability is everywhere but it cannot be measured independently of the relevant circumstances. Politics and ontology intertwine like fire and inflammability. This can seem like the interaction between activity and potentiality (or effects and tendencies, or dispositions and qualities, or execution and capacity). In fact, the interactions between *energeia* and *dunamus* are akin to the movements of fire: it ignites the inflammable while also affecting the inflammability of things. Ontology is about inflammability, and therefore nothing is safe from political fire. The inspiration can be found in Heraclitus' doctrine of the *polemos* (more below) and its connection with fire. Heraclitus has that "[f]ire in its advance will judge and convict all things" (see, for example, 2009, fr. 66). But fire mingles with spices, he adds, and takes the flavor of them. It is as if political fire can inflame anything; there are things that set the stage for the fire—but they are no less combustible material.

In the fire view, ontology and politics dwell rather in pyrotechnics. The friction between them is no longer a matter of grounding, not even of reversed grounding. But rather an issue of how the inflammable is ignited. It is also no longer a question of territories—whether politics has an outer boundary. It is not that ontology reigns over things (or objects, or events, or intensities) while politics rules elsewhere. There is a politics of things (and of objects, events, intensities). But also, there is ontology of these things too. They are combustible. Ontology and politics get mixed, as fire knows no borders, no scope separations. To be is to take a political stance—it has a measure of inflammability and therefore is political fuel. To be is to be up for political grabs. There is no room for ontology separated from the realm of politics and yet they are contingently distinct one from the other. Ontology is made of combustible materials. As a consequence, nothing is immune to politics and no political outcome ceases to be up for grabs.

When we consider fire—and not bedrock—we escape the issue of grounding. Also, we avoid the subsidiary issues of layers, realms, priorities, mon- or pan-*archy*. Fire spreads by catching from one thing to the next. It is about contact, not about established orders. The non-reckoned inflammability of things lie in their capacity for politics. No order is alien to its surroundings. So, no movement of the planets or constitution of the particles is tested once and for all. It depends on what comes along. And it would be no good to appeal to a general ontology that maps what is possible and what is not. Or rather to postulate all-encompassing laws ruling over what is possible. This would be again to crave for bedrock. Once ontology is placed within pyrology, there is no appeal to an ultimate layer. Unless this ultimate layer can itself be burned.

ONTOLOGY AND POLITICS MEET ON FIRE

In order to flesh out the fire view I will now draw on some ideas developed within the speculative turn. In general, these ideas tend to open spaces to the contingent in ontology. They see the world as made more of interactions and change and less of stability and fixed structures. One could see them as building on the idea of an ontology without much appeal to necessary connections (or necessary beings). They are anarcheological in the sense that they make room for the ungoverned. They can be placed in the fire view because they somewhat contrast with ontologies that appeal to grounds.

A first idea about how to understand the connection between ontology and politics in terms of fire comes from Process Philosophy. Whitehead's (1929) guiding metaphysical idea is that reality has few ready-made items and they recombine themselves in processes that sustain and are sustained. Much of what happens to the characters of the world—the actual entities that form its *dramatis personae*—depends on processes ignited by how things take on others. Souriau (2009) introduced the vocabulary of *instauration*: something exists if and only if it has been constantly brought about by something else. Existing things are in a network or a crossroad of sponsors. And whatever sponsors can also blow things up—supporting alliances can be unmade, standing lifelines could be disrupted, and current networks can be dismantled. Existence is not independent from whatever else exists. Everything is at risk when anything can affect the support of anything else: the existence of something depends on what else happens to exist. As with combustible materials, flames can come from anywhere. Souriau's conception of existence as *instauration* appeals to an act of sponsoring. There is no existence without a sponsor. Existence never stands alone. Therefore, existence is not independent of anything else. One way of understanding the lesson of process philosophy is to think that everything is a creation of something else—everything ends up being implicated on everything else. It is about an interrelatedness of all things, a holism with no sense of whole apart from that of an assemblage of things, of things contingently placed together. Everything is connected to everything through actual alliances and sponsoring networks—and nothing like internal, necessary relations.

Process philosophy makes the vocabulary of ontology very close to that of politics—the processes (negotiations, alliances, tests, etc.) are common to both. Ontology is somehow about the political transactions among whatever exists—not only human groups but living beings, objects, materials and forces. Latour (1984), drawing mainly on Souriau's conception of existence, puts forward an ontology of testing procedures. He starts out with a principle of *irreduction*—which he calls "a prince who doesn't govern"—stating that things *by themselves* are neither reducible nor irreducible to any other thing. For Latour, it follows that reality is what resists *testing* (or rather what has resisted so far). Reality doesn't get certificated. Further, nothing on its own resists the different test procedures—everything relies on supporting alliances. We rely on the matter of our body, we rely on our tools, they rely on energy transmission, and energy transmission relies on pressure and temperature. Importantly, it is a chain that knows no privileged *ex-nihilo* starting point. There is no reality beyond the processes of negotiation, of crafting alliances and of relying on support. There is no reality beyond what is combustible by the trails of fire—no reality is politics-proof.

The image of ontology promoted by process philosophy is one where there are no transcendent principles or forces (or laws or fixed ingredients) that shape reality. In other words, there is no ontological bedrock. Further, there is no bedrock hauntology as there is no lack of ontology—existence is immanent to what exists. This lack of transcendence is akin to many ways of thinking popular in the twentieth century—including those championed by Heidegger and Deleuze. In contrast with the first,[6] process philosophy promotes a robust ontology guided by the idea that all things are thrown in the world with no prior purpose or definite transcendent role—a generalized *Geworfenheit*. There is no transcendent element that guides, grounds or gives flesh to what there is. Similarly, there is nothing supporting politics like bedrock—ontology and politics are alike on-fire, the difference between them lying only in what is burnt now and what is inflammable. We can take politics to be the former and ontology to be the latter but there is no constitutional difference between them. Like fire, inflammability is to be tested by combustion (and the power of protective alliances). The difference in inflammability, in any occasion, is what guides the flames.

A second idea to flesh out the fire image comes from geophilosophy, tectonics, and a conception of materialism according to which matter is a vibrant repository of potentialities with a histo-

---

[6] It is interesting to compare Heidegger's word "gestiftet" with Souriau's "instaurer." In both cases, it is an act that brings forward existence—an act that sponsors it.

ry of folds and layers. Iain Hamilton Grant contrasts materialism to the many sorts of *somatism* that hold that there is nothing beyond bodies—for instance, Harman's insistence that there is nothing beyond objects (see the debate in Bryant, Snircek, and Harman (2011)). Grant draws on Schelling in seeking a philosophy of nature capable of providing a continuation to a tradition that goes back to Plato's conception of physics where the main focus is ontogenesis and not a physics of all things (objects, already formed structures like bodies or governments or mobs or ideas) as Aristotle would understand it. Grant also finds in Schelling the idea of a natural history that underlies both what exists and what is politically at stake. Natural history is a geology of folds and layers that makes what is possible conditioned on what has taken place in the past—whereas matter is itself unconditioned, *das Unbedingte,* also translated as unthinged. It belongs in a transcendental level, in the sense of Schelling's nature as transcendental, as the condition of possibility for everything. Matter here is inflammable, it is about what can be done with a material that is saddened with potentialities. There is a material element undermining the core of anything—politics is always possible because matter itself has no nature, nature is nothing but history.

Jane Bennett's (2010) vital materialism provides a framework for a political ecology of things. She believes our time and our political concerns are taking us towards matter and objects. The appeal to ecology is itself an interesting element of a taste for fire. Guattari's (1989) seminal concern with how politics emerges from a confluence of an ecology of the *socius*—the practices, the institutions, the habitus etc.—an ecology of subjectivity—desires, fears and management of drives—and an ecology of fauna and flora and objects. The three ecologies interfere in each other, each one of them make the others possible. Whatever takes place in one of those ecologies is echoed and spread through contagion. There is no fixed structure in any of the three scopes, neither is there a hierarchical order between them. Change can come from each of the three realms and spread throughout. Bennett conceives of matter as a repository of capacities for composition that cannot be exhausted by its deployment in any particular configuration of things. Here it is worth mentioning that politics meets ontology in fire at least in some sense in the ontology of plastic put forward by Catherine Malabou (2005). She also holds that there is a common component to everything and holds that this then has a high degree of plasticity; which she contrasts with elasticity: plastic has no archaic shape to which it tends back to, its form just shrift endlessly. Malabou's ontology of plastic is not presented as a variety of materialism, but it shares with it the idea of a common component that is not in itself determining of anything but, like fuel, carries potentiality. In general, the appeal to matter can be something different than the appeal to bedrock; it could be the basis of a universe with no determinate form. Even though in important senses contemporary materialisms differ from process philosophy, in both cases we can find elements to see ontology and politics meeting in fire. They in fact meet in matter—which is at once ontological and political—but matter is intrinsically combustible. It is fuel lent to what there is; no passive constituent.

A third idea to flesh out the fire comes from absolute facticity as put forward by Meillassoux (2006). While Grant's materialism takes matter as a repository of folds and layers and process, philosophy sees a state of affairs in terms of alliances and resistances actually in place, the thesis of absolute facticity holds that nothing prevents nothing from turning into something entirely other—the ruling principle is the principle of unreason. Meillassoux (2006) argues that we should draw from Hume not a thesis about the limit of our capacity to access the world—correlationism, that maintains that we cannot know (or even think) of anything beyond a correlation between us and the world—but rather simply that there is no sufficient reason for anything. It should follow that everything is contingent, nothing is held the way it is based on needs of any sort, things are the way they are out of no necessity. He argues that instead of embracing a humility from Hume's attacks on how reason (aided or unaided by experience) can reach the world, we should rather proceed to find in the facticity of all things an absolute that reason can attain. All things are factual— this is the only absolute. The absence of grounding precludes the possibility of bedrock of any kind holding and framing political action. Politics and ontology meet in facticity. Here there is no inflammability before the work of fire and everything can catch fire—anything is therefore equally inflammable. There are no more than sudden flames—or rather *ignis fatuus*, those fires that look like a flickering light and that disappear when looked closely. There is nothing beyond the factual combustion of something—nothing but the inflammability of everything.

POLEMOS AND INFLAMMABILITY

The fire view contrasts vividly with the bedrock one. Ontology is no longer seen as the realm of the ready-made but rather as something that fuels politics while entangled with it. The fire view is made especially plausible if we put aside a separation between politics and nature and regard the latter as equally affected by the stuff politics is made of: disputes, conflicts, contagion, persuasion, alliances, negotiations. Nature is a realm for politics. Nature is full of political agents and it is part of human politics, as the history of technical objects attest. The ontology of inflammability can be seen as the ontology of problems: as such it is simply the landscape where politics takes place. It captures the smoothness, the vulnerability, and the difficulties ahead of any political alliance or dispute. The notion of *polemos*—and its corresponding ontology of polemics—can help understand that.

Heraclitus has arguably worked within the fire view. His fragments (see, for example, 2009) present an image of the world as filled with interactions, flows, and self-animation. Fragment 53 introduces the *polemos* as what made some slaves while making some masters. But the *polemos* is not presented as a *ex-nihilo* creator—but rather also what made some gods while making some mortals. Slavery, but also mortality, is driven by the *polemos*. It bridges together how things are and how we relate to them. It appears as the vulnerability of all alliances. All things come to being through *polemos*, says fragment 80. It is the force of dispute, the engine of all *polemics*. The force of *polemos* is that of disruption that can come from anywhere. It is no fixed *arché* but rather an element of displacement and disturbance that acts as an insurance against any ontology (or politics) of fixed ingredients. It is a force that has no fixed ontological status, no fixed place in any chart of beings. Heidegger (see Heidegger & Fink [1979]) translates *polemos* with a German word for dispute, *Auseinandersetzung*—what moves out to another position. It is an interesting way to portray controversy. *Polemos* is dissolution. It belongs to a realm of displacements, negotiations, disputes, and frictions that stops nowhere short of ontology itself.

I have recently been part of an effort to uncover new fragments of Heraclitus (see Bensusan et al. [2012]). It was an anarcheological effort, in the sense of the construction of a version that contrasts with the settled one. According to this new legend, Heraclitus survived for millennia, but didn't remain fully faithful to himself. He lived to be a world-traveler and aged to cherish his widespread anonymity. Due maybe to his mountain herbs, he had the strength to leave Ephesus for good and to live for millennia. Our work considered his late output, mainly his last texts from his days in Deir Al Balah, Gaza, before the bombings of 2009. Rumor had it that he was planning a second edition of his book on *physis* to be published in the several languages he then spoke. He used to say that in him lived those philosophers who didn't intend to have a grip on things but who would rather approach things on tiptoes. The manuscript that he was carrying with him in his last years disappeared after the Israeli attack and no more than about two hundred new fragments remained. Some of these new fragments provide an *aggiornamento* of the doctrine that the *polemos* ties ontology and politics together. Heraclitus' account of the *polemos* brings together ontology and politics and encompasses some of the ideas I rehearsed in the previous section. His account is both an alternative to the bedrock image and to all efforts to make politics alien to ontology.

Polemos is presented as a political plot inside everything. It is not something that can be contemplated from the outside as it also acts through our awareness of it. It is thoroughly situated. It is as if Heraclitus were saying that no matter is immune to fire—one can maybe contemplate things from beyond the inflammable, but one wouldn't then be able to breathe there. Among the many ways the *polemos* finds to spread its disruption, our knowledge of it is one of them. He writes:

130.[7] Whenever something comes about, a *polemos* comes about. Then there is politics.

131. *Polemos* often lies where we don't expect. It lies not only in the catapults, but also in the surprise that meets the *polemos*, in the temptation for *polemos* and in the knowledge of *polemos*.

Polemos cannot be controlled through knowledge because it is present in the very cage that attempts to capture it. Any exercise in ontology takes on a political stance. The *polemos* is the force of resistance against the establishment of realms and dominions. It is a vulnerability to fire and an incapacity to be merely following

---

[7] These recent fragments by Heraclitus were found in different versions in different languages. Anarcheology, of course, deals always in a plurality of versions and refrains from trying to single them down. Here I chose one amid different versions of each fragment. The ones marked with a star are considerably different from what was published in Bensusan et al. (2012).

orders. It is the spark of things, rather than what subjects them. Heraclitus has several fragments on the *polemos* and an-*arché*:

138b. The powerful of the time end up claiming that the *polemos* is asleep. It sleeps, but doesn't obey.

155. I keep meeting people that act as if disputes are about poles. Polarization distorts the *polemos—polemos* has no poles. Its force lies in the sliding of the poles. . . . only when we get tired, we choose sides.

178.* There are no *archés*. What we take to be *archés* are often no more than the slowest things to change—like a turtle that would hold the world or the laws of nature that would guide the world. Slow things are not always metronomes setting the pace for the orchestra. Often, they are other instruments. *Polemos* can also be slow. It is just about a lack of *archés*—it is an an-*arché*.

198.* . . . [On the other hand,] attachment to *archés* springs from an interest in control: find out who is the boss and cut deals with him. But no empire lasts because no realm lasts. Not even the realm of all things. There is no principle that could rule out any other beginning. Bacteria, worms, and viruses as much as roaches and rats didn't surrender to the alleged human victory over the animal world. Human gestures are themselves full of anomalies that resist the humanizing principle imposed to all things. The humanizing principle is the compulsory adherence on which people are forged out of whoever is born from a human womb. . . . Still, no principle can prevent the monster coming out. All that can be done to keep the monster at bay is to protect the *archés* with armies and leave all the exceptions unarmed.

252. The *polemos* doesn't do anything, but it doesn't leave anything done either.

259.* The *polemos* is no demiurge. It is closer to a blind molester.

Polemos is a capacity to disrupt. To say that it is not in our heads but rather among things is to say that there is no non-slippery core to anything. Fragment 145 says:

> 145. It is quite common to exorcise the *polemos* from the
> world by holding that each thing has its core. A core is a
> conquered territory where battles have already been
> fought and everything is properly trained and tamed. In
> order to persuade us that the world is rid of any *polemos*,
> we posit a world that has no more things than the ones
> that seem to be still. And then we can say, with the sort of
> philosophy that has been most popular in the last centu-
> ries, that *polemos* (and all polemics) is in our heads.

In contrast, Heraclitus sees *physis* as *polemos*. It lies in the
weaknesses of the arrangements. Disruption is not therefore an
incident, but rather what he prefers to see as styles of acting in an
ontological plot. He diagnoses what is lost in the interpretation of
physis as a realm of natural laws:

> 141. When *physis*, which is *polemos*, was replaced by a
> realm of laws—and nature stopped being strong to become
> merely ruling—it became an instrument of order and pro-
> gress. What was left of the *polemos* itself was then thrown
> into a realm of chance.

> 157b.* Nature, but not *physis*, is no more than our scape-
> goat.

> 271.* [It often seems as if we are] taming nature in order to
> tame people. The world is presented as a universe of servi-
> tude—a universe of unavoidable servitude. So people fight
> for concessions. [But, in fact,] they have nothing to lose
> other than their ontological chains.

There are no hierarchies (no -*archies*) other than the ones determined by the existing alliances, by the current political configuration of things. Here the fire view is clear: politics shapes ontology
as much as ontology shapes politics. Heraclitus takes necessity
and contingency to be equally up for grabs, not derived from *archés* and not held by bedrocks.

> 196.* . . . While the river changes, it changes what it drags
> and what can swim in it. Nothing is necessary or contin-
> gent once and for all. The flowing of the river changes not

only what there is but also what there possibly is. No law is immune to flooding. Some of them are just too costly to challenge at the moment.

Heraclitus' conception of the ontological as something that has little to do with fixity in itself and his suspicion concerning the politics of bedrock ontologies are expressed by fragments like the following:

210. While everything is connected to everything, there is no whole

212. Borders are where the war stopped. Being? It cannot be anything but a cease-fire.

213. [They say, someone says] that words are prejudices. So are things.

223. There is *polemos* in the midst of it all.

237.* I hear people asking what the world is made of. It cannot be made of anything but of world, I want to say. They want a list. There are things that cannot be in a list. I guess they are asking for an end point to what can be acted upon. They are asking for the unmovable. I suspect this is because they would like to find a source of activity that makes anything else inanimate. They want to be rid of their possibilities to act. They want to delegate. The world is not made of delegated actions.

277b.* Thought cannot strip off the garments of the world. It is itself a piece of garment. Nothing, not even the world, is ever fully naked—nor is it fully clothed. *Physis* loves to hide itself—it would dread to be fully unveiled. Thought has nothing to do with the naked universe. *Physis*, and the *polemos* that infests it, live rather in the undressing.

The activity of making ontological claims is itself political. It is a political activity—an intervention on how things are. Ontology is not in the description, but rather it is in the performance of describing things. It fits no narrative; it requires rather a gesture, and a situated one. Ontology is not about faithful accounts, but about teasing the world. Heraclitus writes:

222. A friend once explained to me that ontology is politics
viewed from above. I never stopped thinking about that.
But I feel the vertigo.

147. In the beginning there was no politics. Neither was
there *polemos*. Nor was this the beginning.

228.* . . . No description of the world can afford not to stir
it. Don't read me as if I am saying that there are *polemos*
or *logos* or anything. I don't deal in catalogues. Everything
can be ripped apart. When I talk about what there is, I
want to unlock something. The unlocking is what matters.
What matters is what escapes from one's words.

286. When I talk about the *polemos*, I'm not describing the
underground of things, I'm finding one amid many ways
to bury them.

286a. . . . I don't do geology, I dig tunnels.

286b. Words are actors. They perform different characters
in different acts. They carry through at most a style
throughout. *Polemos* is no character in the plot nor is it the
director behind the scene—it is no more than a style of acting.

Heraclitus argues against the privilege of substantive nouns over
articles, pronouns and adverbs. He also argues against taking the
world to be no more than a formal architecture. It won't do to
consider the difference between reductionism and non-reduc-
tionism, or between monism and pluralism, without considering
the difference between saying that everything is a rock and saying that everything is fire. While not in the business of taking
everything to be one thing, not even fire or *polemos*, Heraclitus
points at the difference between an ontology inspired by layers of
rock and one that draws on flames. His gesture would rather
mostly be one of asserting the *polemos* as something that cuts
across ontology and politics. At the same time, he aims to avoid
fire to be thought of as lava which will ultimately solidify and,
instead, point at the ubiquitous molten rock.

Fire is not like earth; it spreads, it doesn't ground. In a fire ontology, contagion matters more than support and subjection. It is
also about contact: nothing catches fire at a distance. Fire has to

go and spread itself. Fire is a testing procedure that discovers unsuspected distances between things. It unveils empty gaps between fragments assembled by testing the strength of the alliances. Whenever anything relies on anything else, there is a sort of inflammability between them. To rely on something is to entertain a *vinculum*—a bond, a chain, a link. There, ontology and politics meet on-fire.

Hilan Bensusan lectures at the department of philosophy of the University of Brasília. He has a Ph.D. from Sussex (England) and has recently been a visiting researcher at the Universities of Granada, Nottingham, Paris 8 and Madras at Chennai. In the last two years he has published in *Acta Analytica, Speculations, IJPS, Daimon, O-Zone* and the *Croatian Journal of Philosophy*. His current researches revolve around the politics and the metaphysics of contingency and immunity, bringing together speculative and analytic contributions. He maintains the blog *No Borders Metaphysics* at http://anarchai.blogspot.com.

REFERENCES

Ahmed, Sara (2006). *Queer Phenomenology: Orientations, Objects, Others*. Durham: Duke University Press.
Alaimo, Stacy and Susan Hekman, eds. (2008). *Material Feminisms*. Bloomington: Indiana University Press.
Aristotle (1924/1953). *Aristotle's Metaphysics*, trans. D. Ross, 2 vols. Oxford: Clarendon Press. (Greek text: *Aristotelis Metaphysica*, ed. Werner Jaeger. Oxford: Oxford University Press.)
Bennett, Jane (2010). *Vibrant Matter: A Political Ecology of Things*. Durham: Duke University Press.
Bensusan, Hilan, Leonel Antunes, and Luciana Ferreira (2012). *Heráclito—Exercicios de Anarqueologia*. São Paulo: Idéias e Letras.
Bogost, Ian (2012). *Alien Phenomenology, or What It's Like to Be a Thing*. Minneapolis: University of Minnesota Press.
Brassier, Ray (2007). *Nihil Unbound: Enlightenment and Extinction*. New York: Palgrave Macmillan.
Bryant, Levi, Nick Srnicek, and Graham Harman, eds. (2011). *The Speculative Turn: Continental Materialism and Realism*. Melbourne: re:press.
Bryant, Levi (2011). *The Democracy of Objects*. Ann Arbour: Open Humanities Press/MPublishing.
Delanda, Manuel (2002). *Intensive Science and Virtual Philosophy*. London: Continuum.

84 | HILAN BENSUSAN

Deleuze, Gilles (1968). *Difference et Répétition*. Paris: Presse Universitaires de France.

Deleuze, Gilles & Félix Guattari (1980). *Mille Plateaux*. Paris: Minuit.

Ellis, Brian (2002). *The Philosophy of Nature*. Montreal: McGill-Queen's University Press.

Guattari, Félix (1989). *Les Trois Écologies*. Paris: Galilée.

Grant, Iain Hamilton (2006). *Philosophies of Nature After Schelling*. London: Continuum.

Haar, Michel (1993). *Nietzsche et la Métaphysique*. Paris: Gallimard.

Harman, Graham (1999). *Prince of Networks: Bruno Latour and Metaphysics*. Melbourne, re:press.

Heidegger, Martin and Eugen Fink (1979). *Heraclitus Seminar*, trans. Charles Seibert. Tuscaloosa: University of Alabama Press.

Heil, John and Charles Burton Martin (1999). "The Ontological Turn." *Midwest Studies in Philosophy* 23: 34–60.

Heraclitus (2009). *Fragments*. London: Penguin.

Kripke, Saul (1972). *Naming and Necessity*. Oxford: Blackwell.

Latour, Bruno (1984). *Guerre et Paix des Microbes*, suivi de *Irréductions*. Paris: Anne-Marie Métailié. English translation: *The Pasteurization of France*, trans. A Sheridan and J. Law. Cambridge, MA: Harvard University Press.

Latour, Bruno (2012). *Enquête sur les Differents Modes d'Existence*. Paris: La Découverte.

Lewis, David (1986). *On the Plurality of Worlds*. Oxford: Blackwell.

Negasterani, Reza (2008). *Cyclonopedia: Complicity with Anonymous Materials*. Melbourne: re:press.

Nietzsche, Friedrich (2008). *Human, All Too Human*, trans. Helen Zimmern. New York: Barnes & Noble.

Malabou, Catherine (2005). *La Plasticité au Soir de L´écriture*. Paris: Leo Scheer.

Meillassoux, Quentin (2006). *Aprés la Finitude*. Paris: Seuil.

Mumford, Stephen (2004). *Laws in Nature*. London: Routledge.

Parisi, Luciana (2004). *Abstract Sex: Philosophy, Biotechnology, and the Mutations of Desire*. London: Continuum.

Protevi, Jon (2013). *Life, War, Earth*. Minneapolis: University of Minnesota Press.

Serres, Michel (1990). *Le Contrat Naturel*. Paris: François Bourin.

Shaviro, Stephen (2009). *Without Criteria: Kant, Whitehead, Deleuze, and Aesthetics*. Cambridge, MA: MIT Press.

Souriau, Etiene (2009). *Les Différents Modes D'existence*. Paris: Presse Universitaires de France.

Viveiros de Castro, Eduardo (2009). *Métaphysiques Cannibales*. Paris: Presse Universitaires de France.

Whitehead, Alfred (1929). *Process and Reality*. New York: Macmillan.

Williamson, Timothy (2004). "Past the Linguistic Turn?" In Brian Leiter, ed., *The Future for Philosophy*, 106–128. Oxford: Oxford University Press.

Woodard, Ben (2012). *Slime Dynamics*. Winchester, UK" Zero Books.

Woodard, Ben (2013). *On an Ungrounded Earth: Towards a New Geo-philosophy*. Brooklyn: punctum books.

Anarchist Developments in Cultural Studies
ISSN: 1923-5615
2013.2: Ontological Anarché: Beyond Materialism and Idealism

Schellingian Thought for Ecological Politics

Ben Woodard

ABSTRACT
Given the re-engagement of ontology in recent developments in theory
at large (whether under the auspices of Speculative Realism, New Materialism, the affective, nonhuman, inhuman, or otherwise), the relation
between ontology and politics requires serious renegotiation. In particular, the assertion that any form of ontology implies or even necessitates a
particular form of politics (or a politics whatsoever) needs to be closely
examined. This essay takes on Schelling's *Naturphilosophie* as a form of philosophy more amenable to thinking through ecological politics through a critique of the aforementioned strategies. This is done through an analysis of
Iain Hamilton Grant's recuperation of Schelling's work against other
dominant interpretations.

KEYWORDS
Schelling, Speculative Realism, New Materialism, Jane Bennett, Hasana
Sharp

0: INTRODUCTION

Given the re-engagement of ontology in recent developments in
theory at large (whether under the auspices of Speculative Realism, New Materialism, the affective, nonhuman, inhuman, or otherwise), the relation between ontology and politics requires serious renegotiation. In particular, the assertion that any form of
ontology implies or even necessitates a particular form of politics
(or a politics whatsoever) needs to be closely examined.

The central works of Jane Bennett and Hasana Sharp to be
discussed below break ground for such a project as they have

both pursued the constructions of a materialist politics with Spinoza and Deleuze as their central theoretical reservoirs. Given this and the ongoing environmental crisis (a short leap given the celebration of Spinoza and Deleuze by ecological theorists broadly), this essay will interrogate the ecological purchase of Bennett and Sharp's projects and contrast it with the possibility of a Schellingian politics of nature based on the interpretation of Schelling by Iain Hamilton Grant and Arran Garre.

Schelling, it will be argued, provides a methodological split which Spinoza and Deleuze lack, a split which better serves to develop an ecological politics that takes seriously the continuity of, yet difference between, thinking human and nonhuman agencies. Whereas Spinoza's system of parallel naturalism relates mind to nature via a vague correspondence of degree (i.e., a rock is a little minded whereas a human is far more minded), for Schelling there is a real unity between mind and nature. For Schelling, mind cannot grasp the totality of being and furthermore, mind creates a second nature for itself.

Given the relation of ontology and politics laid bare by the recent theorizations noted above, as well as the character of those redrawing the relation through Spinoza and Deleuze, this ecologically friendly formation of politics clangs against the iron of Žižek's Hegelianism (armored with cautionary Lacanian quips) as well as the minoritarian limitations and tactical uncertainties of Deleuzian politics (bolstered by the obscure power of becoming-whatever). That is, I would argue that Sharp and Bennett are steps in the right direction in that they are less subjectivist (as Žižek's Hegelianism seems to be) and more concerned with particular actualities (than the latter Deleuzian politics-of-becoming often seems to be). By subjectivist I mean overly concerned in determining the ontological nature of the subject to necessitate political change. Subjectivism, in my sense here, is to be read as an ontologically sophisticated form of voluntarism. This is not all that surprising given both Sharp and Bennett's connections to the materialist feminisms of Grosz, Bradotti, Haraway, Barad and others. However I believe that Sharp and Bennett (as well as scores of others) are held back by a particular relationship of ontology to politics engendered by their commitment to flat ontologies.[1]

---

[1] Both practitioners of Object-Oriented Ontology/Philosophy (OOO/OOP) and New Materialism adhere to flat ontologies; however, they do not mean exactly the same thing for each group. Generally, flat ontology means that no particular entity or set of entities has ontological privilege

Against such flatness I want to argue that Schelling provides a model of philosophy that emphasizes ontological stratification (caused by a freedom at ground as a metaphysical or transcendental dynamic) and gives both freedom and constraint to thought that politics can adapt locally. Such a model, I will argue, is particularly relevant to ecological politics writ large.

1: NEW MATERIALIST POLITICS: SPINOZA BETWEEN SHARP AND BENNETT

The recent work of Jane Bennett and (even more recently) Hasana Sharp has brought materialism into a close association with politics. That continental thought is geared towards the political is nothing new. But the fact that these arguments are necessitating or at least suggesting a politics from the point of view of ontology *is* new.

While several theorists (most notably, and recently, Graham Harman[2]) have pointed out that the term materialism has all but lost meaning because of its diffuse activation, the materialism discussed here is one of a particular provenance. While, at least, with regards to politics and the relation of philosophy and / or theory to politics, materialism summons particularly Marxist visions, the materialism I wish to engage here is that of Gilles Deleuze which, in turn is pulled from the so-called Prince of Immanence himself: Benedictus Spinoza. This association reintroduces the just-elided specters of Marxism, as Spinoza's naturalism and heretical parallelism were inspirational not only to Marx himself but to Marx's most important philosophical source, Hegel (who famously claimed that all must pass through Spinoza). It is not surprising that the May '68ers—Marxist to various degrees as students of Al-thusser (Balibar, Badiou, Ranciere, and others)— were also affected by Spinoza. But the use of Spinoza here is to follow the more Deleuzian tract, a thinker of roughly the same era but who was, at least ostensibly, more anti-humanist and less psychoanalytically interested than many of his contemporaries.[3]

---

over any other. For a specific account of the differences, see Ian Bogost's *Alien Phenomenology, or What It's Like to Be a Thing* (Minneapolis: University of Minnesota Press, 2012).

[2] While Harman has made this point many times, the most focused example is most likely Graham Harman, "I Am Also of the Opinion that Materialism Must be Destroyed," *Environment and Planning D: Society and Space* 28.5: 772–790.

[3] For a historical explication of the relation of psychoanalysis and huma-

However, even Deleuze's Spinoza brings with it a Marxist weight, as Deleuze himself worked with and on Marxist texts (with his works co-authored with Guattari as well as in the most revered non-existent book *The Grandeur of Marx,* the latter was published at the time of Deleuze's death). This is compounded by numerous secondary works on Deleuze (most notably the texts of Michael Hardt and Antonio Negri) that are political syntheses of Marx, Deleuze, and Spinoza.

But the Spinoza and Deleuze of Jane Bennett and Hasana Sharp is less Deleuze's Spinoza as a Marxist, than one which utilizes Spinoza's naturalism as the well-spring for political action. This is an odd move given not only the feminist credentials of the two authors (as nature has far too often been the bear trap of passivity in which women are ensnared) but that politics is taken to be inferred from a particular reading of nature, whether that nature is couched in terms of agency, materiality, or becoming.

This is not to say that Bennett and Sharp pull only from Spinoza and Deleuze's reading of Spinoza but that their models draw heavily on them and, in so doing, suggest a particular definition of nature, a particular relation of nature to politics which, in turn, suggests a particular relation of thought to nature. It is on this latter issue which I believe Schelling provides the best alternative to Spinoza and to Deleuze. But first it will be important to outline both Bennett and Sharp's use of Spinoza and Deleuze's Spinoza.

Bennett's *Vibrant Matter* is subtitled *A Political Ecology of Things* and thus emphasizes not only nature by the political ramifications of human agents being tied to a nature of things but also the political ramifications of human agents being tied to further agencies known and unknown. Bennett argues that thinking politics in such a way makes sense given the fact that "our powers are thing power[ed]."[4]

Furthermore, Bennett argues that one way of accessing such thoughts resides in a strategic anthropomorphism which finds materialities over ontological distinct categories of beings.[5]

In other words, Bennett seeks to highlight the kinds of physical and energetic materiality shared between kinds of beings instead of arguing for a fundamental separateness between beings.

---

nism in Post-War France, see Julian Bourg's *From Revolution to Ethics: May 1968 and Contemporary French Thought* (Montreal: McGill-Queen's University Press, 2007).

[4] Jane Bennett, *Vibrant Matter: A Political Ecology of Things* (Durham: Duke University Press, 2010), 11.

[5] Bennett, *Vibrant Matter,* 99.

In terms specifically relevant to the parameters of this paper, Bennett attempts to bring together ecology and politics. Bennett asks what the relationship of politics is to ontology and whether politics can be considered an ecology, a kind of relationality between human and nonhuman agents.[6]

While I appreciate Bennett's goals and choices of examples I have to wonder if her ontological reservoirs are doing the work she wants them to do without undermining her project from the beginning. This of course assumes that ontological justifications are more than operational rhetorics; and, if they are operational rhetorics, they have serious consequences for the forms which politics (or at least political theory will take). For instance, Bennett quite strongly dismisses epistemological concerns because they are, she argues, inherently self interested.[7] This collapses the possible ontological results of an epistemological project (where a concern with how the self accesses the world can over-focus on the self and forget the world at large). However I do not believe this is necessarily the case. In other words, Bennett's approach covers over the need for epistemology in damning epistemology as a self-interested project. Questioning our access to materiality, however, does not mean that that materiality must be inert or that our access gives it life, it merely notes the capacities as well as the limitations, of our own grasp on any kind of materiality, whether human or nonhuman.

One way of seeing the issue here is to examine Bennett's strategy of strategic anthropomorphism. Bennett's anthropomorphism, while useful as a tactic, covers over her disregard of 'cold' (or not politically open) ontology on the one hand and her dismissal of epistemology on the other. This creates a problem as the inclination to anthropomorphize then appears as a natural tendency which retroactively justifies the ontological choices Bennett makes for her politics via the pivot of strategic anthropomorphism. If this anthropomorphism was a full fledged methodology, it would be far less problematic. Bennett suggests that to have this strategy in place of an epistemological apparatus produces encounters which trigger impersonal affects and which further lead to new knowledge of (or perhaps new connections with) the vibrancy of things.

This vibrancy, which is Bennett's articulation of the agency of matter, points to a deeper tension which exists between a thing's vibrancy or power, and the human receptivity or the purported

---

[6] Bennett, *Vibrant Matter,* 100.
[7] Bennett, *Vibrant Matter,* 3.

thinkability of the underlying metaphysics, the connection between, yet difference in, powers and things. The question becomes: Does material immanence adequately account for the powers of things in relation to immanence, and yet is it also separate from affectivity? Spinoza's politics are combinatorial or ontologically or formally ecological because Spinoza's monism speaks of a world as a single substance in which things that exist as apparently separate entities are in fact only modes of that singular substance. I would argue that it is a performative contradiction to abandon epistemology yet still claim to have strategies. Buoyed by feminist texts, one could argue that affect has in effect become the new epistemology.

Hasana Sharp's text *Spinoza and the Politics of Renaturalization* sets up a similar project as Bennett's but draws from further back historically because she draws mostly from Spinoza and less from Deleuze.[8] Furthermore, instead of drawing political lessons from vibrant matter, Sharp pulls a concept of nature from Spinoza which she believes not only works against typical usages of nature (in terms of confining normativity) but furthermore suggests that Spinoza's naturalism offers a powerful reservoir for addressing ecology, animal rights, and feminist issues.

Sharp argues that these critiques grow out of Spinoza's ontological flatness and that this leads to a kind of philanthropic posthumanism much along the same terms of Jane Bennett's project (2, 4). While Sharp brings up the problems with deriving a politics from metaphysics, she wholeheartedly endorses the Deleuzian procedure of equating her project of Spinozistic renaturalization with joy by connecting it to a sense of agency (10, 14). This agency, Sharp continues, is affective; she thereby makes affect as such into a trans-individual network of being that is inherently a joyful ground for politics (24–25).

To give Sharp her due, she addresses the problems of attempting politics in nature as a kind of constraint; she also argues that understanding material causes is no doubt necessary for any political enterprise when she writes: "An adequate grasp of the causes and conditions that make oppression the cause often emerges in the process of fighting it" (34, 83). Despite these moments of borderline pragmatism, Sharp, like Bennett, sees affect as a kind of networked system of knowledge which can thereby replace epistemology. Sharp ends her book with a claim that De-

---

[8] Hasana Sharp, *Spinoza and the Politics of Renaturalization* (Chicago: University of Chicago Press, 2011); hereafter cited parenthetically by page number.

leuze and Guattari's Spinozist inspired immanence can lead to a naturalistically charged form of politics. The question becomes whether it is merely the Deleuzian form of ontology (or more broadly theory) that seems non-importable to politics, or could it be that assuming any kind of direct relation whatsoever is a grievous stitching of *is* to *ought*?

In the last year there have been numerous outbreaks of political discussions surrounding Speculative Realism and Object Oriented philosophies within the blogosphere. These disputes, of which there are too many to track, have often centered on the separation of ontology from politics. The surgical nature of this separation has been a concern for adherents to, as well as opponents of, speculative realism and its splinter groups since the beginning of its online presence (starting in 2007). While the critiques simply question the possibility of such a connection, the responses have been diverse. Levi Bryant, who has spoken most outwardly for Object Oriented thinking in this regard, has argued that the separation is one of conceptual coherence that to combine the way things *are* with the way things *should be* is egregious. Other responses, and the one I am making here, are more in line with the work of Ray Brassier (and to a lesser extent Iain Hamilton Grant), in that ethics or politics (or other normative dimensions) should not decide ontology any more than ontology should decide them.[9] But, unlike OOO/OOP, the separation is one where naturalism gives over to realism and/or rationalism in that a change happens that is different in kind. This shift is untenable for thinkers of OOO/OOP as all things must be on the same ontological plane in their existence as objects. The foregoing engagement with Schelling is ultimately motivated by such critical verticality. In other words, a vertical or graduated approach to ontology and ethics is not necessarily a hierarchical one just as a horizontal or ontologically flat approach is not inherently democratic.

2: SCHELLING'S NON-POLITICS

There are three solid nails in the coffin of the very possibility of a Schellingian politics. First, Schelling rarely if ever openly talked about politics and was brought in to quell the radical upstart of

---

[9] See Ray Brassier's *Nihil Unbound: Enlightenment and Extinction* (London: Palgrave Macmillan, 2007) as well as Iain Grant's *Philosophies of Nature after Schelling* (London: Continuum International Publishing Group, 2006).

the young Hegelians in the name of a Christian political conservatism. Second, given Schelling's opposition to Hegelianism, his politics automatically appears as a kind of anti-Marxism or anti-dialecticism. Third, the dominant pseudo- political use of Schelling, and perhaps the only well known political or even partially political use of Schelling, is from Slavoj Žižek, and it falls into the subjectivist problem mentioned above.

2.1: FIRST PROBLEM: HISTORICAL CONTEXT AND REACTIONS

From the outset it is difficult to get beyond the very reasons Schelling gave the Berlin lectures due to which he received such poor reviews and responses from the young political upstarts of his time. The situation was a mix of social desperation (to fill Hegel's absence, having recently died) as well as appeasement (to the conservative Christian rule of Germany at the time).

In a letter penned to Schelling, the King's ambassador to Munich, C. J. Bunsen, informed Schelling, in stormy language, that he must set off for Berlin and take the chair of the recently deceased Hegel (his once rival and former friend and roommate) in order to dispatch the "dragonseed" of Hegelian pantheism which had been fostered there by the recently dead dialectician.[10]

Alberto Toscano in his essay "Philosophy and the Experience of Construction," gives an excellent account of the manner in which Schelling gave his Berlin lectures:

> In 1841, with the blessing of the Prussian state, the aged Schelling climbed the rostrum of the University of Berlin to denounce the errors and shortcomings of the Hegelian dialectic and reveal the contents of his own positive philosophy. This intellectual episode has gone down in the annals of the history of philosophy principally on account of the audience that came to listen to this last survivor of the golden age of idealism, speaking from the post that once belonged to his philosophical nemesis, Hegel. Kierkegaard, Bakunin, Feurbach, Marx's friend Arnold Ruge, and Friedrich Engels were amongst them.[11]

---

[10] F.W.J. Schelling, *The Grounding of Positive Philosophy* (Albany: State University of New York Press, 2007), 6.
[11] Alberto Toscano, "Philosophy and the Experience of Construction," in *The New Schelling*, ed. Judith Norman and Alistair Welchman (London: Continuum, 2004), 106.

In his essay, Toscano questions what a return to Schelling means given that Schelling's return to the stage in Berlin served as negative inspiration for the projects of the young Hegelians[12] and provided examples from both Engels, Marx, and Kierkegaard of the complaints of those that accused Schelling of being a puppet of the state, and a very highly paid one at that. However, as Bruce Matthews' excellent research has shown, this historical caricature is misleading and must be read as Schelling was expecting it to be read, in one form or another, as a way to attack Hegel's system (as he had begun to do in an introductory remark to Hubert Beckers translation of Victor Cousin's 1834 *Essays on French and German Philosophy*).[13]

If one can get beyond this and search Schelling's work for gems of political insight, then one will find that little are likely to be found. Few have addressed Schelling's contradictory uses of state politics, though, somewhat surprisingly, Jurgen Habermas is one exception. In his essay entitled "Dialectical Idealism in Transition to Materialism: Schelling's Idea of a Contraction of God and its Consequences for the Philosophy of History," Habermas states that "Schelling is not a political thinker" and that what is instead present in Schelling are three incompatible deductions of the function of the state.[14] As Habermas shows, to draw political ramifications from Schelling is tricky, to put it lightly.

But before getting too deeply into the political possibilities of Schelling, it would be prudent to first address the problematic relation of Schelling to Hegel and Idealism.

2.2: SECOND PROBLEM: SCHELLING AS ANTI-HEGEL

This problem could also be put as follows: why Schelling over Hegel? This is a particularly salient question given Žižek's valorization of Hegel's system as politically useful. Schelling is often thought to be merely the protean misstep between Fichte and Hegel. The immediate question that can be raised is whether Schelling's late critiques of Hegel share goals with Marx's famous inversion of Hegel.[15]

---

[12] Toscano, "Philosophy and the Experience of Construction,"109.

[13] Schelling, *The Grounding of Positive Philosophy*, 8–9.

[14] Jurgen Habermas, "Dialectical Idealism in Transition to Materialism: Schelling's Idea of a Contraction of God and its Consequences for the Philosophy of History" in *The New Schelling*, ed. Judith Norman and Alistair Welchman (London: Continuum, 2004), 43.

[15] See Bruce Matthews' "Translator's Introduction" to *The Grounding of*

This is compacted by the fact that several of the thinkers present at Schelling's lectures adapted his critiques of Hegel. Whereas Marx and Engels lamented Schelling for being too idealist and Christian, the former issue is false in practice (as Schelling clearly passed through idealism and consistently tried to break out of it starting at least as early as the System of Transcendental Idealism). Schelling's religiosity is the more damning critique, though it is difficult to separate from the pragmatic political constraints of his time. Furthermore, Schelling, despite or even because of his religious moorings, has been referred to as a realist (as in the case of John Laughland's *Schelling versus Hegel*).[16]

Yet the specter of Schelling's idealism seems to continue to haunt critiques of him. Wesley Phillips in "The Future of Speculation?" attempts to simultaneously critique Schelling, Iain Hamilton Grant's reading of Schelling, as well as the use of speculation by Speculative Realism broadly; yet, I would argue, this reading fails in all attempts and instead defends Hegel's concept of history as better than Schelling's.[17] However, Phillips seems (in the end) to turn Schelling's materialism into a crude physicalism that is then seen as less potentially political than Hegel's endless history and a possible speculative materialist history stemming from Hegel's purportedly more concrete and more political notion of materiality. Phillips argues that the crux of this relies on Hegel's negation of the negation (the pivotal synthesis of the dialectical process).

In the end, the fundamental difference between Hegel and Schelling is that consciousness determining history against and with other consciousnesses is the central ontological agency for Hegel, whereas for Schelling the past, or nature, or the real unilaterally, determines the trajectory of thought and action because of its un-prethinkability.[18] Where Phillips erroneously casts

---

Positive Philosophy.

[16] See John Laughland, *Schelling versus Hegel: From German Idealism to Christian Metaphysics* (Farnham: Ashgate, 2007). The relation of politics to religion is further complicated by biographical notes from Schelling's early life at the Turbingen Seminary (where he famously roomed with Hegel and Holderlin). Some accounts suggest that Schelling was a rebel and wrote on the border of heresy, whereas Laughland suggests, based on the accounts of the instructors, that Schelling was a goody goody.

[17] See Grant's *Philosophies of Nature after Schelling*, as well as Wesley Phillips, "The Future of Speculation?" in *Cosmos and History: The Journal of Natural and Social Philosophy* 8.1 (2012): 289–303.

[18] "Unprethinkable" is the preferred translation of Schelling's term "das Unvordenkliche." The term addresses not simply what precedes the

Schelling (and in particular Grant's use of Schelling as physical-ist), as materialist in a non-political or anti-political way I would argue that Schelling's realism (however strange it appears) makes him more politically useful than Hegel.

Andrew Bowie has pointed out that there are moments of a nascent ecological politics in Schelling's work, particularly with regards to *Naturphilosophie* and Schelling's distanciation from his former mentor Fichte whose pure ego-centered idealism Schelling had grown tired of. What is most problematic is that Schelling's realism is not a realism of things but a realism of powers and grounds, which are neither things nor non-things.

Even in Schelling's most idealistic phase, there are traces of a materialist (if not realist) connection. In the *System of Transcendental Idealism* Schelling discusses the possibility of a practical philosophy which follows necessarily from his Fichtean-inspired transcendental idealism. Towards the end of the text Schelling attempts to flesh out how it is that the practical can even be connected to the ideal in order to form a thought of the practical in which the subject appears to be the productive center of the universe.[19] Schelling writes:

> That which is to be intuited as operating upon the real, must itself appear as real. Hence I cannot intuit myself operating upon the object immediately, but only as doing so by means of matter, though in that I act I must intuit this latter as identical with myself. Matter, as the immediate organ of free, outwardly directed activity, is the organic body, which must therefore appear as free and apparently capable of voluntary movements.[20]

Grant argues that matter, in Schelling's case, must be read in its most radical Platonic sense, as the darkest of all things that consistently resists philosophical interrogation, the reef on which so many thinkers run their thoughts aground.

Here Bennett's fondness for body over object takes on a different meaning: rather than pointing towards the deepness or limit of her strategic anthropomorphism, it instead shows a non-foundational concept that itself is a ground but since it is not a

---

emergence of thought in terms of temporal sequence but that which may be beyond the very capacity of thought as we understand it.

[19] F.W.J. von Schelling, *System of Transcendental Idealism* (Virginia: University Press of Virginia, 1978), 184.

[20] Schelling, *System of Transcendental Idealism*, 185.

ground in any formal sense (having abjured epistemological solidity) the body becomes a self-grounding materiality or a construction constructed in a way outside of, or means otherwise alien to, knowledge.

It is for precisely such reasons that Grant's anti-somatic reading of Schelling is so important.[21] Given the power-based consistency of Schelling's theory of nature—which is ultimately a speculative field physics—Grant argues that Schelling's speculations are fundamentally anti-somatic and anti-Aristotelian. By holding to an anti-somatic model of nature Grant's theory of knowledge itself becomes a process and not necessarily an ossifying capture or overly artificial construction.

If there is another reason why the young Hegelians balked at Schelling (despite his obvious anti-Hegelianism), is it possible that it was Schelling's call for a more pragmatic or at least engaged form of thinking the positive (what has been variously aligned with hermeneutics, deconstruction, and theology)?

2.3: THIRD PROBLEM: ŽIŽEK'S PSYCHOANALYTIC SCHELLING

The flight from the pragmatic brings us to the third problem: that of clearing the brambles Slavoj Žižek has placed on Schelling aligning him with his larger Lacanian-Hegelianism and with his use of Schelling as a figure to prove Hegel's strength through Schelling's failures namely by showing the superiority of Hegel's idealism in relation to necessity and contingency versus Schelling's appeal to actuality and reality.

In a footnote in *The Metastases of Enjoyment* Žižek assaults Schelling's critique of Hegel's logic:

> According to Schelling, Hegel's error resides in his endeavor to deduce the contingent fact of existence from the notion: the pure notion of a thing can deliver only *what the thing is*, never the *fact that* it is. It is Schelling himself, however, who thereby excludes contingency from the domain of the notion: this domain is exclusively that of necessity—that is to say, what remains unthinkable for Schelling is a *contingency that pertains to the notion itself.*[22]

Žižek claims that Schelling wrongfully critiques Hegel's notion

---

[21] See Grant's *Philosophies of Nature after Schelling*.
[22] Slavoj Žižek, *The Metastases of Enjoyment: On Women and Causality* (New York: Verso, 2005), 51n11.

for its lack of contingency, responding that Schelling is unable to accept contingency within the notion. But in so doing Žižek overlooks the fact that the necessity at work for Schelling is one of endless becoming, a becoming so unhinged that it is unprethinkable, that it cannot be mentally quarantined or mediated via reflection. Contingency (and hence political possibility for our purposes here) in thought for Schelling (and by connection the raw possibility of a politics if not its proscriptive program) lies in instances of cognition being unable to ever fully grasp the idea as it is.[23] I will discuss this more below in relation to Spinoza.

Furthermore, following the above quotation, Žižek argues (in relation to Lacan) that Schelling's philosophy (in relation to Lacan) only thinks the irrational drives of the real whereas Hegel's logic relates directly to mathemes which operate at the level of the Lacanian Real. Žižek effectively psychologizes the irrational drives or will of Schelling's philosophy thereby making the propulsive force of both contingency and necessity in Schelling's work subjective, perhaps even more so than Hegel's. While Žižek cautiously qualifies his labeling of Schelling's philosophy as "naive psycho-cosmic speculations," the weight of the prefix psychoclearly overrides the purportedly dogmatic or naïve cosmic work of Schelling in Žižek's view.[24] To throw Schelling's speculations in with any pre-critical dogmatism forgets the alliance that Schelling attempts to forge with the sciences on the whole. Instead of highlighting the materialist motions of Schelling, Žižek argues that Schelling puts the emergence of logos as that which speaks towards the imbalance in nature.[25] Put otherwise, Žižek takes the material instability that Schelling places in Nature and translates it into psychoanalytic terms, which disregards Schelling's relation to science as well as Schelling's critical approach to Kant's philosophy.

It is important to note, as Iain Hamilton Grant does, that, in Schelling, thought is nature's attempt to become an object to itself which is always a failed maneuver. There is nothing special (at least ontologically) about thought (it remains a part of nature). Since thought, for Schelling, is a part of nature and does not lord over it, the relation of contingency and necessity becomes a part of nature and not a problem of thinkability or logic. Ultimately the central difference between the materialisms of Žižek and that

[23] Žižek, *The Metastases of Enjoyment*, 51n11.

[24] Slavoj Žižek, *The Fragile Absolute, or Why is the Christian Legacy Worth Fighting For?* (New York: Verso, 2000), 85.

[25] Žižek, *The Fragile Absolute*, 88.

of Schelling, is that for the former thought is self-grounding whereas, for Schelling the very question of ground is an open question (the ground of ground is an issue of nature and not one of thought since thought, as one of many products of nature, cannot capture its own conditions). Or, as Schelling states, the grounds of consciousness lay outside of consciousness.[26] In kind, we can say that ontology makes politics possible but it cannot lord over its form.

3: SCHELLING AND SPINOZA

In his youth, Schelling concluded a 1795 letter to his then friend Hegel, stating "I have become a Spinozist." Despite his epistolary enthusiasm, Schelling's published remarks on Spinoza are generally far more measured.[27]

In his *Naturphilosophie* stage, Schelling defines his philosophy of nature as a Spinozism of physics[28] and notes Spinoza's struggle with the subject-object relation.[29] In the *System of Transcendental Idealism,* Spinoza is mentioned only as an example of dogmatism.[30] In the 1810 Stuttgart Seminars, Schelling distinguishes the *Naturphilosophie* from Spinoza's theories which maintain a parallelism, a mechanical physics, and ignore God's personality (i.e., his difference from Nature).[31] Schelling makes similar remarks in the 1815 draft of the *Ages of the World* (104–105). Finally, Schelling spends much of the closing movement of his 1842 Berlin lectures critiquing Spinoza's concept of God though ultimately praising Spinoza's necessitarian argument for God.[32]

Two texts omitted from this list are *The Philosophical Investigations into Human Freedom* and Schelling's lectures *On the History of Modern Philosophy,* both of which devote more substantial discussion to Spinoza.[33] In both texts Schelling's praise for and

---

[26] Schelling, *System of Transcendental Idealism,* 101.

[27] Quoted in Frederick Beiser, *German Idealism: The Struggle Against Subjectivism, 1781–1801* (Boston: Harvard University Press, 2008), 472.

[28] F.W.J. Schelling, *First Outline of a System of the Philosophy of Nature* (Albany: State University of New York Press, 2004), 117, 194.

[29] Schelling, *Ideas for a Philosophy of Nature,* 53–54.

[30] Schelling, *System of Transcendental Idealism,* 17.

[31] F.W.J. Schelling, *Idealism and the Endgame of Theory,* trans. Thomas Pfau (Albany: SUNY Press, 1994), 214.

[32] Schelling, *The Grounding of Positive Philosophy,* 206.

[33] See F.W.J. Schelling, *Philosophical Investigations into the Essence of Human Freedom,* trans. Jeff Love and Johannes Schmidt (New York:

criticism of Spinoza orbit his notion of necessary unity being, which, through its association with the divine, positively defines it as totalizing, creative and unthinkable, but negatively as erasing God's personality (i.e., difference from nature as productive, as *natura naturans*). How does this relate to the political? Threaded throughout Schelling's discussion of Spinoza's philosophy is a critique of immanence and, in relation to this, a critique of the quietism that relates immanence to Spinoza's mechanical parallelism. The overall effect of this mechanical immanence is what Schelling calls, following Goethe, a calming effect. Schelling writes:

> Spinozism is really the doctrine which sends thought into retirement, into complete quiescence; in its highest conclusions it is the system of perfect theoretical and practical quietism, which can appear beneficent in the tempestuousness of a thought which never rests and always moves.[34]

But how does immanence as a lesser form of being play into this?

For Spinoza, God is perfect and creates out of the necessity of that perfection, whereas for Schelling freedom, at least as the creative capacity of nature, pre-exists God, since, otherwise, God would be rife with evil or, on the other hand, would be static and lifeless. Furthermore, Spinoza's parallelism, as Hasana Sharp describes it, is that of a parallel naturalism (i.e., mind and extension do not interact but merely mirror the affects which cross both). Schelling's approach appears similar except that instead of attempting an absolute immanence (a formulation which, I believe, Schelling would find oxymoronical), Schelling seems to describe immanence as being punctuated by bouts of the transcendental. But, because Schelling sees being as always escaping thought as well as preceding it, this transcendental is not a stable transcendence guaranteeing human efficacy over nature but one which marks a break between regimes of immanence, between the distinct stratifications of being which are re-presented in our thinking and which our thinking can transgress within limits. Spinoza's thinking, on the other hand, because of the strictly main-

---

SUNY Press, 2006), as well as F.W.J. Schelling, *History of Modern Philosophy* (Cambridge University Press, 1994).

[34] Schelling, *History of Modern Philosophy*, 66.

tained parallelism, can only think being as being in thought, or what he refers to as immanent being.[35]

While Schelling's essay on human freedom has been, in my opinion, over-emphasized, it is the essay which receives the most attention in Schelling's corpus (in Heidegger, Nancy, Žižek, Bloch and others) to the disregard of all else. In part, this can be justi-fied by the all-too-often cited 'protean' nature of Schelling, of the figure of Schelling as he who could not make up his mind, and hence why this peculiar transitory text is so focused on. But for our purposes here it is important to discuss the relevance of Spi-noza in particular.

In *The Philosophical Investigations into the Essence of Human Freedom,* Schelling defends Spinoza from the charges of panthe-ism but attacks him (in ways similar to Jacobi, i.e., charging him with nihilism) as a fatalist or determinist not because of putting God into nature but for making the will (that source of freedom) a thing; that is, by explaining it in terms of extension.[36] Schelling seems to suggest (as is unsurprising given his comments above on Spinzoa in the *Naturphilosophical* texts) that Spinoza's system could be saved by giving it an injection of dynamics.[37]

In this regard Schelling, on the one hand, seems to see himself as less of a realist than Spinoza, in that Spinoza too freely gave freedom to non-human entities. Yet, at the same time, Schelling levels the following critique at Kant in that Kant should have ap-plied freedom to things in themselves:

> It will always remain odd, however, that Kant, after having first distinguished things-in-themselves from appearances only negatively through their independence from time and later treating independence from time and freedom as cor-relate concepts in the metaphysical discussions of his *Cri-tique of Practical Reason*, did not go further toward the thought of transferring this only possible positive concept

---

[35] Schelling, *History of Modern Philosophy,* 65.
[36] Schelling, *Philosophical Investigations into the Essence of Human Freedom,* 20.
[37] Schelling, *Philosophical Investigations,* 21. While Schelling's use of dynamics is too complex an issue to fully grasp given the space available, it is central to the discussion, as for Schelling nature is fundamentally a source of movement. Spinoza's system is for Schelling too closed and too mechanical to allow for movement to take place. For Schelling dynamics is the science that most closely grasps the importance of addressing the centrality of movement for philosophy.

of the in-itself also to things; thereby he would immediately have raised himself to a higher standpoint of reflection and above the negativity that is the character of his theoretical philosophy.[38]

From this, Markus Gabriel argues that the higher realism suggested by Schelling is in fact a form of Hegelian objective idealism.[39] Given the demands of Schelling's *naturphilosophie*-as-will and as the ontological unity of the philosophy of identity, how is it that the 'higher realism' of Schelling is the force of the subject all the way down and not (in a more realist vein) that freedom is a name for a more deep-seeded dynamism which exceeds the subject.

In a daunting footnote in *the History of Modern Philosophy* following Schelling's dissatisfaction with Kant dismissing the possibility of knowing the super-sensual Schelling writes:

[I]f one had to distinguish a *Prius* and *Posterius* in sensuous representation, then the *true* Prius in it would be what Kant calls "thing in itself"; those concepts of the understanding which it shows itself as affected by in my *thinking* are, according to Kant himself, precisely that by which it first becomes object of my thinking, thus is able to be experienced by me; the *true* Posterius is, then, not, as he assumes, that element which remains after the concepts of the understanding have been removed, for rather, if I take these way then this is the being . . . which is unthinkable, *before* and outside the representation, it is thus the absolute *Prius* of the representation, but the true *Posterius* is precisely this Unknown (which he himself compares with the x of mathematics).[40]

Schelling, in the above quote from the *Freedom Essay* and here from *On the History of Modern Philosophy*, indirectly addressing the patchwork problem of the 2nd edition of the *Critique of Pure Reason*, seems to be wondering why Kant did not grant the non-sensible the pure dynamics of nature and then, on top of this, assume that once removed of their experiential sheen, that the

---

[38] Quoted in Markus Gabriel and Slavoj Žižek, "Introduction: A Plea for a Return to Post-Kantian Idealism," in *Mythology, Madness, and Laughter: Subjectivity in German Idealism* (London: Continuum Books, 2009), 4.

[39] Gabriel and Žižek, "Introduction."

[40] Schelling, *History of Modern Philosophy*, 104.

concepts would be not only thinkable but more than thinkable: *actual.*

In this sense, Spinoza's conceptualization of freedom boils down to the virtues of humans (to the degree which we can balance our power which stems from our essence in relation to exterior causes) but in the context of either the realm of either extension or the realm of thought. For Schelling, freedom is the dynamism that is creation (of both thought and nature) and is constrained by the way in which that creation has laid down the sediment of actuality. That is, for Spinoza freedom is a combinatorial game, whereas for Schelling it is a simultaneous wrestling with time and the ideal absorption of time against the limits and constraints of material existence into the past and into the future.

What then, from the historical material, can be extracted of at least the ontological base of a Schellingian politics? Given the name of Schelling in place of Spinoza and / or Deleuze, what kind of vital materialisms could one create, what kind of politics of nature or naturalization could create that do not weigh too heavily on *is*-ness determining *ought*-ness?

4: GARRE AND GRANT

While Schelling's numerous systems could be taken as significantly disjunctive phases, this, as Iain Hamilton Grant has pointed out, overlooks the themes which run throughout his work, a theme which is directly tied to his non-systematicity.[41] In an early letter Schelling writes:

> Nothing upsets the philosophical mind more than when he hears that from now on all philosophy is supposed to lie caught in the shackles of one system. Never has he felt greater than when he sees before him the infinitude of knowledge. The entire dignity of his science consists in the fact that it will never be completed. In that moment in which he would believe to have completed his system, he would become unbearable to himself. He would, in that moment, cease to be a creator, and would instead descend to being an instrument of his creation.[42]

This is coupled with Grant's assertion throughout his *Philosophies of Nature after Schelling* that the main focus of Schelling's

---

[41] See Grant's *Philosophies of Nature after Schelling,* 3.
[42] Schelling, *The Grounding of Positive Philosophy,* 3.

work is that being precedes thinking. The strongest basis for this trajectory is Schelling's non-concept of the unprethinkable. By this Schelling means that there is something (yet not even a thing) which is not even unthinkable but rather *unprethinkable*; this means that it is totally outside of thought which may or may not become thinkable in the future. This non-concept, which Heidegger takes and translates into purely hermeneutic terms, is what drives Schelling to try his hand at different systems. Schelling is less a protean thinker in this regard than he is a prismatic thinker of the same unthinkable and unprethinkable being which precedes thought. It is this problematic which also forces Schelling to have a divided approach to philosophy, whether the system of identity or the *Naturphilosophical*. While multiple approaches to philosophy are addressing the same field (in terms of the unthinkable, thinkable, and the manifestations of both in the other to various degrees) it does not suffice to collapse the approaches into a more general materialism given the unthinkability of nature in the last instance on the one hand (which dynamics comes closest to addressing) and the over-thinkability or reflexity of the transcendental project on the other hand. In other words, to collapse both into the phrase materialism, says little about the critical positions and different kind of impacts both the real and the ideal have.

Two theorists (though there are many more) who have brought Schelling into the present are Arran Garre and Iain Hamilton Grant. While the former is overtly political in his use of Schelling, the latter is not political but has also done the most to make Schelling a materialist or realist in the ways similar to which Bennett and Sharp have done with Spinoza. It is my hope that combining them will bring Schelling into the debate about the relation between politics and ontology.

Garre has utilized Schelling in numerous works to discuss ecological problems and the concepts of nature. In his extensive essay "From Kant to Schelling To Process Metaphysics," Garre argues that Schelling's philosophy should be less associated with the project of German Idealism and more so connected to Process Philosophies such as those of William James and Alfred North Whitehead. At the level of content, Garre goes to great lengths to show how Schelling's ideas in his *Naturphilosophie* in particular prefigured concepts such as emergence and field physics. Furthermore, Garre argues that Schelling's concept of nature and of humanity's relationship to it provide the possibility of a global ecological civilization. What exactly that entails is left unclear.

Garre admits that he is (at least partially) following Andrew Bowie's lead in terms of reading Schelling's *Naturphilosophie* as a hermeneutics of nature. At the same time, Garre utilizes throughout his essay Iain Hamilton Grant's *Philosophies of Nature After Schelling* as book which argues for the centrality of nature to Schelling's project.

A serious point of contention, however, is apparent in Garre's concern that Grant grossly misreads Schelling's relationship to the Copernican revolution. As counter evidence, Garre cites pages from *The Grounding of Positive Philosophy*, where Schelling heaps praise upon Kant. However, the pages that Garre cites precede roughly one hundred pages of Schelling critiquing Kant. Furthermore, from a young age to his twilight years Schelling asserts the importance of Kant (similar to his comments on Spinoza) but believes that while Kant found a form or methodology that works (the critical or negative philosophy), it nonetheless works best as an academic discipline, as a philosophy which investigates itself and that cannot adequately address nature outside of us. Contra Garre, Schelling's unending assertions that being precedes thinking is *de facto* contradictory to even a kid-gloved handling of the division of the noumenal and phenomenal in Kant's critical system.

Garre's comments on Schelling may be in part due to Grant's abjuration of the political (and serious criticism of the ethical) in Schelling opposed to Bowie's reading as well as many others. However, what Garre does not acknowledge is that the focus on *The Philosophical Investigations* reads a Kantianism (or Hegelianism or Fichteanism) into Schelling which violently undoes the radical premise of his system: namely that freedom is a natural fact and the cause of and material from which most of the world is built is unknown and a smaller fraction is fundamentally unpre-thinkable.

While the difficulties of this system in many ways led Schelling back into theology, from which he began, this is not a necessity. Even Schelling himself would say so. As Bruce Matthews expertly demonstrates in his introduction to *The Grounding of Positive Philosophy,* Schelling's theological adherence is a decision, it is (drawing a connection to CS Peirce) a form of abductive logic, or what is in many ways an educated guess. Abductive logic was, for Peirce, *the* maxim of pragmatism.[43]

---

[43] Incidentally Garre wrote a piece on the semiotics of climate change utilizing Schelling and Peirce. But Garre concludes by attempting to connect Schelling and Peirce to Ellis Lovelock's Gaia theory. I do not see

The discussion of pragmatism, combined with a radical theory of nature, brings us back to the philosophies of Bennett and Sharp because their use of Dewey. While Bennett's use of Dewey is interesting, it becomes difficult to see (as already noted) how Bennett can grant humans the capacity of arbitration over (or at least within) the parliament of things. It is here where epistemology appears as a necessary means (the only means) for constructing ontological politics. Schelling's epistemology, as Mathews has shown, is strange, as it relies on abductive inference as well as capacities of knowing which Kant found less than stable; particularly intuition. But Schelling's productive intuition is a kind of construction of a second nature, in which not only concepts but concepts combined with a productive intuition (an expanded empiricism, as he calls it in *The Grounding of Positive Philosophy*) which involves both authentic and emphatic knowing.[44] Humans are not lords of nature but "autoepistemic organs of nature's self organizing actuality."[45] This does not eradicate the capacity nor the responsibility of humanism regards to nature but makes the fact of being human a fact produced by nature.

5: CONCLUSION

As Garre and Bowie have suggested, Schelling's approach to nature demands a thinking of nature that is rational as well as affective. This is unsurprising given the inability of either a plethora of scientific data as well as ethical and emotional pleas to force serious change.

We may question the ease with which politics can be installed as an ecology given the instability of the human element, but it remains true that our ideas of ontology of metaphysics affects the political whether we intend this or not. So if we are going to pursue political ontologies, this cannot merely be a cover for avoiding issues of *ought* in the guise of issues of *is*. For Žižek, it would not be an exaggeration to claim that German Idealism (bound to Lacan) has been more and more construed as a body of knowledge most concerned with the genesis and operation of the sub-

---

the political force of this. See Arran Garre, "The Semiotics of Global Warming: Combating Semiotic Corruption," *Theory and Science* 9.2 (2007): http://theoryandscience.icaap.org/content/vol9.2/Gare.html.

[44] Bruce Matthews, "Translators Introduction," in Schelling, *The Grounding of Positive Philosophy*, 80.

[45] Bruce Matthews, *Schelling's Organic Form of Philosophy: Life as the Schema of Freedom* (Albany: SUNY Press, 2011), 9.

ject, that strange unknown X which we live inside. I think this is a far too limited image of German Idealism at large and it misrepresents Schelling's work in particular. Schelling is the German Idealist most concerned with the material world, with nature as productivity *and* as a collection of products. Politically, this may have been less appealing in a time where the material crippling of the world through environmental degradation was an unimaginable impossibility; this is simply no longer the case.

While political ontology is a sensible salve to this predicament, it begs several questions. While the ontological democracy of Jane Bennett, Hasana Sharp and others is tempting, I do not believe it adequately accounts for either the capacity nor the responsibility of human beings in a world of things produced by a raw, chaotic, productivity known as nature; a nature that then subsists in a complex network of things through and around us. Schelling's articulation of what could be called a transcendental dynamism attempts to probe the relation between the ontological and the normative, between nature being the face of the ontological dimension of freedom and freedom (in a transcendental sense) being a derivation of that nature that in turn appears as a kind of symmetry break in the productivity of nature. Transcendental dynamism is that which attempt to explain how nature lays down a new set of conditions in which nature operates by different rules broadly construed that are mentally apprehended for us.

What do I mean by this? The transcendental is not an airy concept sewn from gossamer thread floating about us. Grant, following Schelling, makes the transcendental that which gives grounds, that inaccessible process which determines grounds of existence whereby being itself is thought of as a pure productivity stemming from unprethinkable chaos. As Iain Hamilton Grant argues in "Movements of the World," transcendental philosophy focuses on attempting to find the universal "morphogenetic field" from which all objects and subjects are derived.[46] This field is only ever force or motion[47] from which things derive, a derivation which cannot be one of kind (as only forces can interrupt forces) but the result of which is a vertical wasteland of objects, a graveyard of stratifications.

While our capacity to apprehend these objects, or the ways in which we think them may seem to make the world flat, such flatness does not account for the thick skin of time layered over each

---

[46] Iain Hamilton Grant, "Movements of the World: The Sources of Transcendental Philosophy," in *Analecta Hermeneutica* 3 (2011): 15.
[47] Grant, "Movements of the World," 16.

object, nor for the very different grounds of production for each. Affectivity and connectivity cannot account for pragmatic access (as well as awareness of) of ecological problems. The derision of local engagements in that they do no directly challenge the system at large (whether statist, capitalist, or otherwise) tends to overlook this point. Local engagement is not *the* answer, nor is it worthless. This is why for Schelling philosophy must be systematic but never a single system that is closed and completed. This makes no sense if reality is by its very nature dynamic, and thought must be as organized as it can be without becoming mechanical to the point of failure. How can politics be different?

Ben Woodard is a Ph.D. student in Theory and Criticism at the University of Western Ontario. He is the author of *Slime Dynamics* (Zero Books, 2011) and *On an Ungrounded Earth: Towards a New Geophilosophy* (punctum books, 2013).

Anarchist Developments in Cultural Studies
ISSN: 1923-5615
2013.2: Ontological Anarché: Beyond Materialism and Idealism

Ontological Anarché
Beyond Arché & Anarché

Jason Harman

ABSTRACT

I analyze the contemporary notion of a world without preordained principle, ground, or substance and argue that this inversion of the tradition of metaphysical thinking remains parasitic on metaphysics. I show that ontological anarché is firmly oriented around the notion of arché, which entails a process of denial and asceticism by its proponents. In moving beyond the tragic opposition of arché and anarché, I suggest we turn to the work of Jean-Luc Nancy. Nancy helps to undermine the traditional opposition of *something* and *nothing,* arché and anarché, by demonstrating the co-originality of the two *together* in being-*with.* I conclude that the proper notion of the modern human community is precisely that its ground or arché is not the ground, principle, or, substance of the premodern era but rather *spirit* or *relationality:* the *com-* of community.

KEYWORDS
ground, principle, substance, post-foundationalism, democracy, community

This essay examines an ambivalence that lies at the heart of the notion of *ontological anarché*. This ambivalence arises from the conflict between an active and actual (i.e., positive) political projects espoused in much anarchist thinking and the negative *denotation* that accompanies the word anarchy. Anarchy, as is well known, proceeds from the confluence of the privative affix *an* and the Greek root *arché*, which can be translated variously as rule, ground, principle, or foundation. Placed together, an-archy signifies the absence of a preordained order through which to guide action. In the past, anarchy merely represented one political regime among many; it could be compared and contrasted with the great and ubiquitous *arché* mon-archy: the rule of one. However, in recent times anarchy has gained a deeper metaphysical or ontological status thanks to the decline of metaphysics ushered in by Nietzsche and Heidegger and proceeding into our *post-modern* present.

In this vein, anarchy signifies not simply a *style* of politics but the very predicament (or scandal) of politics itself. Politics, and political regimes, exist precisely because of the absence of *arché* that defines our ontological existence. My interest in this topic lies specifically within the context of the metaphysical or ontological embrace of a world without foundation (without arché) by political philosophers on the French Left (Castoriadis, Lefort, Manent, Abensour, Rancière, etc.). This article aims to demonstrate that what has been called "post-foundational" thinking (Marchart, 2009), is essentially *ontological anarché*, and that the latter, despite its pretensions, maintains hidden commitments to the onto-theological project of foundational or principled (archic) thought. As such, *post-foundational* thought, or *ontological anarché*, manifests itself as essentially the mirror-image of that which it seeks to oppose. Following my demonstration of this tragic reversal, I will conclude with a brief discussion of the work of another contemporary Leftist political philosopher, Jean-Luc Nancy, who aims to reposition ontological anarché in such a way as to move it beyond the arché/anarché divide (entangled as it is with other modern dichotomies like dogmatism/skepticism) in order to rethink human communities as the product of a paradoxically *principled anarchy.*

The burgeoning fascination with ontological anarché can be traced to the 20th century. With the collapse of the totalizing meta-narrative of communism, coupled with the decay of capitalist liberal-democratic multiculturalism, the West witnessed a revival of a politics of *radical democracy.* The metaphysical makeup that sustains much of the new philosophy of radical democracy, whether in the formative thought of Cornelius Castoriadis and Claude Lefort, or their successors Miguel Abensour and Jacques Rancière, is the thought of a *cosmos* without order, an ontology that is fundamentally *anarchic.* As Castoriadis put it, the enterprise of modernity, almost universally attributed to René Descartes, was shackled to a delusion that concealed the ontological fact that "there is not and cannot be a rigourous or ultimate foundation of anything" (1995: 87). Sharing in this sentiment, the embrace of anarché—at least at the metaphysical level—has reached new heights among contemporary French intellectuals.

One can immediately sense the attractiveness—the temptation—that ontological anarché presents the weary and disappointed theorist. Having been successfully strung along for millenia with ever-changing regimes of order—God, Reason, History— the notion that all of these are merely varying types of *illusion* seems quite revelatory, even emancipating. Not only may we then reject the entire history of Truth as metaphysical superstition, we may finally cease looking for order altogether. Cosmos is, in actual fact, chaos. Quite similarly, truth is *doxa* (opinion) and *doxa* is power. This is the new *post-modern* formula that undergirds ontological anarché.

Yet the turn toward an ontological anarchism as an escape from the legacy of 20th century totalizing thought is fraught with difficulties. Castoriadis, for one, accepts anarchism as a sort of *tabula rasa* that lies beyond good and evil: if there is no foundational arché then all action is equally arbitrary (1995: 106, 161). According to him, the only possible purveyor of a criterion can be found in those who constitute a given social-historical milieu: a group he calls the *demos* (1995: 105–106, 109). Yet, the actions of the demos themselves are essentially beyond judgment (save by a future *demos*) and as such Castoriadis can offer no hard and fast ethical rules. The only ethical principle of his an-archic political philosophy is the mandate of disclosing the *demos* as the constituent members of any and all human creation: whether in the form of politics, economics, or jurisprudence.

Castoriadis' brand of radical democracy, grounded on the abyss of an ontological anarchism, has become popular in contemporary discourse. It functions as a critic of representative and totalizing systems which serve to conceal how the whole of society is responsible for creating and legitimating the vast matrix of socio-historical artifacts. His intellectual colleague, Claude Lefort, approached the same problem from a different angle, one undoubtedly influenced by his own mentor, Maurice Merleau-Ponty (1968: 211). Lefort (2000) proposes "savage democracy" (see Moyn, 2005: xx) which his student, Miguel Abensour, links directly with anarchy in an essay published alongside the English translation of the latter's *Democracy Against the State*; "savage democracy," according to Abensour, resists and rejects all notion of principle which would violate the essential purity of its groundlessness (2011: 123–124).

This abrupt passage from rigid order to absolute and essential disorder, however, belies a concern that is at least as old as the very project of post-foundationalism or ontological anarchy. This concern is expressed in "Letter on Humanism" by Martin Heidegger in his critique of the existentialism of Jean-Paul Sartre, where he posits the *tragic* problem at the heart of the matter, namely that "the *reversal* of a metaphysical statement *remains a metaphysical statement*" (1993: 232). In Heidegger's mind, Sartre's existential humanism was merely replacing belief in God with an equally opaque belief in "man" (1993: 226). In the eyes of Christopher Watkin, Sartre was not dethroning religion but imitating it (2011: 2). Yet, imitation, or perhaps better, *substitution*, is not the only form of upholding an allegiance to *archic* thought. One can also forgo the chain of substituting one metaphysical principle for another by renouncing metaphysics itself, and in so doing, maintain a connection to *archic* thought by more subversive and subconscious means. Watkin names this process "residual atheism" (2011: 6)—a concept which we may easily convert to *residual anarchism*—and its duplicitous nature is most clearly shown by the paradoxical notion of *negative theology*.

The concept of *negative theology* arises from the philosophy of religion that, in some ways, is a counterpart of modern anarchist thought. As Hegel and others make clear, what lies at the heart of the modern experience of Christianity is *the death of God* (Hegel, 2006: 468). As such, Christianity is essentially "a religion for departing from religion" (Gauchet, 1997: 4). Yet, this departure which Sartre and others have interpreted as a rejection of the *archic* onto-theological *cosmos* takes the form of trading the notion of a *present* God for an *absent* one. This switch (from presence to absence) is far less radical than it first seems: in both cases, thought is still firmly entrenched on the original subject (e.g. God, truth, arché). As Henri Bergson reminded us a century ago,

> a non-existent can only consist, therefore, in *adding* something to the idea of this object: we add to it, in fact, the idea of an *exclusion* of this particular object by actual reality in general. To think the object A as non-existent is first to think the object and consequently to think it existent; it is then to think that another reality, with which it is incompatible, supplants it. (2005: 310)

Bergson shows us that the grammar of non-existence involves maintaining the conception of the very object whose existence is to be denied. In the case of ontological anarché, despite the explicit denial of the premise (arché), anarché implicitly retains an orientation around ground, foundation, or principle (arché). In

the words of Nietzsche, the followers of an ontological anarchism have merely divested themselves from the "church"—the
outward appearance of archic thought—but have yet to abandon
the "poison" (2006: bk. 1, §9)—the hidden nectar or kernel of
archeism that runs through the veins of ontological anarché.

The source of the problem lies in the terms of the controversy
itself. Ontological anarchism, far from being a radical alternative
to the modern paradigm, is very much rooted in the same dichotomous structure as its predecessors. Indeed, one can trace its lin-
eage from the high modernism of figures like Max Weber—who
famously posited the fact/value distinction—to the post-meta-
physical thinkers who espouse an anarchic ontology. The mod-
ernist gulf separating what-is (ontology/metaphysics) from what-
ought (ethics/morality), which first destabilized the latter realm in
the name of pure scientific rationality (positivism), later expanded
to envelope that which it had originally safeguarded. How could
one seek objective scientific truth without recognizing the implicit valuation, passion, or drive that lies behind such a pursuit? The
end result of this post-modern destabilization is not merely a political anarchism that takes the form of collective legislating on
values or nomos (laws) that exist within the framework of an
ordered and regimented natural world (a cosmos). Instead, it is
the dawn of a thoroughly ontological anarchism which finds itself beyond the reach of any stabilizing factor (a chaos).

Pierre Manent, another figure of the post-foundational group,
explains that the chaotic abyss that late modernism has opened
should be neither shunned nor bridged. Rather, he tells us that it
is our profound and heroic task to stand face-to-face with this
nothingness, this nihilism which is "not only our curse but also
our duty" (Manent, 2000). Politically, it means to embrace the
arbitrary legislation of Castoriadis' demos and the savage democracy of Lefort. The ancient ethos of courage, then, returns as the
cardinal political virtue, and it signifies the ability to stare un-
flinchingly into the abyss. Yet, was it not also Nietzsche who
warned us of the dangers inherent in such an act (2001: pt. 4,
#146)? In our case, the danger results from a tragic reversal that
weaves together subject and object, infusing nihilism into the
heart of the courageous hero.

The drama of the tragic reversal, captured by Aristotle as the
heart of the ancient plays of Aeschylus, Sophocles, and Euripides
(1984: ln. 1452a22–24), returns with the metaphysical substitution
of arché with anarché. This process of reversal completes the teleology of modernism. The abyss resulting from the de-structuring

of values and facts leads not to yet another set of values—for that would be contradictory—but rather to the celebration of the abyss as our tragic destiny, as we witnessed with Manent. In this regard, ontological anarchism is predisposed to take the form of a negative theology that binds itself to the withdrawal of the Absolute/archic and constitutes itself in mourning for this powerful absence. Indeed, by situating itself precisely on the negative 'an' of an-archism, the legatees of modernism have constructed for themselves an essentially reactive metaphysics that is parasitic on the history of archic ontology.

In place of the variety of principles that have substituted and signified presence—the core of archic thought—ontological anarchism pivots around absence. There, absence becomes every bit as much of a foundation (an arché) as the varied incarnations of presence ever were. In Sartre, the abandonment of humans by God leads to a brand of Promethean humanism where the role of God is downloaded to us mortals (2004: 352). Yet, as Heidegger points out, this exchange or reversal, imports the metaphysics of the former into the latter. Humanism becomes pregnant with unthought assumptions which provide the hidden ground of Sartre's onto-political project (1993: 226, 232).

Similarly, the central place of human self-determination or autonomy in the thought of the post-foundationalists belies a metaphysics of production and valuation. Rather than radically revaluing value—as Nietzsche commends us—the thought of human self-production or auto-poiēsis carries out the modern capitalist dream of the self-made man. However, by destabilizing the values that originally complemented modernism, by disclosing them as essentially empty and vain, humanity finds itself driven further and further into nihilism.

We are tasked, according to the thinkers of radical democracy with building a world, with owning the values we instill, whilst simultaneously acknowledging that all values are equally valueless. As such, the world envisioned by ontological anarché, captivated as it is by the value-producing faculty of the imagination and the social imaginary, resembles the dystopian limbo featured in Christopher Nolan's 2010 film, *Inception*. There, the imaginary world created by Mal and Cobb crumbles and vanishes away like castles made of sand. Moreover, this reality leads the deranged wife of the protagonist, Mal, who is haunted by the presentiment that her world is ultimately false (or arbitrary), to commit suicide in order to wake to the truth.

Perhaps contemporary post-foundational philosophers would

object that such an action bespeaks a lack of courage to come to terms with the radical contingency, anarchy, or falsity that has become the substance of the post-modern world. Yet, as long as these terms (contingency, anarchy, falsity) exist as a couple with their opposites (necessity, arché, truth), through which they are defined, the presence of one will entail a longing for the absent other. Following Bergson, we can affirm that "the act by which we declare an object unreal therefore posits the existence of the real in general" (2005: 310). If we return, briefly, to *Inception*, we can note that prior to Mal's anxiety over the valuelessness or falsity of the world, she embraced her imaginary world only by forgetting or suppressing the fact of its falsity. As such, the dreamworld exists for Mal either as real and therefore archic or as false and therefore as a remnant or residue (to borrow from Watkin) of the real. In either case, the dreamworld is entangled with ontological arché. In this way, *Inception* depicts both trajectories that are nascent within our (post)modern epistemology. The embrace of ontological anarché requires either a concealing, as Heidegger saw in Sartrean humanism, or an increasingly maddening flight from the clutches of the abyss egged on by an "unquenchable craving for the Absolute" (Lánczi, 2010: 95).

Ultimately, both embracing and fleeing an anarchic world is essentially tragic. Furthermore, the notion that one can courageously stand midway between these two tragic poles, occupying the magical midpoint that Aristotle called sophrosyne (moderation), is to commit the very act of hybris (hubris) that ancient tragedy preys upon. One can take, for example, Aeschylus's Agamemnon where the eponymous tragic hero attempts to navigate between his duty to express humility before the gods and his wife's demand, on behalf of the polis, for his exaltation following the Greek victory in the Trojan War. Needless to say, this juncture leads to his tragic demise.

Despite the grim dilemma that ontological anarché opens before us, it still compels our attention simply because we can no longer fool ourselves into believing a return to a pre-modern hierarchical model of being (God, human, animals) or politics (the ancient cycle of monarchy, aristocracy, democracy) is a solution to our current predicament. There is no way to re-enchant a disenchanted world. Indeed, in those moments where such recourse has managed to seduce a population (e.g., in the totalitarian movements of the early 20th century), the cure has proven far worse than the original disease.

If regression is out of the question, and the brute acceptance of anarchic or savage being and its political counterpart, savage democracy (Lefort/Abensour), contains two perilous and equally tragic alternatives, it appears that modernity leaves us with an insoluble problem. It is at this point where the thought of Jean-Luc Nancy commends itself. Nancy (2010) speaks of a paradoxically "principled anarchy" (p. 66)—or archic-anarchy that overcomes the dichotomic trap established by our modern bipolar condition. Rather than seeking comfort in the oppressive regimes fortified by tradition and the transcendent idols called God, Reason, the Good, etc., or risking the savage democracy of a world without principles or meaning, Nancy suggests overcoming the very choice itself. Such a choice, he argues, misapprehends the fundamental nature of human existence as being-with: a condition which is neither singular nor plural (Nancy, 2000: pp. 7, 42).

By understanding ontological anarché as having eclipsed the central dichotomies of modernity—operating neither as anarchic or archic nor through an originary founding of society on either the individual subject (as king) or the collective subject (as demos)—Nancy opens a new way of understanding anarchism that is not constrained by the libertarian / communitarian divide. Indeed, this principled anarchy or archic-anarchism may prove to be the essential turning point in re-grounding political sovereignty in a world that remains hesitant at leaping head-first into the abyss of the savage democracy constituted by ontological anarché, but that must come to grips with the failure of utopian communism and our eroding liberal-democracies.

According to Nancy, we must be wary of dodging the commitments of modernism by simply choosing otherwise. Watkin, we might recall, notes that such a maneuver employs a form of asceticism or self-denial that defines itself in juxtaposition to that which it decries. Asceticism, no more than the blatant substitution of one arché for another, a strategy he calls parasitism, surpasses the trap of modernity (2011: 11). Nancy's ontological solution avoids both parasitism and asceticism and yet reclaims the function of (archic) foundation. Following a Hegelian motif, Nancy asserts that ontology properly understood is not an archic substance but spirit. Arché is thus restored but not as a thing—a foundation, ground, or principle—but rather as relation. In The Creation of the World or Globalization, Nancy plays with the notion of the anarchic abyss as nothing, which he reads as a special type of thing that is not: "it is that very particular thing that nothing [rien] is" (2007: 102).

Similarly in The Inoperative Community, Nancy argues that

what he is speaking about

> is a groundless 'ground' less in the sense that it opens up
> the gaping chasm of an abyss than that it is made up only
> of the network, the interweaving, and the sharing of sin-
> gularities: *Ungrund* rather than *Abgrund*, but no less ver-
> tiginous. (1991: 27)

Here the distinction between the German *un* and *ab* with the root
grund [ground] goes to the heart of our problematic regarding
ontological anarché. Nancy's distinction operates on the difference between the strictly negative *ab* of *Abgrund*—denoting absence—and the less antagonistic *un* of *Ungrund*, which denotes
instead dissimilarity. In this way, Nancy means to suggest a sublation of the dichotomy of ground and abyss that confounds modern (and post-modern) metaphysics.

What makes Ungrund distinct from Abgrund is the fact of relation. Nancy circumvents the dichotomous logic of presence and
absence by making the relation he calls being-with central to ontology. The with of being-with, or, alternatively, the com of
community, speaks neither of a primordial togetherness (a demos
or society or collective) nor of an ex post facto association of disparate and atomized individuals (as envisioned by liberal-democratic philosophers in the tradition of the social contract). Nancy
achieves this by realizing that the abyss that underlies all attempts at founding an ontological or political order is essentially
ambivalent. As I have tried to demonstrate, the contemporary
interpretation of this abyss does not account for this ambivalence
and reads the concept strictly as nothingness, lack, disorder, or
chaos: the negation of the cosmological arché. This pure negativity opens the door to nihilism, as Pierre Manent is well aware.
However, rather than attempt to moderate or barter with nothingness, as Manent suggests, Nancy finds in the abyss itself an
essentially positive meaning. It is this insight into nothingness
that enables Nancy to determine that nothing is identical to the
common—an object that is incomparable to demos, society or
collective. Rather, the common is the spacing which is always
between singular beings, relating them and hence implicating
singularity alongside plurality.

On account of its status as space, the common is clearly nothing: a lacuna, the void. However, it is that because it is always
already implicated in the bodies of the singularities themselves.
There is no spacing outside of singularities nor any singularities

outside of spacing. For this reason, it is perhaps more productive to speak of Nancy's no-thing as the with of being-with or the 'com' of com-munity. In this manner, we are disabused of the pretence of an originary lacuna that necessitates a contingent or arbitrary society. In its place, we see the co-originality of no-thing and some-thing—forever upending the philosophical question as to why there is something rather than nothing. As such, ontological anarché loses its meaning as a tabula rasa from which all artifice is equally arbitrary, and instead gains a positive ethical imperative: relationality. Relationality, of course, is hardly the archic telos espoused by the metanarratives of old, but neither is it nothing. Instead, it is the trace and measure both of the democracy we have and the democracy-to-come.

It is the contention of this article that the notion of ontological anarché acts as a siren song to call us back to the tyrannical logic of arché through the pretence that an inversion of this logic will lead to a fundamentally different outcome. At the same time, however, ontological anarché can allow for exploring paths beyond the contradiction created by the dichotomies of modern logic. In undertaking this alternate path, beyond the polarity of arché and anarché, we have the chance of salvaging value from the nihilism of our postmodern condition. To realize the value of being-with, of com-munity, as the essential creator of all sense and signification, is to move from an abstract and vapid ontology of nihilistic value-production to an ethics and politics of world— or community—creation. It is the latter which strikes me as the proper course for contemporary ontological and political anarchism.

Jason Harman is a recent graduate of the *Social & Political Thought* program at York University in Toronto, Canada. His interests revolve around the intersection of philosophy, religion, and politics. His dissertation, *The Politics of Tragedy: The Reversal of Radical Democracy*, explores the revival of Greek tragedy as a contemporary program of democracy by members of the post-Heideggerian Left. This notion and its proponents are criticized in favour of a more Hegelian approach based on a reinterpretation of the works of Nietzsche, Kierkegaard, and Hannah Arendt. Jason is also an Assistant Editor of *Theoria & Praxis: International Journal of Interdisciplinary Thought*.

REFERENCES

Aristotle (1984). "Poetics," in *Complete Works of Aristotle: The Revised Oxford Translation*, trans. Ingram Bywater. Vol. 2: 2316–2340. Princeton: Princeton University Press.

Abensour, M. (2011). *Democracy Against the State: Marx and the Machiavellian Movement.* (Blechman, M. and Breaugh, M., Trans.). Cambridge: Polity.

Bergson, H. (2005). *Creative Evolution.* New York: Cosimo, Inc.

Castoriadis, C. (1995). *Philosophy, Politics, Autonomy: Essays in Political Philosophy.* New York: Oxford University Press.

Heidegger, M. (1993). "Letter on Humanism." In *Basic Writings: from Being and Time (1927) to The Task of Thinking (1964)* (Krell, D.F., Ed.). New York: HarperCollins. 217–265.

Gauchet, M. (1997). *The Disenchantment of the World: A Political History of Religion.* (Burge, O., Trans.). Princeton: Princeton University Press.

Lánczi, A. (2010). "Democracy and Moral Relativism in a Post-secular World: Reclaiming Obligation." In *From Political Theory to Political Theology: Religious Challenges and the Prospects of Democracy* (Losonczi, P., and Singh, A., Eds.). New York: Continuum. 85–100.

Lefort, C. (2000). *Writing: The Political Test.* (Curtis, D.A., Trans.). Durham: Duke University Press.

Hegel, G.W.F. (2006). *Lectures on the Philosophy of Religion: The Lectures of 1827 (One Volume Edition).* (Hodgson, P.C., Ed.). New York: Oxford University Press.

Manent, P. (2000). "The Return of Political Philosophy." *First Things* 103 (May 2000): 15–22; www.firstthings.com/article/2007/01/the-return-of-political-philosophy-39.

Marchart, O. (2009). *Post-Foundational Political Thought: Political Difference in Nancy, Lefort, Badiou and Laclau.* Edinburgh: Edinburgh University Press.

Merleau-Ponty, M. (1968). *The Visible and the Invisible, Followed by Working Notes.* (Lefort, C., Ed.). Evanston: Northwestern University Press.

Moyn, S. (2005). Savage and Modern Liberty: Marcel Gauchet and the Origins of New French Thought. *Constellations* 15(3): 406–420.

Nancy, J.-L. (2000). *Being Singular Plural*, trans. R.D. Richardson and A.E. O'Byrne. Stanford: Stanford University Press.

Nancy, J.-L. (2007). *The Creation of the World or Globalization.* (Raffoul, F., and Pettigrew, D., Trans.). Albany: State University of New York Press.

Nancy, J.-L. (2010). "Finite and Infinite Democracy." In *Democracy in What State?* (Allen, A., Ed.). New York: Columbia University Press. 58–75.

Nietzsche, F. (2001). *Beyond Good and Evil: Prelude to a Philosophy of the Future.* (Norman, J., Trans.). New York: Cambridge University Press.

Nietzsche, F. (2006). *"On the Genealogy of Morality" and Other Writings.* (Diethe, C., Trans.). New York: Cambridge University Press.

Sartre, J.-P. (2004). "Existentialism is a Humanism." In *Existentialism: From Dostoevsky to Sartre* (Kaufmann, W. Ed.). New York: Plume Penguin Group. 345–368.

Watkin, C. (2011). *Difficult Atheism: Post-Theological Thinking in Alain Badiou, Jean-Luc Nancy and Quentin Meillassoux.* Edinburgh: Edinburgh University Press.

Anarchist Developments in Cultural Studies
ISSN: 1923-5615
2013.2: Ontological Anarché: Beyond Materialism and Idealism

Critique of Static Ontology and Becoming-Anarchy[1]

Salvo Vaccaro

translated by Jesse Cohn

ABSTRACT

The following article was written by Salvo Vaccaro and translated by Jesse Cohn. The article raises the following question: Is anarchism a philosophy? Moreover, is anarchism, as a philosophy, foundationalist?

KEYWORDS

ontology, foundation, Adorno, reconciliation, Deleuze, becoming

Anarchism and philosophy [*Anarchisme et philosophie*]. Let's start by questioning the status of the connective "and" [*et*]. Or is the *and* perhaps a copula, an "is" [*est*]? In both cases, it will be necessary above all to understand the two polar terms of this statement, and then to weave a relationship between them, the nature of which will tell us what this "and/is" [*e(s)t*] indicates. It seems that understanding what *anarchism* is represents an easier task, rather than understanding what *philosophy* is in our Western conceptual milieu (from before Plato to the present). But is this so? Let us address this last question.

There are many definitions of *philosophy;* I will consider only three of them. The first definition posits a coincidence between philosophical knowledge and knowledge as such, i.e., knowing

---

[1] This paper originally appeared as: "Critique de l'ontologie étatique et devenir-anarchie," in Jean-Christoph Angaut, Daniel Colson, Mimmo Pucciarelli (s.d.), *Philosophie de l'anarchie* (Lyon: Atelier Création Libertaire, 2012).

things for what they are; not the analysis of the activity of think-ing as a material substrate (today, we would call this the *hard-ware*), but the analysis of the constructions of thought that serve to situate the object on the basis of its content (i.e., the Aristotel-ian categories as *software*). This definition has the merit of re-minding us of our continuity with antiquity, the cosmology of the Renaissance, and Kant, who innovates only in the *critical* attitude he imparts to this philosophical analysis. When this philosophical analysis "leases" (to use a contemporary term) the criteria of veri-fication belonging to the scientific order, for the precision of the exact sciences transposed onto the plane of thought, then the philosophy of modernity is first and foremost epistemology.

The second definition proposes to go further than this cogni-tive activity, which no longer agrees to limit itself to deciphering the reasons for the reality of experience (by the use of logic or the senses), in order to project itself beyond: *metà fusikà*. In fact, metaphysics studies, exclusively through the logic of reason—although somehow edified by an affinity with what we might define as *theology*—all that goes beyond the mere reception of the senses, in order to find, beyond sensation, a spirit, an idea, the visibility of which (a tautology in Plato) provides the real key to the understanding of reality because it illuminates the original apparatus that animates it, that gives it existence and allows it to be reproduced.

The third definition in this brief overview is, finally, the spe-cific activity of philosophy that seeks the substance of each thing contained in the objects of thought, a substance by unique neces-sity that is hidden behind what appears, what is given. In short, ontology seeks being [*être*] behind the existant [*étant*], a deep background that lies behind it, at the cost of the inadmissibility of its thinking existence, so anything short of its pure existence as existant [*étant*].

Surely you will have noticed that I didn't intend to approach the question of the term "philosophy," which is generally traced back to the love of wisdom, φιλος [*philos*] and σοφος [*sophos*] in Greek. But Reiner Schürmann, in a note that I cannot fully ana-lyze in this paper, states that "Philein [φιλειν] signifies here not 'to love,' but 'to appropriate,' (*suos* [σφος], in Latin, *suus*, in French *sien*). The *philosophos* is the one who pursues a knowledge in order to make it his own."[2]

---

[2] Reiner Schürmann, *Broken Hegemonies*, trans. Reginald Lilly (Bloom-ington: Indiana University Press, 2003), 635n26.

Let us pause for the moment and turn our attention to the other side of the polarity, anarchism. Is anarchism a philosophy? Is it an independent philosophy, or is it contained within a particular school? It is difficult to contain all the protagonists and all the propositions that can be visibly traced back to the anarchist idea within just one body of doctrine in the singular, *anarchism*. Indeed, the plurality of thought and thinkable anarchisms makes it difficult to reduce or return them to unity such that we could identify it within a single discipline of thought that is philosophy. So I say that anarchisms cannot be reduced to a form of thinking which is philosophy, even if in some passages anarchism seems to echo some philosophical considerations. If, for example, we take ethics as the focal point of the dynamics of thought, then we would be further encouraged to think that the plural variants of anarchism could be integrated within a certain ethical conception, tied to an individual and collective behavior as a kind of material precondition for each political hypothesis under the sign of anarchism.

But then, what is this plural anarchism? If we look at it in its historical-material genesis, it arises within the political sphere. It emerged in a thoroughly politicized context, emerged in sharp contrast to the modern, secular tendency to depoliticize society and its constituents (the term *actor* betrays the tacit and servile acceptance of its spectacularization, well before Guy Debord's subtle diagnoses). Of course, the rather visible influence of the Enlightenment might lead us to rethink this "placement" of anarchism within the domain of political ideas in order to give it a philosophical halo instead, but it is almost impossible to detach the anarchist idea from the historical movements that have embodied it, all politically aimed at overthrowing not just one historical political regime, but rather a form inherited for centuries, in order to inaugurate an associative and emancipated form of life.

But is it a form of political thought, i.e., a theory, a philosophy of politics? Or is it only a discursive practice, as in Foucault, which is in equal measure theory and practice? Several elements point towards the latter account, elements that could be interrogated by an interesting and very useful genealogical research (quite far from the kind of historical-archival reconstruction which predominates among anarchists). Above all, the singular condition according to which the stratification of the anarchist idea in general terms only gives us the figure of a theoretical thinker who, even in his biography, coincides with the figure of a militant activist. Apart from Godwin and Stirner, in our "pantheon" there is not one anarchist theorist who was not an active protagonist in the history of the political movement. It is as if most agreed on the legitimacy of the act of theoretical reflection, without running the risk of an uncritical and hagiographic exaltation of the singular human figure, but on condition that it be brought down from the ivory tower, set within the plural domain of common mortals, of activists operating within praxis as the primary site of verification and truth-telling, according to the success or failure of political strategies and tactics, just like everyone else in a particular historical and social context.

Since the quantity of documents of all kinds that characterize the cultural production of plural anarchism reflects the discursive practice that feeds on political analyses, on theoretical considerations, of course, but also on pamphlets, leaflets, articles in the endless press that signaled the golden years of the anarchist movements, whose members were mostly subaltern individuals bordering on cultural illiteracy, although very attentive to the cultural dimension—more so than today, when we certainly observe a rise in the cultural competences of each, at least in the rich and powerful planetary North.

Doubtlessly, then, plural anarchism, understood as a *discursive formation*, contains the elements of a theorization of pure politics, so to speak, i.e., infinite and not contingent: the critique of statism (not only of the state-form), the negation of authority constituting a given, as well as some sophisticated levels of self-reflexive theorizing about its own epistemic categories that could almost make it belong to a certain idea of political philosophy. But these singular attitudes do not signal, in my view, the corpus that is emblematic of anarchism and its plural flesh-and-blood historical actors. On the contrary, if we just look at one of the reasons that plural anarchism today speaks haltingly within the social arena of the rich and powerful world of the West, it is likely because it presents this specific element: the ultimately stifling, self-referential conditions of the cultural reproduction of anarchism and its movements, which appears fearful or reluctant to contaminate itself by mixing with and incorporating, through a few filters of critical re-elaboration, certain varieties of thought and practice that come from other, neighboring but distinct cultural contexts that are possessed of many affinities as regards motives, perspectives, goals and objectives.

At the end of this rapid double exposition of philosophy and anarchism, we feel that the status of this *and* lies in a disjunctive conjunction. If we juxtapose their descriptions, we cannot fail to see how the spark that ignites philosophical thought is visible in *astonishment as the motivating force of cognitive contemplation*, although the detonating fuse that activates anarchist discourse (theoretical and practice at once) is represented, recalling Hannah Arendt here, in *rage as the motivating force for transformative action*. The experience of the injustice, the lying, the arrogance of power is the *prius movens* of anarchist action, and this is reflected in the ethics that it connotes: the privative *a* that negates, as its primary postulate—a kind of unfounded *incipit* of theoretical perspective, but often so profound as to impel a radical turning point in life—the authority towards which, purely in the negative, anarchism orients itself. Of course, it would be too complicated to analyze in brief the ways in which the historical movements have conjugated this "originary rage," ranging from ironic invective to insurgency, from spontaneous revolt to (more or less) organized revolution.

The negative approach of anarchism, as signaled by the privative *a*, also produces, in my view, another bifurcation of philosophical reflection. Just by the act of excusing itself, in the first place, from the contingent task of offering a proposal for the organization of a society without domination, a task that is also consigned to the real movements, anarchism presents itself as *infinite* in the spirit of its thought. The anarchist proposition, indeed, is not susceptible to counter-factual negation on the historical plane: the fact that no society, ancient or modern (Clastres' regression to preliterate societies is debatable), has ever achieved an anarchic phase in its existence does not present a theoretical weapon against anarchism, which posits the negation of authority, with all this entails on the institutional and social plane, regardless of the finitude of history. Thus its spirit is infinite, certainly, but in a way that would be dangerously "analogous" to the metaphysical search for a foundation of being [*statut de l'être*] if anarchism were to seek a kind of "counter-foundation of being [*contre-statut de l'être*]" with which to legitimize the negation of authority, not in the very fact of being able to think it, but because a "fundamentally-virtually-anarchic-being" is thinkable.

Instead, the most critical and dissonant contemporary philosophical thought has now abandoned every metaphysical pretension, at least in its more politically radical statements, situating its own research within a trans-generational *finitude* of the human (and even the post-human) that examines the psychological effects of existence at a singular and collective level, from a political standpoint that owes nothing to any theology, seeking to give the contingent space of life its greatest meaning and value, to lend as much aid as possible to the daily adventure between the prenatal *nihil* and the postmortem *nihil*.

When I point to the perilous nature for anarchist thought of a "counter-foundation of being," what I am really distancing myself from is the search for an ontology of being that could confirm the anarchist hypothesis by setting it upon a base that has truth as its platform. This is the fate of any ontology as a conceptual operation, short of a pluralistic declination (Deleuze) or a historico-social declination (Hacking). Ontology is that particular branch of philosophical reflection which looks for the stability of being *qua* being, i.e., where the object of research is specifically twisted towards a transcendental abstraction, toward an essence that is invisible to the existence, which is to be anchored to something immobile, to a deep substrate, so that it will stay firmly rooted in a fixed, immutable, predestined condition, which is precisely being *qua* being, not the existence, which is always changing in relation to the historical-conceptual conditions of thought.[3]

Ontology is a moment of philosophical reflection that signals that we are leaving behind the naturalistic and physical account of the things of the world in order to construct a single hidden essence (Parmenides) that is to be brought into the light of truth. This is the Greek etymology of the word "truth," *a-letheia*, unveiling, as if the philosophical thought that seeks the origin of the world in the facts of nature carried the vice of concealment in itself, the concealment of the meta-physical, which goes beyond the mere sensible appearance of a world perceived by the easily deceived and deluded senses, while the ability to reason becomes infallible in relation to sense-perception, but such that this is the preserve of an elite of philosophers, of course, whom Plato really intended to be not only cultural but political leaders.

The philosophical approach thus reveals its political intentionality, i.e., in the first place, ensuring knowledge of the world not to those who possess five senses *naturaliter*, so to speak, thus without any specific competencies, but really to those who have a faculty of reason (*logos*, not *noos*, always available to everyone as pure *spirit*), the exercise of which becomes, for the first time, the result of a specific training, a specific domestication, through the

---

[3] "It is no longer being that is divided into so many categories, arranged into an ontological hierarchy, distributed into specific beings assigned to a fixed place; rather, ontic differences are distributed in a smooth space, open to being": Véronique Bergen, *L'Ontologie de Gilles Deleuze* (Paris: L'Harmattan, 2001), 19.

schools of thought, the techniques of rhetoric and sophistry, etc.

At the same time, to know the world means to control it, as we can see from the German word *ver-stehen*, *Verstand* ("understanding," "concept"), both a *comprehension* of the world and a *grasping* of the world; thus, the relationship between power and knowledge appears from the very beginning of a specific disciplinary knowledge such as metaphysical philosophy and, at its heart, the search for an ontological foundation of being. This search has a political purpose: to conceal the eternal tension between thought and world, transforming it into a war, a particular twisting of the conflict in a field of tension that can be appropriated by someone, the victor of thought, we might say, as Heraclitus reminds us when he posits *polemos* as father and king of all things. The doubling of *polemos* takes the name of *stasis*, which in Plato (*The Republic*) means precisely a state of (internal) war:

> In my opinion, just as we have the two terms, war [*polemos*] and faction [*stasis*], so there are also two things, distinguished by two differentiae. The two things I mean are the friendly and kindred on the one hand and the alien and foreign on the other. Now the term employed for the hostility of the friendly is faction, and for that of the alien is war. . . . We shall then say that Greeks fight and wage war with barbarians, and barbarians with Greeks, and are enemies by nature, and that war is the fit name for this enmity and hatred. Greeks, however, we shall say, are still by nature the friends of Greeks when they act in this way, but that Greece is sick in that case and divided by faction, and faction is the name we must give to that enmity.[4]

Today, if we tear away the veil of concealment, we can see *stasis* as the thematic root of the "state," of "statism" as a principle of stability, stability conceived as immobility, the product of a violent appropriation under the sign of a war of conquest, the originary myth of the violent foundation of the state and of political power.[5]

---

[4] Trans. Paul Shorey, in Plato, *The Collected Dialogues of Plato*, ed. Edith Hamilton and Huntington Cairns (Princeton: Princeton University Press, 1973), 709.

[5] Jean-Pierre Vernant, *Myth and Thought Among the Greeks*, trans. Janet Lloyd and Jeff Fort (London: Routledge & Kegan Paul, 1983); *Myth and Society in Ancient Greece*, trans. Janet Lloyd (New York: Zone Books, 1988).

Ontology traces the metaphysical horizon of this entirely philosophical-political course within which to anesthetize the entirely reducible tension between thought and world, to anesthetize the constitutive excess of thought with respect to the world-as-it-is and of the world with respect to the thought-that-conceptualizes-it, to anesthetize what Derrida calls the *aporia* founding the void over which the history of Western thought has raised its crowded mausoleum. Indeed, ontology posits an origin in a dimension that is unverifiable, incorruptible, untouchable—in a word, non-contingent—which renders possible the long trajectory of philosophy's account not only of the interpretation of the world, but also of its transformation, long before the famous Marxian theses on Feuerbach.

Seeking the ontology of being means seeking to install an essence at the moment of the *arché* of the world, either as originary principle or as the leader dictating the sense [*sens*—in French, both "meaning" and "direction"] of the philosophical account of being. The *arché* is present all at once and in every case, apart from any historical contingency, but far from the human senses, trusting to the *logos* as the sovereign operation of capture: the *logos*, then, not only as a faithful and thus a true account, but the *logos* as the selection intended to determine the supra-historic, eternal and metaphysical truth of the world and of all that will be contained in it. Being *qua* being is stable, hidden in the depths of public invisibility (to attain the light of the Enlightenment, it will be necessary to publicly break through this screen of invisibility), resting upon bases that are stable, thus statist, polemical (warlike) by definition, that is to say political, in order to render senseless any other possibility of thinking beyond the *arché*. A stubbornly anti-an-archic mortgage [*hypothèque*] of thought: here is the statist dimension of ontology, the only one that can be articulated within Western metaphysics.

Seeking a position in a conflict of ontological narratives (Ricoeur) means starting a war of truth under the pyramidal sign of hierarchy. This account, which succeeds in attaining a hierarchically superior position by setting the immobile stance of being on a foundation bolstered by the public recognition accorded to an accredited philosophy, will have the right to present itself as a single, nonconvertible (albeit certainly revocable) truth, only on condition that it fight on the same battlefield, the arena where what is at stake is the position of hierarchical superiority: a paradigm of sovereignty, to paraphrase the political effect of Kuhn's epistemological tension. Ultimately, determining the static being means appropriating a sovereign position from which to hierarchically control the entire framework of meaning that includes what is offered as digestible within the paradigm of metaphysical truth and that at the same time excludes, without further appeal, that which does not seem subject to domestication by means of the ontological search, relegating it to the status of a mad thought, utopian, crazy, beyond the pale, because it is unthinkable and impossible, because it is denied by the ontological truth of being.

I think that the *archic* effect of the philosophical search for an ontological foundation for being that would overdetermine the relationship of the being with the lifeworld not only tends to produce metaphysical tension, but it also hides within its subtlest folds a thought extended and aimed at a horizon of salvation and emancipation. Here I will refer to the concept of "reconciliation" (*Versöhnung*), found not only in the dialectic in Hegel, with the debt relative to his surpassing in a materialist key in Marx, but also as the final horizon of Critical Theory with Adorno.

Observers with viewpoints and intentions as different as those of Carl Schmitt and Hans Blumenberg have noted the proximity of the categories of modern political reason to a medieval theological semantics. Giorgio Agamben claims to find a strong analogy between the external forms of the Church's liturgical styles and specific political organizations. Secularization is literally the transposition onto the earthly plane of the transcendent devices linking the being of corporeal beings to the fate of the spirit, entrusted to the kingdom of heaven rather than to the terrestrial *civitas*. While salvation takes place entirely in the afterlife, according to classical political theology, modernity secularized this device—leaving the formal logic unaltered, while displacing emancipation onto the terrestrial plane. This is accomplished by means of a Copernican revolution that, displacing the cosmological framework from which it starts, concludes its vibrant trajectory in the dialectic of political revolution, which is simultaneously the heir to the historical materialist inversion of Hegel's dialectic.

For Adorno, therefore, reconciliation becomes the horizon of each counter-factual case of the qualitative transformation of existence, although fundamentally incomplete and ephemeral, in the direction of a dialectic of self-surpassing the split between nature and society, particular and general, world and subject, "a kind of non-violent excess of that abyss . . . a free agreement of multiple non humiliated in his own singularity."[6]

---

[6] Albrecht Wellmer, "Verità, parvenza, conciliazione," in *La Dialettica*

"Reconciliation" refers to the theoretical point where a synthetic unity of the multiple becomes possible, a "nonviolent synthesis of the diffuse,"[7] according to Adorno, which reconciles a subject broken by a bourgeois individualism obsessed with disciplinary knowledge (knowledge that is both disciplined and disciplining, reflecting the division of labor as an intellectual level, and thus reduced to a commodity itself, as Alfred Sohn-Rethel argues), in order to recompose a happy identity between his cooler, more sober subjectivity and the world of "undamaged" life, to paraphrase the subtitle of *Minima Moralia:*

> Either the totality comes into its own by becoming reconciled, that is, it abolishes its contradictory quality by enduring its contradictions to the end, and ceases to be a totality; or what is old and false will continue on until the catastrophe occurs.[8]

Moderno-Postmoderno: La Critica Della Ragione Dopo Adorno, ed. Albrecht Wellmer and Fulvio Carmagnola (Milano: Unicopli, 1987), 88, 90 ["Truth, Semblance, Reconciliation: Adorno's Aesthetic Redemption of Modernity," in *The Persistence of Modernity: Essays on Aesthetics, Ethics, and Postmodernism,* trans. David Midgley (Cambridge: MIT Press, 1991)].

"What Adorno's notion of reconciliation, however, has in common with the theological one is the flavour of something *fundamentally disjunctive* from the historical world *as we know it.* Reconciliation means for Adorno, when measured by empirical reality, something that is *radically* transcendent, which on the one hand falls itself under the taboo on representation, but on the other hand, if it is not to be entirely void, must become the object of a hope that needs at the very least a negative explication. . . . Adorno's emphatic idea of reconciliation, were one to take it literally, casts a shadow over his work by putting the historical world in a messianic perspective which threatens to level the difference between barbarism and that betterment of society that is humanly possible": Albrecht Wellmer, "Adorno and the Difficulties of a Critical Reconstruction of the Historical Present," speech given on the occasion of the awarding of the Adorno Prize in Frankfurt, 2006, trans. Frederik van Gelder.

[7] Theodor W. Adorno, *Aesthetic Theory,* trans. Robert Hullot-Kentor (London: Continuum, 2004), 189.

[8] Theodor W. Adorno, *Hegel: Three Studies,* trans. Shierry Weber Nicholsen (Cambridge: MIT Press, 1999), 79. See also Richard Wolin, "Utopia, Mimesis, and Reconciliation: A Redemptive Critique of Adorno's Aesthetic Theory," *Representations* 32 (Fall 1990): 33–49, and Iain McDonald, "'The Wounder Will Heal': Cognition and Reconciliation in Hegel and Adorno," *Philosophy Today* 44 (Supplement 2000): 132–139.

"Reconciliation," finally, is the name Adorno wants to give to the road to the ideal state of justice pursued by critical theory, which dialectically strips politics of the task of realizing it,[9] in order to make it true through a permanent movement of negation. This is precisely what Adorno called negative dialectics, which he entrusts only to art, first of all—to the sense of aesthetic judgment that does not need to have hierarchy because reason and mimesis meet—and secondly, to philosophy:

> The only philosophy which can be responsibly practised in face of despair is the attempt to contemplate all things as they would present themselves from the standpoint of redemption. Knowledge has no light but that shed on the world by redemption: all else is reconstruction, mere technique. Perspectives must be fashioned that displace and estrange the world, reveal it to be, with its rifts and crevices, as indigent and distorted as it will appear one day in the messianic light.[10]

Reconciliation, thus, is the reconstruction, in a future anterior, of an originary condition for which we will nostalgically develop grief, loss, lack; this originary condition will be recomposed as an emancipatory dimension, a freedom that is tightly restricted to a path of liberation that recovers the identitary unity of being and world—just like Hegel's Absolute Spirit, the poorly-disguised heir of theological salvation on a spiritual level, but endowed with the political and conceptual power of the dialectical system. The reconstruction of lack evokes the stamp of Christianity upon Western thought that Nietzsche denounced: as the Fall, according to the doctrine of original sin, forever loses the garden of Eden, so the ontological insufficiency of the human condition blocks the way to the anarchic non-place, whose realization is projected ever further away, beyond the anthropological wager concerning the goodness of man (Rousseau), beyond the political gamble of an uncertain revolution, to be found only in a recompositional, nostalgic key, just like the resurrection in the Christian model. Thus, reconciliation does not present itself as a multi-potential

---

[9] "[E]ven if his negative dialectics carries with it an ethical message that can be decoded, this message cannot be translated into an account of justice and its relation to law": Drucilla Cornell, *The Philosophy of the Limit* (New York: Routledge, 1992), 181.

[10] *Minima Moralia: Reflections from Damaged Life,* trans. E.F.N. Jephcott (London: Verso, 2005), 153.

process that is to come (Derrida), but as an event to be recovered. In this sense, hegemony over the path of liberation outweighs the creative practice of freedom, unwittingly confirming the figure of modernity where even critical theory wished to take a distance from it in order to recuperate it at a deeper level: the priority of the method of thinking over the object of thought, which, politically speaking, means what Habermas never ceases to repeat: the strong character of the unfinished project of modernity signals the impossibility of making the condition of freedom objective, at the cost of an infinite and endless conflict, just as Freud had predicted about analysis. Hence the retreat into a depoliticized position where the neutralization of the conflict revolves around the rules of the game, around methodological procedures, in which freedom finally becomes a dependent variable of the rules rather than a creative invention on the model of artistic genius. On the artistic conception, the conflict between different styles, being left to the an-archic judgment of taste, need not be resolved hierarchically; there is no need to close off the creative tension once and for all on the basis of a master canon of taste.

The dialectic of reconciliation is then perverted into its hierarchical subjection, its archic configuration, in which a unitary identity between being and world is pursued, expressible as the competence of a hegemonic subject, whether in thought or in practice, to dictate the rules of the game (those rules which outline in advance the path of liberation). The political battle between Marx and Bakunin is echoed each time in order to signify a methodological difference between two political theories, both of which are aimed at liberation, but which are both perhaps unconsciously victims of the trap of modernity, which designates a shared fictitious horizon. Being and world are reconciled through the success of the dialectic, ending the story once it has arrived at the terminus. Today, fortunately, this is no longer thinkable within a critical perspective that is more attentive to the dialectic of Enlightenment criticized by Adorno and Horkheimer, which Adorno himself saw as presenting itself just *as* the dialectic . . . *of* dialectics, so to speak, without specifying in what sense the strong anchoring the negative could have pushed the reconciliation ever further away, without any terminal, definitive, historical closure.

The problem with Hegel's system and its pursuit of the unknown, however, is that in seeking reconciliation with actuality, through the speculative 'is', it normalizes the flows of life, of thought, of becoming, of evolution, and does so by constantly reducing them to an equilibrate state. In the face of the most extreme, violent tensions and discordance, it persists in positing reconciliation and harmonization.[11]

The more lasting effect of the philosophical search for an onto-logical style of thought can be found in the identitarian vice by which we accord an immobile essence to what we accord a proper name. The scope of ontology, in fact, is this form of thought by which we block the flow of time in substance, i.e., that which arises *below* the flux, to be valorized as a noun. Therefore, the ontological operation of substantivating beings and the terrestrial things surrounding them produces a blockage of time, frozen, crystallized in the proper name whose stability conceals and hides the flow of time, this passage from the nothingness out of which we all came to the nothingness into which we are headed. To offer a vital meaning to this passage, which is finally our existence, the only one available to us (and for this reason demanding so much attention and care), would mean valorizing the fullness of life against the destiny of death. The price of this signification is the commodification of life, of its anarchic flow, without any origin other than the fortuitous nothingness, and without predetermined direction, unless this identitarian meaning does not substantivate the becoming of the living into a stable, closed form-of-life, the nomination of which becomes the goal of the control effected by apparatuses of domination.[12]

Gilles Deleuze often invited us to destabilize the ontological operation of the substantivation of being by displacing the names that freeze identity into something static, so as to steer not only the style of thinking but also political existence, both singular and plural, in the direction of the mobile diagram of *becoming*. Although Deleuze proposes an ontology of difference, articulated by

---

[11] Keith Ansell Pearson, "Deleuze Outside/Outside Deleuze," in *Deleuze and Philosophy: The Difference Engineer*, ed. Keith Ansell Pearson (London: Routledge, 1977), 5.

[12] On the contrary, "it is essential to overturn the primacy of substance, of the selfsubsistent or identical, and so too any infinite being that transcends and governs the world of finite beings and becoming. It is necessary to situate an originary web of difference from which individual identities both appear and dissolve" (Nathan Widder, "The Rights of Simulacra: Deleuze and the Univocity of Being," *Continental Philosophy Review* 34 (2001): 446.

the arrangement of various concepts such as immanence, multiplicity,[13] heterogeneous intensities, univocity, become a "connection between fluxes,"[14] which inaugurates a nomadic thought that evades any statist mortgage: "Being, the One and the Whole are the myth of a false philosophy totally impregnated by theology."[15] Rather, for Deleuze,

> The One is said with a single meaning of all the multiple. Being expresses in a single meaning all that differs. What we are talking about is not the unity of substance but the infinity of the modifications that are part of one another on this unique plane of life.[16]

---

[13] "Recognising multiplicities is to admit that being is incapable of subsuming becoming": Mark Halsey, "Ecology and Machinic Thought," *Angelaki* 10.3 (2005): 46. Tom Lundborg thinks the idea of becoming "as an unlimited movement without beginning or end," "movements of becoming that cannot be actualized or translated into what *is*": "Becoming, in this sense, does not have a pre-determined goal. It presents only a 'flow of life' that can take on new paths and create new ways of thinking and perceiving. For Deleuze, then, the task is to articulate and make thinkable this process by which there is an event of difference that does not fall back on identity and similarity but affirms the creative and productive elements of the event": Tom Lundborg, "The Becoming of the 'Event': A Deleuzian Approach to Understanding the Production of Social and Political 'Events,'" *Theory & Event* 12.1 (2009): 3).

[14] Philip Goodchild, *Gilles Deleuze and the Question of Philosophy* (Cranbury: Associated University Presses, 1996), 92. For a lexical interpretation of the concept of *becoming* in Deleuze, see Stéfan Leclercq and Arnaud Villani, "Devenir," in *Le vocabulaire de Gilles Deleuze*, ed. Robert Sasso and Arnaud Villan (Nice: Centre de recherches d'histoire des idées, 2003), 101–105, and Cliff Stagoll, "Becoming," in *The Deleuze Dictionary*, ed. Adrian Parr (Edinburgh: Edinburgh University Press, 2005), 21-22.

[15] Deleuze, *Logic of Sense*, 279. "Now we can see as well that that instability and play is not given to us from outside our own reality but is constitutive of that reality. It works from the inside, producing reality from within reality, rather than creating it from elsewhere. The fourth idea in the passage on Heraclitus is that 'becoming is the affirmation of being.' Here again, we need to take the term 'being' in the second Heraclitean sense, not as a matter of stable identities but as a matter of whatever it is that founds those identities. If becoming is the affirmation of being, it is the affirmation of difference in itself, of a pure difference that is not reducible to the identities, the actualities, that present themselves to us": Todd May, "When is a Deleuzian Becoming?" *Continental Philosophy Review* XXXVI (2003): 148.

[16] Gilles Deleuze and Félix Guattari, *A Thousand Plateaus: Capitalism and*

Becoming is not a category of metaphysical thought which is simply substituted, as such, for being; it is an *evacuation* of the identitarian relation between world and thought—"pure becoming without being (as opposed to the metaphysical notion of pure being without becoming)," as Žižek says[17]—in order to eliminate any disciplinary strategy that would establish the monadic isolation of a single substance over things and ways of thinking:

> to participate in movement, to stake out the path of escape in all its positivity, to cross a threshold, to reach a continuum of pure intensities where all forms come undone, as do all the significations, signifiers, and signifieds. to the benefit of an unformed matter of de-territorialized flux, of nonsignifying signs. [...] There is no longer anything but movements, vibrations, thresholds in a deserted matter.[18]

Within this movement of thought, we will immediately identify the first passage—stripping the concept of "foundation" of any meaning:

> What needs a foundation, in fact, is always a pretension or a claim. It is the pretender who appeals to a foundation, whose claim may be judged well-founded, ill-founded, or unfounded. . . . [T]he simulacrum . . . renders the order of participation, the fixity of distribution, the determination of the hierarchy impossible. It establishes the world of nomadic distributions and crowned anarchies. Far from being a new foundation, it engulfs all foundations, it as-

---

Schizophrenia, trans. Brian Massumi (London: Continuum, 2008), 281.

[17] Slavoj Žižek, *Organs without Bodies* (New York: Routledge, 2004), 9.

[18] *Kafka: Toward a Minor Literature*, trans. Dana Polan (Minneapolis: University of Minnesota Press, 1986), 13. "The 'machinic' in Deleuze's thought refers to this dynamic process of unfolding subjectivity outside the classical frame of the anthropocentric humanistic subject, re-locating it into becomings and fields of composition of forces and becomings. It is auto-poiesis at work as a qualitative shifter, not merely as a quantitative multiplier. Becomings are the sustainable shifts or changes undergone by nomadic subjects in their active resistance against being subsumed in the commodification of their own diversity. Becomings are un-programmed as mutations, disruptions, and points of resistance": Rosi Braidotti, "Affirming the Affirmative: On Nomadic Affectivity," *Rhizomes* 11/12 (Fall 2005-Spring 2006): http://www.rhizomes.net/issue11/braidotti.html; see also Rose Braidotti, *Transpositions: On Nomadic Ethics* (Cambridge: Polity, 2006).

sures a universal breakdown, but as a joyful and positive event, as an *un-founding*.[19]

Of course, the flux of becoming-life is channeled into contingent modalities and forms in order to assemble and articulate existences, but these arrangements are presented as mobile and reversible, open to the contingency of other arrangements that open up new meanings, different each time and never immobile. The diagram of becoming is clearly opposed to the program of statism, i.e., to the individuation of a final horizon toward which we will address the *telos* of historical time. This is the risk courted by a certain metaphysics of anarchy, this idea of a final fulfillment of human effort in the triumphant achievement of a state of total freedom, a post-emancipatory condition that, as Simon Critchley puts it, would mystically reconcile the anarchist idea with the "conflict-free perfection of humanity."[20]

To take up an account of the multiple senses of becoming would mean, following Deleuze, to disable the powerful statist idea of a need to trust in an invisible essence behind the appearance of being of life; it would mean dismissing the idea of an eternal order because it has been made real in a substantial and substantive dimension of the world-as-it-is; it would mean taking up a perspective that slips out of virtually every knot of being-thus-and-not-otherwise; it would mean inexorably detaching oneself from a "bellicose" idea of coming to attain, to seize, to capture, to maintain in a lasting and stable condition, even as an idea, a "state" of anarchy in the sense of a realized, achieved society;[21] it would mean accepting an ethical stance of the plural relationship (and not the individual atom) as the mobile foundation

---

[19] Gilles Deleuze, *Logique du sens*, 294 and 303 [*Logic of Sense*, 292 and 300]. "There has only ever been one ontological proposition: Being is univocal. . . . the essential in univocity is not that Being is said in a single and same sense, but that it is said, in a single and same sense, *of* all its individuating differences or intrinsic modalities. . . . It is said of difference itself. . . . Univocity of being thus also signifies equality of being. Univocal Being is at one and the same time nomadic distribution and crowned anarchy": Gilles Deleuze, *Différence et répétition* (Paris: PUF, 1968), 52–53, 55 [*Difference and Repetition*, trans. Paul Patton (London: Continuum, 2004), 44–45, 47]).

[20] Simon Critchley, "Mystical Anarchism," *Critical Horizons* 10.2 (2009): 282.

[21] Here, I extend the brief considerations I made in "Anarchie in-finie," published in *L'anarchisme a-t-il un avenir?*, ed. Renaud de Bellefon, David Michels and Mimmo Pucciarelli (Lyon: ACL, 2001), 531–538.

of each historical fact and thus of each collective solution, each properly *political* solution to the many problems we encounter in social life, because every identitarian form-of-life contains at least two or more singularities that intertwine; it would mean practicing open and indeterminate processes in which one experiments with hypotheses of becoming-freedom and becoming-liberation as conflictual opportunities (and therefore more than just one politics at two moments) to spin the identitarian circle of substantivation, i.e., the self-referential closure of the established and constituted order (whatever the juridical forms in which this can and shall be given).

Let me conclude with a remark made by Gilles Deleuze that, in my opinion, bears on our case: "If we've been so interested in nomads, it's because they're a becoming and aren't part of history; they're excluded from it, but they transmute and reappear in different, unexpected forms in the lines of flight of some social field."[22]

Salvo Vaccaro (b. 1959) is a Professor of Political Philosophy at the University of Palermo where he also teaches Political Science. He is now Vice-President of Social Solidarity and Human Rights at the University of Palermo. He is interested in critical responses to modernity (inspired by anarchist thought) and the Frankfurt School (Adorno and Benjamin). Recent publications include: *Pensare altrimenti: Anarchismo e filosofia radicale del Novecento* (Eleuthera, 2011), *Il governo di se, il governo degli altri* (with S. Marceno; duepunti, 2011), *L'onda araba: I documenti delle rivolte* (Mimesis, 2012), *Il buco nero del capitalismo* (zero in condotta, 2012), and *La vita oltre la biopolitica/La vie au de la de la biopolitique*, "La rosa di nessuno" (Mimesis, 2013).

Jesse Cohn lives in Valparaiso, Indiana, where he teaches literature, theory, and popular culture; translates anarchist texts, engineering documents, and anthropological papers; edits encyclopedias and anthologies; and researches the radical histories and uses of culture. In all respects, he aspires to be a good "relay."

---

[22] Gilles Deleuze, *Negotiations, 1972–1990*, trans. Martin Joughin (New York: Columbia University Press, 1995), 153.

Anarchist Developments in Cultural Studies
ISSN: 1923-5615
2013.2: Ontological Anarché: Beyond Materialism and Idealism

Three Scandals in the Philosophy of F. W. J. Schelling
Ontology, Freedom, Mythology

Jared McGeough

ABSTRACT

This paper examines the philosophy of F. W. J. Schelling as a precursor to a theory of ontological *anarchē*. Contesting Mikhail Bakunin's dismissal of Schelling early in *God and the State* as an "idealist," as well as the later Schelling's reputation as a conservative and stooge for the Prussian government, I propose a different reading of the historical and ideological context which shapes Schelling's arrival in Berlin. Where standard-issue histories of philosophy often frame the Berlin period as a *gigantomachia* between the "conservative" Schelling and the "radical" Hegel, this narrative neglects Schelling's prior reputation as an anti- or non-establishment thinker. I then go on to examine three "scandals" proper to Schelling's philosophy, including his conception of philosophy and of nature as "unconditioned," his attempt to think a "system of freedom," and his subsequent deconstruction of origins in the *Ages of the World*. I argue that Schelling's turn to sciences such as geology to help explain cosmic origins in the *Ages* represents an initial effort at what Quentin Meillassoux (2008) calls "ancestral" thinking, that is, the task of thinking a world prior to *archē*. Finally, I focus on Schelling's transition from negative to positive philosophy in his philosophy of mythology, and how it forms a critical response to the Hegelian "philosophy of essence."

KEYWORDS

Friedrich Schelling, anarchism, ontological anarche, German Idealism, Quentin Meillassoux, Speculative Realism, Mikhail Bakunin, G. W. F. Hegel

This essay finds its starting point in two rather singular, but suggestively connected, remarks. The first refers to the future direction of anarchist theory in Jesse Cohn and Shawn Wilbur's 2010 paper, "What's Wrong with Postanarchism?" Under their fourth point of contention, Cohn and Wilbur argue that post-structuralist criticisms of "classical" anarchism tend to situate the latter within the reductive categories of "humanism," "rational-ism," and "Enlightenment." This in turn creates an artificially monolithic conception of both the history of such terms and of anarchism itself, "as if there was no significant developments in ideas about subjectivity, truth, or rationality" after Descartes (Cohn and Wilbur, 2010: 5). One of the many suggestive possibili-ties Cohn and Wilbur proceed to excavate from the lacunae with-in the post-anarchist project is a suggestion to take up what "[Mikhail] Bakunin might have learned from Schelling's call for a 'philosophy of existence' in opposition to Hegel's 'philosophy of essence'" (Cohn and Wilbur, 2010: 5). The second remark also appears in a much earlier essay by Jürgen Habermas (1983, 2004). Explicating the consequences of Schelling's thought for a materi-alist philosophy of history, Habermas writes that although Schel-ling is "not a political thinker," his writings nonetheless contain "barely concealed anarchistic consequences" (Habermas, 2004: 43, 46).

This essay takes up Cohn and Wilbur's and Habermas' re-marks so as to disclose the "anarchistic consequences" within Schelling's "philosophy of existence," which, I argue, must be read as a theory of ontological *anarchē*. This *anarchē* begins to emerge as early as Schelling's 1799 *First Outline of a System of the Philosophy of Nature* and continues to shape Schelling's philoso-phy throughout the rest of his career, from the 1809 *Philosophical Investigations into the Essence of Human Freedom* and the unfin-ished drafts of the *Ages of the World* (1811, 1813, 1815) to the Ber-lin lectures on the philosophy of mythology and revelation that Bakunin attended in the 1840s. Though standard histories com-monly acknowledge Schelling's influence on Bakunin, the for-mer's potential contributions to the history of anarchism have been almost entirely overlooked, not least because of Bakunin's own dismissal of Schelling in *God and the State* (1871, 1882). In that text, Bakunin labels Schelling an idealist who, along with Descartes, Spinoza, Leibniz, Kant, Fichte, and Hegel, fails to acknowledge that "*facts are before ideas*" and, as such, cannot properly explain the emergence of the living existence of matter from the perfection of the divine Idea (Bakunin, 2009: 9). On the one hand, by lumping Schelling together with such thinkers un-der the catch-all of an "idealism" that is simply, as he says, "wrong," Bakunin ironically anticipates what Cohn and Wilbur later criticize as post-anarchism's reductive approach to the history of ideas. On the other hand, Bakunin's criticisms of idealism are in fact already a prominent feature of Schelling's middle- and late-period work, in which Schelling also criticizes his contemporaries' reluctance to "acknowledge the priority of Realism" (Schelling, 2001: 107). In short, Bakunin's criticism, which eventually turns towards a post-Hegelian vision of the real as rational, fails to acknowledge Schelling's own explicitly stated transition from "negative" to "positive" philosophy, or as Karl Jaspers puts it, from "rational *a priori* science" to a "science of actuality": "In negative philosophy we proceed to the ascent of the highest idea and we attain it only as an idea. Positive philosophy leaves us in actuality and proceeds from actuality" (Jaspers, 1986: 98).

At the same time, I want to suggest that Schelling's significance for anarchist theory extends well beyond Bakunin's (mis)readings of him. An anarchistic reading of Schelling today necessarily occurs in the context of a certain return to Schelling already undertaken by post-Marxist theorists such as Habermas and Slavoj Žižek (1996), as well as speculative realists such as Iain Hamilton Grant (2008). For such thinkers, Schelling serves as an important precursor for their own attempts to re-conceptualize what materialism and materiality mean today. In particular, this reconceptualization takes place through a rigorous return to German Romanticism's still under-recognized contributions to a philosophical materialism that proceeds from a sense that Being is always *an-archically* non-identical with itself.

In what follows, I wish to pursue how Schelling's philosophy represents a thoroughgoing attempt to think an ontological *an-archē*, an ontology that anticipates and responds very precisely to the desire to think beyond the opposition between idealism and realism. Before pursuing this argument, however, I first propose a different reading of the historical and ideological context which shapes Schelling's arrival in Berlin. Where standard-issue histories' of philosophy have framed Schelling's Berlin period in terms of a *gigantomachia* between the "conservative" Schelling and the "radical" Hegel, this narrative is, at best, an oversimplification that short-changes Schelling's own prior reputation as an anti- or non-establishment thinker. I then go on to discuss the salient features of Schelling's philosophy of existence as a philosophy of ontological *anarchē*, including his conception of philosophy as a mode of "unconditioned" thought that contests the positivism of Enlightenment sciences, his paradoxical attempt to think a "system of freedom" and his subsequent deconstruction of cosmic origins in the *Ages of the World*. In particular, I suggest that Schelling's turn to such sciences as geology to help explain cosmic origins in the *Ages* represents an initial (though incomplete) effort at what speculative realist philosopher Quentin Meillassoux (2008) calls thinking "ancestrality," that is, the task of thinking a world prior to thought, and therefore prior to the *archē* by which subjectivity establishes the world as its objective correlate. In turn, I contest Meillassoux's dismissal of Schelling to suggest that the *Ages* agrees with certain aspects of speculative realism, although he also departs from it in other ways. Finally, I focus on Schelling's transition from negative to positive philosophy in his philosophy of mythology, and how it forms a critical response to the Hegelian philosophy of essence.

HISTORICAL CONTEXTS: SCHELLING IN BERLIN

In 1841, the recently appointed German Minister of Culture hired a 65-year-old Schelling to take up the Chair of Philosophy at the University of Berlin, a full decade after the death of Schelling's former roommate at the Tübingen seminary, Hegel. Schelling's arrival in Berlin has become something of an academic legend, much of which had to do with the makeup of Schelling's audience rather than the actual content of his lectures. Indeed, the "imposing, colourful" group attending Schelling's inaugural talks on the philosophy of mythology and revelation, so vividly recounted by Friedrich Engels in 1841, included a veritable who's who of the nineteenth century's most influential philosophical minds, including Engels himself, Soren Kierkegaard, Otto Ranke, Alexander von Humboldt, and of course, the young Bakunin (Engels, 1841). High expectations from both conservative and radical quarters of German intellectual and political society preceded Schelling's arrival. According to the King's Munich ambassador C. J. Bunsen, with whom Schelling negotiated a lucrative salary and the promise of freedom from the royal censors, Schelling was not merely a "common professor" but "a philosopher chosen by God" (cited in Matthews, 2007: 6). King Wilhelm IV himself perceived Schelling as a means to stamp out the "dragonseed of Hegelian pantheism" that had taken root within the student population (cited in Matthews, 2007: 6).

The King's comment speaks to a broader crisis about the ultimate status of religious faith in German culture, a crisis that had begun with Kant's critical reduction of faith "within the limits of reason alone," continued with the ensuing controversy over Lessing's pantheism and the growing threat of an atheistic "Spinozism" throughout the 1780s and 1790s, and finally climaxed in Hegel's reduction of faith to logic. In the wake of Hegel's critique of religion, the traditional segments of the German intelligensia perceived Schelling's appointment as nothing less than an attempt to win back the hearts and minds of the nation's youth, so long corrupted by what the King acidly called the "facile omniscience" of the Hegelian system (Matthews, 2007: 7).

Nonetheless, the enthusiasm of Bakunin and many of his like-minded peers was also palpable. In a letter to his family in the summer of 1841, Bakunin writes: "you cannot imagine with what impatience I have been awaiting for Schelling's lectures. In the course of the summer I have read much of his works and found therein such immeasurable profundity of life and creative thinking that I am now convinced he will reveal to us a treasure of meaning" (cited in Matthews, 2007: 13). Similarly impatient, and just as eager to label Schelling a philosophical saviour, Kierkegaard disparaged the Hegelian reduction of life within the massive architectonic of a universal logic, while praising Schelling's desire to reconnect "philosophy to actuality" (cited in Matthews, 2007: 13).

The rest of the story of Schelling's Berlin period, however, is far less auspicious. The *denouement* typically goes like this: the treasure Bakunin so anticipated turned out to be far less than expected, or, perhaps, the treasure discovered was in a currency that was no longer valuable. As Jason Wirth remarks, "in an era when mythology was considered a science, and when science itself was becoming increasingly alienated from its philosophical grounds, the lectures were doomed to be virtually inaudible" (Wirth, 2007: viii), and few in the audience would heed Schelling's own advice to his listeners that "whoever would seek to listen to me, listens to the end" (cited in Matthews, 2007: 5). Abandoning his earlier enthusiasm, Kierkegaard later privately writes that Schelling's lectures were "endless nonsense," while Engels' hysterical *Anti-Schelling* (1841) book publicly attacked the philosopher for criticizing Hegel and called for the Young Hegelians "to shield the great man's grave from abuse." Bakunin would also leave Schelling behind and instead turn towards an intensive politicization of Hegelian negativity that would serve as the theoretical premise for his anarchism; after joining the Young Hegelians, Bakunin then published *The Reaction in Germany*, which ascribed a revolutionary status to the negative as a simultaneously destructive and creative passion (cf. Dolgoff, 1971). This radical return to Hegel, carried furthest in the work of Engels and Marx, would subsequently help establish the philosophical foundations for both the communist and anarchist projects of the nineteenth century.

This story remains somewhat misleading, however, if only because it has been largely dominated by the sometimes extreme representations of Schelling proffered by both the Prussian establishment and the Young Hegelians. Given the King's stated intentions, the left undoubtedly had reason to be suspicious of Schelling for riding to the defence of the Christian orthodoxy that then dominated the upper reaches of the non-secular Prussian state. As Bruce Matthews points out, the Hegelian subordination of religion to logic actively threatened to destabilize the "very center of ideological power that held the state together" (Matthews, 2007: 10). Yet it would also seem that the Young Hegelians effectively swallowed the establishment narrative whole by branding Schelling, as Engels put it, "our new enemy" (Engels, 1841). In turn, the left generated an equally extreme view of Hegel to be defended with a fervour as unquestioning as the establishment's idea of the "god-appointed" Schelling.

This shared characterization of Schelling as a reactionary conservative tends to overlook pertinent historical evidence about Schelling's reputation and his actions towards the Young Hegelians themselves during his tenure in Berlin. On the one hand, Schelling had good reason to procure the King's assurance that his lectures would not be expurgated, since Schelling had already been the victim of censorship in 1838 for openly disobeying the Bavarian government's prohibition against professors lecturing on theological issues. But perhaps the most telling evidence against the characterization of Schelling as a Prussian stooge was his active role in convincing the government to lift censorship of the *Halleschen Jahrbucher*, the main philosophical journal of the Young Hegelians. As Matthews points out, such actions should prompt the question: "if Schelling was a vehicle for reactionary conservatives, why were his lectures such a problem for the conservative government in Munich?," for "even taking into consideration the very real differences between Catholic Bavaria and Protestant Prussia, a philosophy of revelation that could not be taught in a university would not appear to be a philosophy that a conservative theologian would look to for help in combating secular critiques of religion" (Matthews, 2007: 10–11). Moreover, why would Schelling use his influence to *ensure*, rather than limit, the public dissemination of the Young Hegelians' ideas? And why is it the "conservative" Schelling who announces that the greatest task of philosophy in the modern age "is to shrink the state itself . . . in every form," rather than the "radical" Hegel, whose *Philosophy of Right* (1821) hailed the State as an embodiment of Spirit in the political (Schelling, 2007: 235)?

It is not the purpose of this essay to excavate all of the permutations of the historical and cultural debates surrounding Schelling's Berlin lectures; rather, what becomes apparent in our brief discussion of these debates is that both Schelling and Hegel are not simply the names of philosophers whose work can be understood in their own terms, but sites of contest and struggle, struggles which render the ensuing reification of the two thinkers into a simple opposition of conservative and radical deeply misleading. Also apparent is a sense that this narrative and the conceptual opposition that supports it mirrors what Cohn and Wilbur identify as post-anarchism's tendency to take certain notions for granted within their historical accounts of the movement:

> terms taken for granted in much postanarchist critique—
> 'science,' for example—were the explicit subject of com-
> plex struggles within anarchism and socialism broadly. To
> fail to look at this history of internal difference can also
> blind us to . . . other set[s] of forces at work in shaping an-
> archism and socialism as we have had them passed down
> to us. (Cohn and Wilbur, 2010: 4)

Schelling, I here suggest, is a hitherto understudied "subject of complex struggle" within the history of anarchism, one whose role cannot be easily assimilated within a historical logic that would categorize him as an "idealist" (as Bakunin does), and whose conservatism would then re-emerge as the subject of the post-anarchist critique of classical anarchism as a displaced form of essentialism. Instead, our point of departure with Schelling is, as Marc Angenot writes of Proudhon, not an "axiom" but "a sense of 'scandal'—a provocation into thought" (Angenot as cited in Cohn and Wilbur, 2010: 4). What, then, is the "scandal," the anarchic provocation, proper to Schelling's thought?

THINKING UNCONDITIONALLY AND THE SYSTEM OF FREEDOM

The scandal proper to Schelling's philosophy, I would argue, is threefold. The first comes in the form of Schelling's conception of knowledge as "unconditioned," which, I suggest, grants Schelling's overall understanding of the task of philosophical thinking a certain political valence. The second, and more radical, provocation has to do with Schelling's unprecedented attempt to think a system of freedom. The third provocation is what several commentators, such as Joseph P. Lawrence (2005) and Bernard Freydberg (2008), have identified as the untimeliness of Schelling's philosophy, in particular Schelling's turn to discourses such as mythology and religion that seem radically out of step with both enlightened, secular modernity, as well as the conventional dictates of anarchism itself (No Gods! No Masters!).

In his lectures *On University Studies* (1802), Schelling makes a distinction between "positive sciences" and "unconditioned" knowledge. For Schelling, the positive sciences are forms of knowledge that "attain to objectivity within the state" (Schelling, 1966: 78–80). Anticipating Hegel's similar critique of "positive knowledge" as the fiction of something "quietly abiding within its own limits" and therefore unable "to recognize [its own] concepts as finite" (Hegel, 1975: para. 92, 10), Schelling argues that positive sciences take themselves to be systems of knowledge that have been completed or closed, and therefore impervious to change. Hence the sciences officially sanctioned by the state and "organized into so-called faculties" present themselves as completed systems of knowledge, where they in fact merely reflect the values currently sanctioned by the state.[1]

Conversely, in *On University Studies*, as well as in earlier texts such as the *First Outline of a System of a Philosophy of Nature* (1799), Schelling argues for what he calls the "unconditioned character of philosophical knowledge" (Schelling, 2005: 9). In its original German, the "unconditioned" is *das Unbedingt*, literally the "un-thinged," and thus speaks to a radically non-positive / positivistic mode of thinking that resists the conditions under which knowledge is circumscribed:

> The unconditioned cannot be sought in any individual 'thing,' nor in anything of which one can say that it 'is.' For what 'is' only partakes of being, and is only an indi-

---

[1] Schelling's criticism of knowledge "organized into so-called faculties" is a none-too-subtle reaction to Kant's epistemology and Kant's subsequent plea for the government to include philosophy within the German university as a "lower" faculty beneath the traditional or "higher" faculties of Law, Medicine, and Theology. See Kant, *The Conflict of the Faculties* (1992: 23).

vidual form of kind of being.—Conversely, one can never say of the unconditioned that it 'is.' For it is BEING IT-SELF, and as such, it does not exhibit itself entirely in any finite product. (Schelling, 2005: 13)

As *Unbedingt*, the unconditioned can therefore reveal itself only through "negations. No *positive* external intuition of [it] is possible" since it is that which marks what is always in excess of its positive determinations (Schelling, 2005: 19). Redeploying the Spinozist distinction between *naturans* and *naturata*, Schelling sees fixed or instituted forms of knowledge as the product of an originally infinite activity; as such, these products always maintain within themselves an excess that marks a "tendency to infinite development" through which they can be always be decomposed. Yet no decomposition is ever absolute; rather, Schelling characterizes the unconditioned as a Platonic *chora*, not "absolutely formless" but that which is "*receptive to every form*" and hence condition for both the decomposition of fixed forms of thought in order to release the potentiality of recomposing them otherwise (Schelling, 2005: 5–6, 27; Rajan, 2007: 314).

The *First Outline* interprets this process as a dynamic rather than mechanistic materialism that reconstructs Leibniz's monads as products composed by an "infinite multiplicity of . . . tendencies"; hence monads, or whatever generally appears as monadic in the broad sense (unified, simple, whole, a "thing") is only ever "*apparently* simple" since "no substance is simple" (Schelling, 2005: 19, 31). Contrary to the prevailing discourse of positivism and narrowed versions of materialism that began to arise in the 1840s, which dismissed Schelling's *Naturphilosophie* as a wild mysticism, recent critics such as Robert Richards (2002), Arran Gare (2011), and Iain Hamilton Grant have recognized that Schelling's speculative physics is not only full of "citations of the most recent, up-to-date experimental work in the sciences" in his own time, but also pursues a vital materialism that anticipates more recent physics of complexity and self-organizing systems (Richards, 2002: 128; Grant, 2009: 11). Nonetheless, the overall purpose of Schelling's *Naturphilosophie* was less to explain how nature itself functioned than "to allow natural science itself to arise philosophically" (Schelling, 1988: 5)—that is to say, to provide the philosophical or metaphysical framework through which the sciences are pushed beyond their own positivity.

In pursuing this line of thinking, however, Schelling also detects a crucial problem, what Schelling calls "the most universal problem," that will come to preoccupy both his essay on freedom and his book *Ages of the World*: how does the unconditioned or infinite activity submit itself to become determined or inhibited into finite products? The problem, for Schelling, is nothing less than the very problem of *archē*, of discerning the origin, cause, and principle of everything that is: "what cause first tossed the seed of motion into the universal repose of nature, duplicity into universal identity, the first sparks of heterogeneity into the universal homogeneity of nature?" (cited in Krell, 2004: 135). Yet Schelling also admits that his wording of the problem may be imprecise, since it becomes apparent that these initial "sparks of heterogeneity" could not simply be "tossed" into an archaic, pre-existing, self-identical absolute. Rather, Schelling comes to realize that in order to explain the relationship between the unconditioned and the conditioned, infinite activity and finite inhibition, freedom and nature, ideal and material, the latter term must be intrinsic, indeed, "co-absolute" with the former. "If nature is absolute activity," Schelling avers, then "such activity must appear as inhibited into infinity" and thus "no homogenous state can be *absolute*" since "the homogenous is [always already] itself split *in itself*." And this discovery leads Schelling to conceive of the absolute as *originally* split in itself, for "to *bring* heterogeneity *forth* means to create duplicity in identity. . . . Thus identity must in turn proceed from duplicity" (Schelling as cited in Krell, 2004: 139).

Nonetheless, the early Schelling, especially the Schelling of the *System of Transcendental Idealism* (1800), remains idealist in arguing that these purportedly opposed principles of function as complementary and thus arise from an unconscious identity, a "pre-established harmony" that is neither real nor ideal but their "common source" or *archē* (1978: 208). Positing the Absolute as the hidden *archē* behind exterior manifestations of the disjunction of subject and object, Schelling proposes a providential, teleological idea of history that closely approximates Bakunin's view of history in the first chapter of *God and the State*. There, Bakunin argues that while "humanity [is] the highest manifestation of animality," it is also "the deliberate and gradual negation of the animal element" (Bakunin, 2009: 9). This negation, Bakunin continues, is "as rational as it is natural, and rational only because natural—at once historical and logical, as inevitable as the development and realization of all the natural laws in the world" (Bakunin, 2009: 9). In his *System of Transcendental Idealism*, Schelling deploys a similar conception of history as a "progressive . . . revelation of the absolute" which manifests humanity's "first step out of the realm of instinct" and culminates in a "universal constitution," or, as Schelling puts it in *On University Studies*, a "world order based on law" (Schelling, 1978: 209, 199–202; Schelling, 1966: 79). As Schelling writes in his Stuttgart Lectures of 1810, this process effectively alchemizes the materiality of history so as to give birth to "an entirely healthy, ethical, pure, and innocent nature . . . freed from all false being," a description that would appear to link Schelling and Bakunin both to the "uncontaminated point of departure" that Saul Newman criticizes in classical versions of anarchism (Schelling, 1994: 242; Newman, 2001: 32–52).

When Schelling writes his 1809 Freedom essay, however, he returns to the problem of an "original duplicity" at the heart of Being and so instigates what I am calling the second major scandal of his thought: the attempt to think a system of freedom. For if the prevailing opinion has always been that freedom and system are mutually exclusive, Schelling writes, "it is curious that, since individual freedom is surely connected in some way with the world as a whole . . . , some kind of system must be present" (Schelling, 2006: 9). This scandal could also be the theoretical scandal that resides at the very heart of ontological *anarchē* as such—that is to say, ontological *anarchē* is by definition traversed by the paradox of a system whose very principle is the freedom from all principle or system. What is distinctive of anarchism, as opposed to various other political systems that claim freedom as a principle, is precisely the attempt to think what Proudhon famously calls the "union of order and anarchy" as the "highest perfection in society" (Proudhon, 1995: 286). In so doing, Schelling will effectively challenge both the self-founding rationalism that runs through the entirety of the "new European philosophy since its beginning (in Descartes)," which perceives the Absolute as "a merely moral world order," and the equally untenable view of "God as *actus purissumus*" (Schelling, 2007: 26). Indeed, from the outset, Schelling endorses the very realism that Bakunin later champions against the idealists. For Bakunin, idealism bears an unscientific hatred of matter. The "*vile matter* of the idealists," Bakunin avers, ". . . is indeed a stupid, inanimate, immobile thing, . . . incapable of producing anything" and thus requires the external hand of God to set it in motion. Matter thought in this way is stripped of "intelligence, life, all its determining qualities, active relations or forces, motion itself . . . leaving it nothing but impenetrability and absolute immobility" (Bakunin, 2009: 12–13). Similarly, Schelling argues against the tendency of modern philosophy to seek to

> remove God quite far indeed from all of nature. God . . . has entirely different and more vital motive forces in himself than the desolate subtlety of abstract idealists attributes to him. . . . The entire new European philosophy . . . has the common defect that nature is not available for it and that it lacks a living ground. (Schelling, 2006: 26)

In the Freedom essay, Schelling turns to explicate this "living ground" as the very basis for understanding the nature of human freedom itself.

In order to think through the ontological co-existence of freedom and system, Schelling proposes a reinterpretation of a logic of identity that would be capable of bringing these two principles together without subordinating one to the other. According to Manfred Frank (1991), Schelling's ontology is best understood as a theory of predication. The copula "is" that links a subject to its predicate in the identity judgement is conventionally understood as intransitive: static, fixed, or—to make use of a term Schelling often refers to—"dead" in its own self-sameness. Conversely, Schelling understands the copula as transitive, living, creative. The law that differentiates subject and predicate is expressed not as static, but "as what precedes and what follows," "ground" and consequent (Schelling, 2006: 14). Hence the law of identity does not "express a unity which, turning itself in the circle of seamless sameness [*Einerleiheit*], would not be progressive and, thus, insensate or lifeless. The unity of this law is an immediately creative one" (Schelling, 2006: 17). The subject (Being) is the ground of its predicate (existence), and the predicate is the consequence of its ground. However, insofar as the identity of subject and predicate is transitive, Schelling argues that the predicate's dependence on its ground "does not abolish independence, it does not even abolish freedom," since "dependence . . . says only that the dependent, *whatever it also may be,* can be a consequence only that which it is a dependent; dependence does *not* say what the dependent *is or is not*" (Schelling, 2006: 17; emphasis added). Schelling demonstrates how dependence on a ground does not abolish independence through the example of the statement "this body is blue." If we understand the identity relation or the copula as intransitive, then the statement would posit that "the body is, in and through that in and through which it is a body, also blue."

However, Schelling argues that what the statement actually says is only that "the same thing which is this body *is also* blue, although not in the same respect" (Schelling, 2006: 13; emphasis added). Thus to make an identity statement is to already say that what something *is* means that it can also be otherwise.

Though Schelling's discussion of the law of identity may appear abstruse, it has important consequences for his attempt to to understand system as coexistent with human freedom. What the copula reveals is that there can be never any complete system in itself, precisely because the system is nothing other than its own contingency or freedom, nothing other than its own ever-present possibility of being other than it is. In his later 1821 essay "On the Nature of Philosophy as Science," Schelling speaks of this possibility as the "*asystaton*" or a-systematicity always lodged at the heart of system: "the endeavour . . . of contemplating human knowledge within a system . . . presupposes . . . that originally and of itself it does not exist in a system, that it is an *asystaton* . . . something that is in inner conflict" (Schelling, 1997: 210–11). In the Freedom essay and in the *Ages*, this inner conflict is the "contradiction of necessity and freedom," a contradiction without which not only all philosophy but all "higher willing of the spirit would sink into the death that is proper to those sciences in which this contradiction has no application" (Schelling, 2007: 10–11). Thinking unconditionally is precisely not to resolve this contradiction, but to ceaselessly reassert it, since contradiction is the *sine qua non* of life itself.

Schelling thus begins to think of the Absolute itself less in terms of a harmoniously unfolding *archē-telos* than something radically self-divided, "subject to suffering and becoming" (Schelling, 2007: 66). Insofar as "nothing is prior to, or outside of, God, he must have the ground of existence in himself" (Schelling, 2007: 27). This ground is nature or actuality (*wirklichkeit*); rather than a mere concept, the ground is the living basis through which the Absolute creates itself. However, this ground is not rational but a *desire*, the "yearning the eternal One feels to give birth it itself[,] . . . not the One itself but . . . co-eternal with it." As co-eternal with the One, but not the One, the ground is therefore "something in God which is not God himself" (Schelling, 2007: 28). As such, Schelling contests secular-Enlightenment notions that posit rationality as coextensive with the Absolute. Schelling writes:

[N]owhere does it appear as if order and form were what is original but rather as if initial anarchy (*das Regellose*) had been brought to order. This is the incomprehensible base of reality in things, the indivisible remainder, that which with the greatest exertion cannot be resolved in understanding but rather remains eternally in the ground. (Schelling, 2006: 29)

In questioning what precedes the rational organization of the world, Schelling places this organization in question by dissociating *archē* from its traditional association with order and form. As the incomprehensible but "necessary inheritance" of existing beings, Schelling's "initial anarchy" bespeaks an anarchy prior to rational foundations that, appearing to have been brought to order, nonetheless "still lies in the ground, as if it could break through once again" (Schelling, 2006: 29). As the indivisible remainder that conditions order and form, the anarchy of the ground is a negativity that at once precludes freedom to completely free itself from its dark necessity and radically unsettles modern rationality's founding myth of a completely self-founding rationality.[2] Rather, this "irreducible remainder" within the dark ground means that the order of rationality itself emerges "only from the obscurity of that which is without understanding (from feeling, yearning, the sovereign mother of knowledge)" (Schelling, 2006: 29).

Schelling transposes the tortured relation within the Absolute between its self-revelation and the dark ground into the ontological structure of human freedom as such. Human freedom is distinguishable from that of other creatures, Schelling argues, insofar as humans have the capacity for the decision between good and evil. Yet freedom is not, Schelling insists, the ability to choose rationally between alternatives, which presupposes a the *archē* of a subject who chooses. This conception of freedom is actually the death of freedom, Schelling argues, because it treats freedom instrumentally as a means to the subject's ends. For Schelling freedom is not the property of a subject; as Martin Heidegger points out, for Schelling freedom is never *mine*, but rather *I belong to freedom* (Heidegger, 1985: 9). Freedom is therefore never the predicate of the human; rather, Schelling inverts the relation to question the human as a predicate of freedom, which is *an-archicially* "before every ground . . . the primordial ground and therefore non-ground," or what Jason Wirth calls the the "infinite power otherwise than every beginning and ending but given within and

---

[2] On the myth of a self-founding rationality as the "founding" myth of modernity, see Hans Blumenberg's *Legitimacy of the Modern Age* (1985).

thereby dis-completing every beginning and ending" (Schelling as cited in Wirth, 2007: x).

The freedom to which I belong, the radical contingency that my subjectivity *is*, is an ever-renewed struggle between our own particular self-will and the universal will of the Absolute. Where the Absolute "necessarily" reveals itself as order and form by repressing the anarchy of its dark ground, the contingency of human freedom allows for this relationship to be overturned, such that the ground itself can appear as the highest value. Schelling inscribes a proto-deconstructive potential within human freedom as a freedom for evil. In its simplest terms, evil describes the freedom to elevate the individual or the part over the organic harmony of the whole, such as when a part of the body becomes diseased and begins to function "for itself" rather than in harmony with the rest of the organism (Schelling, 2006: 18, 34–38, 66). It would be an oversimplification, however, to see Schelling's conception of evil in simply moral terms, in the sense of evil as that which simply lacks, or is deficient in, the good. As Johannes Schmidt and Jeff Love (2006) point out, Schelling's innovation is his attempt to think the problem of evil as something rather than nothing, and therefore as part of God's very essence. Because evil is associated with the materiality of the ground, it has a "positive, vital force" in which "all the powers that are typically associated with the good, such as rationality, rigour, and probity, come to serve the most brutal and selfish impulses, the ever-varying whims of physical desire" (Schelling, 2006: xxiii).

On the one hand, Schelling's conception of evil overturns prior theological conceptions of evil, and in doing so avoids the metaphysical quandary which fails to explain evil's reality. On the other hand, however, because evil has a kind of vitality, it might also name a more subversive potentiality "that threatens actively to undermine" the "palliative normativity that legitimates the whole" (Love and Schmidt, 2007: xxiv). As such, evil may very well describe a negativity that resists inclusion into the whole and thus forces a rethinking, and potential reorganization, of what legitimizes itself as whole. "Evil" emerges as a potentiality within human freedom that bears a striking resemblance to what Bakunin identifies in the Biblical figure of Satan as "the negative power in the positive development of human animality," the "power to rebel" as a native human faculty (Bakunin, 2009: 10). Indeed, by the time of his 1815 *Ages*, Schelling will criticize the "palliative normativity" of contemporary idealisms that show a "predilection for the affirmative" and deny or repress the existence of "something inhibiting, something conflicting . . . this Other that which, so to speak, should not be and yet is, nay, must be . . . this No that resists the Yes, this darkening that resists the light" (Schelling, 2001: 6). As Joseph P. Lawrence points out, humanity today and in Schelling's time is all too willing to take refuge in the affirmative, whether it be Enlightenment rationality or the incessant Yes of consumer capitalism (Lawrence, 2005: 14–17). Such forces incessantly deny the anarchic ground that serves as the basis for their own freedom in order to re-conceive evil as an external, hence removable, threat to the good. For Schelling, however, freedom necessitates an ever-renewed confrontation with the irreducible remainder of this Other that is always already the other within oneself, an Other that exposes the subject to its radical absence of foundations and that subject "feels his naked impoverishment" before the chaos of eternal creation (Schelling as cited in Lawrence, 2005: 22).

ANCESTRALITY AND THE *AGES OF THE WORLD*

The Freedom essay poses the vexed question of an originating ground that challenges the utopian expectations of modern rationality and introduces metaphysical entanglements that lead Schelling to complicate his earlier idealism. In the *Ages of the World*, Schelling carries these entanglements beyond the question of human freedom and into the fractured origins of the cosmos itself. One useful way of engaging Schelling's concerns in the *Ages* is to see it as an early attempt at what Quentin Meillassoux (2008) has identified with the task of thinking "ancestrality." To think ancestrality, according to Meillassoux:

> is to think a world without thought—a world without the givenness of the world. It is therefore incumbent upon us to break with the ontological requisite of the moderns, according to which to be *is to be a correlate*. Our task, by way of contrast, consists in trying to understand how thought is able to access the uncorrelated, which is to say, a world capable of subsisting without being given. But to say this is just to say that we must grasp how thought is able to access *an absolute*, i.e. a being whose severance (the original meaning of *absolutus*) and whose separateness from thought is such that it presents itself to us as non-relative to us, and hence as capable of existing whether we exist or not. (Meillassoux, 2008: 49)

Ancestrality marks a key concern for philosophy's attempts to understand nature as what Schelling calls the "abyss of the past" (Schelling, 2001: 31). Insofar as empirical science now makes speculative statements about "events anterior to the advent of life and of consciousness," philosophy must in turn create the conceptual tools needed to think this *an-archic* anteriority (Meillassoux, 2008: 20).

In an uncanny parallel of Bakunin's wholesale dismissal of idealism, Meillassoux dismisses "Schelling's Nature," along with "Hegelian Mind; Schopenhauer's Will; the Will (or *Wills*) to Power in Nietzsche; perception loaded with memory in Bergson; Deleuze's Life, etc." as incapable of overcoming correlationism (Meillassoux, 2008: 64). Yet what Meillssoux dismisses in Schelling, namely the latter's earlier view of nature as the "objective subject-object," artificially limits Schelling's position to one that he had substantially modified after 1809. As we have already indicated above, some of Schelling's early attempts to go beyond Kant's correlationism do indeed seek to posit the Absolute as a kind of ur-correlate, the subject-object/object-subject. With the *Ages*, however, Schelling broaches the problem of ancestrality so as to unbind "both [history and nature] from the teleology through which [his earlier] Idealism had configured them" (Rajan, 2007: 319).

In each of the three drafts of the *Ages*, Schelling begins by staging his history of nature as a teleological unfolding of the Absolute through the its past, present, and future (Schelling, 2001: xxxv). Yet, as Schelling passes through three unsuccessful attempts at moving beyond the first book of the past, this teleology gives way to a progressively darker, more traumatic, vision in which both history and ontology are reconfigured around the ancestrality of geology. As Hans Jorg Sandkuhler points out, "the real basis of the theory of the *Ages of the World* is modern geology" (Sandkuhler, 1984: 21). Modern geology, with its discovery of a "deep time" that radically extends the earth's history beyond the time given by Biblical accounts, "defeats *a priori* the prospect of [nature's] appearance for any finite phenomenologizing consciousness" (Grant, 2008: 6).[3] Placed under the sign of modern

---

[3] For a more detailed exploration of the revolution in the earth sciences after the French Revolution, see Paolo Rossi, *The Dark Abyss of Time: The History of the Earth & The History of Nations from Hooke to Vico* (1984) and, more recently, Martin Rudwick, *Bursting the Limits of Time: The Reconstruction of Geohistory in the Age of Revolution* (2006).

geology, whose materiality pushes consciousness beyond its finite origins towards the abyss of the geotemporal past, the *Ages*
marks an early attempt to engage ancestrality as a form of unconditioned thinking what Adorno and Horkheimer call "natural
history," or "the self-cognition of the spirit as nature in disunion
with itself" (Adorno and Horkheimer, 1987: 39).

Schelling's characterization of this "deep time" shifts from the
first to the third drafts of the *Ages.* As Rajan points out, the first
and second drafts of 1811 and 1813 largely repress the *an-archic*
potential within geological ancestrality by understanding the past
in theological and idealist terms, respectively. In 1811, Schelling
still conceives of the "time before the world" as an untroubled
indifference to which the world will ultimately return in the
"completed time" of the future, that is, in quasi-Hegelian fashion,
a time that marks the culmination of all history (Schelling as cited
in Rajan, 2008: par. 8). In that text, the unsettled "rotary movement" of the instinctual life is limited a historical and cultural
stage of development that Schelling, like Bakunin after him, sees
as finished. In the 1813 draft, Schelling actually removes any reference to the "rotary movement" and hence interprets history as
the uninhibited development of Spirit through a "ladder of formations" that will "unfold a complete image of the future world"
(Schelling as cited in Rajan, 2007: 322–23). Conversely, the traumatic figure of the "rotary movement" is not only reintroduced
for the 1815 version, but becomes the very focal point of Schelling's conception of the deep time. Schelling returns to his view
of an "original duplicity" in nature by positing a primordial antithesis of two contesting wills or potencies within the eternal
past, or the ground, of Being itself: a negating or inhibiting force
and an affirming or free principle (Schelling, 2001: 18). These two
wills are not reciprocally exclusive, rather, "they come together in
one and the same because the negating force can only feel itself
as negating when there is a disclosing being and the latter can
only be active as affirming insofar as it liberates the negating and
repressing force" (Schelling, 2001: 19). In turn, the force of these
two contesting potencies or wills therefore "posit outside and
above themselves a third, which is the unity" of the two (Schelling, 2001: 19).

So far, what Schelling imagines appears to be a very orthodox
dialectic in which the negating force, like the negation that serves
as the base or point of departure for humanity's emergence from
animality in Bakunin, constitutes for Schelling an eternal beginning that operates as the ground of an inexorable progression

towards a moment of synthesis: "When the first potency is posited, the second is also necessarily posited, and both of these produce the third with the same necessity. Thereby the goal is achieved" (Bakunin, 2009: 9; Schelling, 2001: 19). However, Schelling immediately deconstructs this synthesis, writing that "having arrived at its peak, the movement of itself retreats back into its beginning; for each of the three has an equal right to be that which has being" (Schelling, 2001: 19). Hence, the rotary movement neither gives birth to any *archē*, since "a true beginning is one that does not always begin again," nor reaches any ultimate conclusion, but continues in a ceaseless displacement of one potency by another. Moreover, since each of the three potencies has an equal right to exist, "there is [also] neither a veritable higher nor a veritable lower, since in turn one is higher and the other is lower. There is only an unremitting wheel, a rotatory movement that never comes to a standstill" (Schelling, 2001: 20). In order to posit the synthesis as above the ceaseless contest of the negating and affirming potencies, this would mean positing the synthesis as an antithesis; hence the former falls back into the very contest is claims to have overcome:

> Just as antithesis excluded unity, unity excluded antithesis. But precisely thereby the ground was given to that alternating movement, to that continuous revivification of the antitheses . . . since neither unity nor antithesis should alone be, but rather unity as well as antithesis. (Schelling, 2001: 36; Rajan, 2008: par. 9)

Schelling's revised view of the role of the negating potency in the 1815 *Ages* lodges an *aystaton* within cosmic history itself, an obliquity within Being to which Schelling compulsively returns as a site of madness and self-laceration that precludes understanding this history as unfolding progressively from *archē* to *telos* (Schelling, 2001: 43, 102, 148). Where in the 1813 version Schelling equated original will with a quiescent "will that wills nothing," in 1815 the annular drive is now "among the oldest potencies," an eccentricity within the very foundations of existence that "seeks its own foundational point" and thus decenters the point of origin itself (Schelling, 2001: 92). At the same time, we have already seen how the rotary motion is not a whole in the sense of a totality in which individual parts are subjected to a principle or *archē*. Rather, as Rajan argues, the rotary motion is a "[self-]critical trope in which the circulation of potencies never allows for a single principle to posit itself without being subject to its own deconstruction" (Rajan, 2008: par. 32).

The "rotary movement" trope in the *Ages* can therefore be read alongside the figure of evil from the Freedom essay. Where the freedom for evil manifested itself in the part's capacity to undermine the normativity of the whole, the rotary motion "commences with a rotation about its own axis," an involution of itself within itself and hence away from whole (Schelling, 2001: 92). The rotary movement is not simply (self-)destructive, but also creative: in its involution away from the normativity of the universal, rotary movements create new wholes that are themselves capable of being deconstructed, pushing forward Schelling's demand "that nothing in the universe be oppressed, limited, or subordinated. We demand for each and every thing its own particular and free life" (Schelling as cited in Lawrence, 2005: 19). At the same time, the rotary motion suggests that the history of the cosmos is a non-linear movement in which the past can never be entirely overcome, since it will always return to force us to re-interrogate its foundations through a continuous revivification of antitheses. For Schelling, this rotary movement is as much epistemological as it is ontological, for whomever wishes to understand the history of the cosmos must face "what is concealed in themselves . . . the abysses of the past that are still in one just as much as the present" (Schelling, 2001: 3–4).

FROM NEGATIVE TO POSITIVE PHILOSOPHY: SCHELLING'S PHILOSOPHY OF MYTHOLOGY

However, insofar as the abyss of the past remains concealed as both history's unconscious and that of the subject, Schelling broaches a fundamental non-knowledge that does not exactly follow the ancestral project as conceived by speculative realism. Perhaps most glaringly, Schelling's explicitly mythopoetic, rather than objectivist, approach to geo-cosmic history runs counter to Meillassoux's "naturalistic" ontology, and his emphasis on mathematics as the basis for a naturalistic, scientific philosophical ontology. Thus appears the third scandal of Schelling's late, ostensibly conservative, philosophy: a recourse to mythology and religion as a viable discourse of ancestrality in the face of both the positivism of his time and the scientism that has rooted itself in our own. Speculative realism takes a resolute stand against any metaphysics that relies on some form of non-knowledge or mystery, which always harbours the temptation to invest this non-knowledge with transcendent divine power. If one allows for any mystical transcendence beyond rational thought, we re-establish an onto(theo)logical *archē* that, by definition, does away with the contingency fundamental to the very idea of a radical democratic politics. For Meillassoux, the ancestral project is at one with that of radical democracy in arguing for what he calls the "necessity of contingency." According to Meillassoux:

> there is no reason for anything to be or to remain thus and not otherwise, and this applies as much to the laws that govern the world as to the things of the world. Everything could actually collapse: from trees to stars, from stars to laws, from physical laws to logical laws; and this not by virtue of some superior law whereby everything is destined to perish, but by virtue of the absence of any superior law. (Meillassoux, 2008: 88–89)

However, Markus Gabriel points out that "despite [Meillassoux's] actual commitment to absolute contingency he believes there must be an ultimate law, a *principle* of unreason that necessarily governs the auto-normalization of chaos" (Gabriel, 2009: 85). Following Alain Badiou, Meillassoux equates ontology with mathematics, a move which Schelling had criticized in Kant's preference for mathematics over philosophy as analogous to the preference for a "stereometrically regular crystal" over the human body because "the former has no possibility of falling ill, while the latter hosts germs of every possible illness" (Schelling, 1997: 212). As such, Meillassoux's approach to speculative realism threatens to become an ideology "that endows 'science' with the magical power of *getting it right*" and thus could be charged with serving "the existential project of making the human being at home in the world" (Gabriel, 2009: 86–87). In turn, although ancestral statements ostensibly divest the world of mythological consciousness they are strictly mythological by definition, insofar as mythology deals precisely with "origins that no one can have been present at" (Cavell as cited in Gabriel, 2009: 89). And if ancestral statements are mythological statements, then a philosophy of mythology can explore ancestrality so as to disclose the necessity of contingency, or ontological *anarchē*.

It is in this context that Gabriel proposes we return to Schelling's late philosophy of mythology. Schelling had already positioned the *Ages* as a mythological poem in which the past is narrated (Schelling, 2001: xxxv), and I have already intimated in previous sections how both the ancestrality of the *Ages* and the Freedom essay's exploration of the system of freedom could disclose the necessity of contingency. But these prior texts remain under the sign of what Schelling calls his negative philosophy, that is, the attempt at a science of the essence and of the concept of beginnings, a science that ascends from necessity to freedom, the real to the ideal, in an attempt to unify these terms in the Absolute. The failure of the *Ages* demonstrated the radical limits of what a negative philosophy could accomplish. At the same time, as Jason Wirth points out, Hegel himself may have helped "reveal to Schelling the limit[s] of negative philosophy . . . by perfecting it" in his *Phenomenology of Spirit* (Wirth, 2007: ix). For in the *Phenomenology*, Hegel articulated the grand march of spirit from its lowest forms in sense-certainty to its highest manifestation in the reflexivity of the Absolute through the inexorable logic of the dialectic. It is with the positive philosophy *qua* philosophy of mythology that Schelling undertakes his most explicit critique of Hegel's philosophy of essence in favour of mythology as a philosophy of existence.

Schelling's critique of Hegel detailed and complex, but it can be said to center on what Schelling calls Hegel's "one mistake" (*von dem Einen Mißbegrif*): his confusion of logical relationships between concepts with actual or existing relationships (Schelling, 1996: 160). In turn, Schelling will argue that Hegel removes the facticity of existence as the basis upon which logic is grounded and reduces the real to logic, which then functions as the totalizing principle for all of knowledge. Hegel, according to Schelling, fails to perceive that negative philosophy or logic can only treat of the possible and not the actual (Schelling, 1996: 135). For Schelling, conversely, the facticity of existence always precedes logic, and it is only from this living ground that one can develop a genuine movement through which the abstractions of logic emerge. By beginning with logic, Hegel thus presupposes an already developed subject that implicitly determines the process (Schelling, 1996: 138, 145). For similar reasons, Schelling also questions the totalizing purview of Hegel's logic; for Hegel subsumes every particular within the circular system of the pure Concept and in doing so, assumes that no extra-logical concepts exist. Yet, as we have already seen, for Schelling the very notion of a system presupposes its *aystaton*, some contingency that makes the system fundamentally incomplete in itself (Schelling, 1996: 144). For Schelling "the whole world lies, so to speak, in the nets of the understanding or of reason, . . . the question is how exactly it got into those nets, since there is obviously something other and something more than mere reason in the world" (Schelling, 1996: 147).

Though it is debatable as to whether Schelling is entirely correct in his assessment of Hegel,[4] the critique itself allowed Schelling to clarify the direction of his positive philosophy. Rather than begin with logic, then, Schelling begins with what he calls the "*unprethinkable*" ground of Being. The *unprethinkable* is pure actuality or facticity, but it is not, as in Hegel, (logical) necessity. Rather, as *unprethinkable* the ground is not preceded by any rationality that would be able to distinguish the conceptual oppositions that would allow it to become thinkable. The *unprethinkable* is neither necessary nor contingent, but the very indifference of necessity and contingency, the groundless ground that the thinkable must presuppose precisely in order to think it. The *unprethinkable*, like the "unconditioned" in Schelling's earlier *Naturphilosophie*, is therefore not directly accessible to concepts since it is the very condition upon which concepts can be articulated. The paradox is that the *unprethinkable* becomes necessary as the condition for thinking only through the movement of thinking itself, and thus simultaneously contingent. This is why Schelling will characterize the *unprethinkable* as "that which is unequal to itself," an "uncanny principle" which cannot ever be fully grasped in reflection (cited in Žižek and Gabriel, 2009: 19–20).

Since the *unprethinkable* is not directly accessible to concepts, it cannot be expressed in the propositional language of reflection but rather expresses itself in and as mythology. What mythology means for Schelling, however, is not simply ancient pre-scientific narratives about the gods. Schelling's interest is not simply in myths but in mythology as such, "the brute fact of [the] existence of a logical space which cannot be accounted for in logical terms" (Gabriel, 2009: 20). For Schelling, myths are not what Hegel identifies as allegories of logic—that is, failed or partial expressions of reason's coming to know itself, delusion, proto-science, or protophilosophy, and so on. Instead, Schelling claims that mythological "ideas are not first present in another form, but rather they emerge only in, and thus also at the same time with, this form. . . . mythology is thoroughly actual—that is, everything in it is thus to be understood as mythology expresses it, not as if something else were thought, something else said" (Schelling, 2007b: 136). Myth-

---

[4] For a more thoroughgoing examination of the Schelling-Hegel debate see John Laughland, *Schelling versus Hegel: From German Idealism to Christian Metaphysics* (2007).

ological content and form are not separable: there is no content that would serve as mythology's hidden *archē*, but rather form and content emerge simultaneously to constitute the "living and concrete differences" that condition the heterogeneity of peoples, differences which are "preserved in language only in abstract and formal differences" (Schelling, 2007b: 40). In this respect, mythology refers directly to the non-reflective ground of "theogonic powers," the very potencies which organize experience itself.

Significantly, one of the mythological figures Schelling emphasizes is Chaos in Hesiod's *Theogony*, a reference which he shares with Hakim Bey's (1993) similarly mythological description of "ontological anarchy." For Bey, ontological anarchy expresses itself mythologically in "the great serpent (Tiamat, Python, Leviathan), Hesiod's primal Chaos, presides over the vast long dreaming of the Paleolithic—before all kings, priests, agents of Order, History, Hierarchy, Law." Likewise, Schelling stresses Chaos' etymological meaning as the "expanse . . . that which still stands open to everything," or what Schelling earlier called the unconditioned (Schelling, 2007b: 30). Chaos thematizes mythology as the necessity of contingency, its dual status as facticity and the unconditioned or the open that constitutes the very coming into being of a world, and whose being can only be proven *a posteriori* once the world is itself manifest. Hence mythology discloses the fundamental inability for Being to grasp itself reflexively; rather, mythology functions for Schelling as the irreducible remainder that remains irresolvable into reason, not in the form of a transcendent *archē* (Meillassoux's worry), but as an exuberance of being itself that exposes us to the radical contingency of our finitude and to the ceaseless creativity of the unconditioned that frees itself from its positivity in an "ongoing process of creative development" (cited in Matthews, 2007a: 5).

CONCLUSION

In many ways, the preceding discussion is something of a prolegomena to an anarchistic reading of Schelling. What I have attempted to do here in explicating the three scandals proper to Schelling's philosophy is to lay the philosophical groundwork by which Schelling can be said to anticipate a theory of ontological *anarchē*. By focusing on this particular aspect of Schelling, I have established a number of threads that bear further examination, including a more thorough account of Schelling's influence on Bakunin, his critical discussions of the state, and his own shifting views of the ideal society. Another potentially rich vein of thinking not addressed here is Schelling's influence on Heidegger, which in turn might yield new readings of Reiner Schürmann's *an-archic* ontology. Undoubtedly, there also remain elements of Schelling's thinking incompatible not only with an anarchistic politics but with contemporary values more broadly, such as his repulsive view of South Americans as animals in the third lecture of his *Historical-Critical Introduction to the Philosophy of Mythology* (Schelling, 2007b: 48); a particularly odd lapse in judgement given Schelling's otherwise respectful treatment of the mythologies of eastern cultures. Nonetheless, Schelling's philosophy does provide a particularly compelling account of the groundlessness of Being which resonates with a number of contemporary concerns, such as the problem of ancestrality and the task of thinking the necessity of contingency as a critical tool against all forms of totalizing ontology.

Jared McGeough received his Ph.D. in Theory and Criticism from Western University in 2011. His dissertation reexamined William Godwin's philosophical and literary anarchism in light of recent developments in post-structural anarchist theory. He has published articles on Godwin and Romantic literature and has been recently invited to edit a special issue of *Literature Compass* on Romantic Anarchism. McGeough has previously taught English literature at the University of Regina and is currently Assistant Professor (LTA) at Concordia University.

REFERENCES

Adorno, Theodor and Max Horkheimer (1987). *Dialectic of Enlightenment*. London and New York: Continuum.
Bakunin, Mikhail (2009). *God and the State*. New York: Cosimo.
––– (1971). *Bakunin on Anarchy: Selected Works by the Activist Founder of World Anarchism* (Dolgoff, Sam, Ed. and Trans.). London: Allen and Unwin.
Bey, Hakim (1993). "Ontological Anarchy in a Nutshell": http://deoxy.org/hakim/ontologicalanarchy.htm.
Blumenberg, Hans (1985). *The Legitimacy of the Modern Age* (Wallace, Robert, Trans.). Cambridge: MIT Press.
Cohn, Jesse and Shawn Wilbur (2010). "What's Wrong with Postanarchism?" *The Anarchist Library*: http://theanarchistlibrary.org/library/Jesse_Cohn_and_Shawn_Wilbur__What_s_Wrong_With_Postanarchism_.html.

Engels, Frederick (1841). "Anti-Schelling," *Marxists Internet* Archive: http://www.marxists.org/archive/marx/works/1841/anti-schelling/index.htm.

Freydberg, Bernard (2008). *Schelling's Dialogical Freedom Essay: Provocative Philosophy Then and Now.* Albany: State University of New York Press.

Gare, Arran (2011). "From Kant to Schelling to Process Metaphysics: On the Way to Ecological Civilization." *Cosmos and History* 7(2): 26–69.

Grant, Iain Hamilton (2008). *Philosophies of Nature After Schelling.* London and New York: Continuum.

Habermas, Jürgen (2004). "Dialectical Idealism in Transition to Materialism: Schelling's Idea of a Contraction of God and its Consequences for the Philosophy of History" (Midgely, Nick and Judith Norman, Trans.). In *The New Schelling* (Norman, Judith and Alistair Welchman, Ed.). London and New York: Continuum. 43–89.

——— (1983). *Philosophical-Political Profiles* (Lawrence, F. G., Trans.). Cambridge: MIT Press.

Heidegger, Martin (1985). *Schelling's Treatise on the Essence of Human Freedom* (Stambaugh, Joan, Trans.). Athens: Ohio University Press.

Kant, Immanuel (1992). *The Concflict of the Faculties* (Gregor, Mary J., Trans.). Lincoln: University of Nebraska Press.

Krell, David Farrell (2004). "Three Ends of the Absolute: Schelling, Holderlin, Novalis." In *Idealism Without Absolutes: Philosophy and Romantic Culture* (Rajan, Tilottama and Plotnitsky, Arkady, Ed.). Albany: State University of New York Press. 135–159.

Laughland, John (2007). *Schelling versus Hegel: From German Idealism to Christian Metaphysics.* Burlington: Ashgate.

Lawrence, Joseph P. (2005). "Philosophical Religion and the Quest for Authenticity." In *Schelling Now: Contemporary Readings* (Wirth, Jason, Ed.). Bloomington: Indiana University Press. 13–30.

Matthews, Bruce (2007). "Translator's Introduction." In Schelling, F.W.J., *The Grounding of Positive Philosophy: The Berlin Lectures* (Matthews, Bruce, Trans.). Albany: State University of New York Press. 1–84.

Meillassoux, Quentin (2008). *After Finitude: An Essay on the Necessity of Contingency* (Brassier, Ray, Trans.). London: Continuum.

Proudhon, Pierre-Joseph (1890). *What is Property? An Inquiry into the Principle of Right and of Government.* (Tucker, Benjamin, Trans.). Marxists Internet Archive: http://www.marxists.org/reference/subject/economics/proudhon/property.

Rajan, Tilottama (2007). "First Outline of a System of Theory: Schelling and the Margins of Philosophy, 1799–1815." *Studies in Romanticism* 46(3): 311–355.

——— (2008). "'The Abyss of the Past': Psychoanalysis in Schelling's *Ages of the World* (1815)." *Romantic Circles: Praxis Series*: http://www.rc.umd.edu/praxis/psychoanalysis/rajan/rajan.html.

Richards, Robert (2002). *The Romantic Conception of Life.* Chicago: University of Chicago Press.

Rossi, Paolo (1984). *The Dark Abyss of Time: The History of the Earth & The History of Nations from Hooke to Vico.* (Cochrane, L. G., Trans.). Chicago: University of Chicago Press.

Rudwick, Martin (2006). *Bursting the Limits of Time: The Reconstruction of Geohistory in the Age of Revolution.* Chicago: University of Chicago Press.

Schelling, F.W.J. (2000). *Ages of the World* (Wirth, Jason, Trans.). Albany: State University of New York Press.

——— (2005). *First Outline of a System of the Philosophy of Nature* (Peterson, Keith, Trans.). Albany: State University of New York Press.

——— (2007a). *The Grounding of Positive Philosophy: The Berlin Lectures* (Matthews, Bruce, Trans.). Albany: State University of New York Press.

——— (2007b). *Historical-Critical Introduction to the Philosophy of Mythology* (Richey, Mason and Markus Zisselberger, Trans.). Albany: State University of New York Press.

——— (1994). *Idealism and the Endgame of Theory: Three Essays by F.W.J. Schelling* (Pfau, Thomas, Ed. and Trans.) Albany: State University of New York Press.

——— (1988). *Ideas for a Philosophy of Nature* (Harris, Errol E. and Peter Heath, Trans.). Cambridge: Cambridge University Press.

——— (1996). *On the History of Modern Philosophy* (A. Bowie, Trans.). Cambridge: Cambridge University Press.

——— (1997). "On the Nature of Philosophy as Science" (Weigelt, Marcus., Trans.). In *German Idealist Philosophy* (Bubner, Rüdiger, Ed.). Harmondsworth: Penguin. 210–243.

——— (1966). *On University Studies* (Guterman, Norbert., Ed., and E. S. Morgan, Trans.). Athens: Ohio University Press.

——— (2006). *Philosophical Investigations into the Essence of Human Freedom* (Love, Jeff and Johannes Schmidt, Trans.). Albany: State University of New York Press.

——— (1978). *System of Transcendental Idealism* (Heath, Peter., Trans.). Charlottesville: University Press of Virginia.

Wirth, Jason (2007). "Foreword." In Schelling, F.W.J., *Historical-Critical Introduction to the Philosophy of Mythology* (Richey, Mason and Markus Zisselberger, Trans.). Albany: State University of New York Press.

Žižek, Slavoj (1997). *The Indivisible Remainder: On Schelling and Other Matters.* London: Verso.

Žižek, Slavoj and Markus Gabriel (2009). *Mythology, Madness, Laughter: Subjectivity in German Idealism.* London and New York: Continuum.

Anarchist Developments in Cultural Studies
ISSN: 1923-5615
2013.2: Ontological Anarché: Beyond Materialism and Idealism

Occult Origins
Hakim Bey's Ontological Post-Anarchism

Joseph Christian Greer

ABSTRACT
Convention concerning the beginning of Post-anarchist discourse locates its origin in Hakim Bey's work in the 1980s; however, no commentator has sufficiently analyzed the thoroughly spiritualized anarchism upon which it is based, termed "Ontological Anarchism," nor the group that promoted it, the Association of Ontological Anarchism. This article draws attention to the ways in which the interface between a starkly postmodern form of esotericism called Chaos Magick and the anarchist tradition produced Ontological Anarchism, and, further, to the implications of this hybridity on the historiography of Post-anarchism.

KEYWORDS
post-anarchism, chaos magick, Hakim Bey, zines, discordianism

INTRODUCTION

Peter Lamborn Wilson once lightheartedly lamented, "Hakim Bey is more popular than I am" (Knight, 2012: 74). What makes this comment humorous is that Hakim Bey is a *nom de plume* for Wilson. What makes this comment *noteworthy* is that Wilson used this *nom de plume* to initiate one of the most innovative developments in the history of twentieth century anarchism. This development, which he termed Post-Anarchism Anarchy (now called Post-anarchism), arose from the confluence of esotericism and anarchism in the 1980s zine network.[1] Thus, in order to under-

---

[1] The category of esotericism should be understood not as a cluster of historically linked occult or hermetic phenomena but rather as an instrument for historians to better understand marginalized spiritual currents

stand the origins of Post-anarchism we must locate it in the context of Bey's work and the specific audience for which he was writing.

While convention concerning the origin of Post-anarchism states that it began in Bey's work in the 1980s (Call, 2010: 10; Newman 2010: 51, 71n.8), no commentator has sufficiently analyzed the thoroughly spiritualized anarchism upon which it is based, termed Ontological Anarchism, nor the group that promoted it, the Association of Ontological Anarchism (AOA henceforth).[2] The aim of this article is to draw attention to the ways in which the interface between a starkly postmodern form of esotericism called Chaos Magick and the anarchist tradition produced Ontological Anarchism, and, further, the implications of this hybridity on the historiography of Post-anarchism.[3] To this end, three related undercurrents run through this article. The first concerns the identification of primary sources with regards to Wilson/Bey and Ontological Anarchism. The second links these esoteric sources to a gap in scholarship on the prominence of esotericism within early Post-anarchist discourse, i.e., Bey's Ontological Anarchism. The third concerns Lewis Call's convincing argument concerning the role of "the Nietzsche effect" in laying the foundation for Post-anarchism (as mention is made throughout the article of Nietzsche's strong influence on the esoteric discourses that predate as well as prefigure Bey's Post-anarchist Ontological Anarchism).[4] The conclusions drawn are likewise

---

which may or may not be related to occultism or hermeticism. See Hanegraaff, 2012 and fn.5.

[2] The title of Leonard Williams's article "Hakim Bey and Ontological Anarchism" suggests that it would have provided some insight into this topic; however, in failing to grasp the spiritual context of Bey's use of Chaos as ontology, the article ends up mistaking Ontological Anarchism for an "artistic practice" and in so doing fails to elucidate Bey's innovative refashioning of anarchism. See Williams, 2010.

[3] The term magick was coined by British occultist Aleister Crowley to separate his spiritual system and writings from the so-called superstitious magic of the occultists whom he considered his competitors. The fact that his term has persisted to this day, as evidenced by the Chaos Magick discourse, testifies to the continued relevance of his approach to spiritual and religious texts and practices. See Crowley, 1992. For an account of Crowley's lasting influence see Bogdan & Starr (eds.), 2012.

[4] Quoting Keith Ansell-Pearson, Call describes "the Nietzsche effect" as the consensus opinion amongst scholars that the most fertile aspect of Nietzsche's work is not so much its content but how its performative

threefold: first, that the history of Post-anarchism cannot be written without considering the contribution of occultism; second, that Bey's work itself will remain misunderstood if the esoteric themes that it addressed, and physical mediums through which it first appeared, remain unexamined; third, through acknowledging the esoteric foundation of Bey's Ontological Anarchism, an even earlier form of Nietzsche-inspired, anarcho-occultism called Discordianism can be read into the multiplicity of discourses that compose the pre-history of Post-anarchism.[5]

At the heart of this article is the correction of an inaccuracy, namely, that Bey's 1991 text, *T.A.Z.: The Temporary Autonomous Zone, Ontological Anarchy, Poetic Terrorism* (hereafter *TAZ*) published by Autonomedia constitutes the origin of Post-anarchist discourse. This is not to deny the centrality of the texts that compose the book *TAZ*, but rather to draw attention to the fact that *TAZ is an anthology of previously published works.* Mistakenly identifying the origins of Ontological Anarchism in *TAZ* effectively neglects the original primary sources which first introduced Bey's idea of Ontological Anarchism, as well as the milieu in which it was initially, developed, critiqued, and revised. The glossy publication produced by Autonomedia in 1991 entitled *TAZ* does not represent the origin of Ontological Anarchism; rather, it is a redacted volume assembled to popularize Bey's work. In order to illustrate the implications of the failure to recognize *TAZ*'s provenance, this article focuses on the Chaos Magick milieu in which Bey first developed Ontological Anarchism.

The *TAZ* text itself is broken into three sections which correspond to three distinct works composed by Bey at various times. The first section of the book is the verbatim reproduction of a prose-poetry zine entitled *Chaos: The Broadsheets of Ontological Anarchy*, first published in 1985. The most rigorous development of Ontological Anarchism followed after the publication of *Chaos* in a number of zines, but most regularly as a series of letters and essays in a Chaos Magick zine from the years 1986–1988. These letters and essays would come to be collected as the second and largest section of *TAZ* and were titled *Communiqués of the Association for Ontological Anarchy.* The essential aspect of this devel-

---

quality deconstructs the logocentric bias of Western thought and reason. See Call, 2001: 51–52.

[5] Debate continues to rage over how to define "occultism" with Marco Pasi's historiographic definition standing out as the most workable. See Pasi, 2012; Hanegraaff, Brach, Faivre, & van den Broek, 2005: 884–889; Hanegraaff: 2012.

opment, as will be shown, concerns the way in which the communiqués were written largely in response to issues prominent in the anarcho-queer-magickal milieu, which heralded Bey's *Chaos* as essential reading for the nascent Chaos Magick movement. The last section of *TAZ* is a collection of writings which focus on the formation of moments where Ontological Anarchism has flourish, termed Temporary Autonomous Zones, and from whence the title of the book is derived. As will be made clear in what follows, *TAZ* was not the primary source from which Post-anarchism originated, and thus, much stands to be gained by both subverting this monolithic origin point and reasserting the radical hybridity of its origins for historians of Post-anarchism and esotericism alike.

As Bey's writings on Ontological Anarchism first appeared in his zine *Chaos*, and developed into "communiqués" published in a number of influential zines, the first section focuses on setting Ontological Anarchism within what Bob Black termed the "marginal milieu" and, in particular, clarifying its relationship to Joel Biroco's influential Chaos Magick zine *Kaos* (Black, 1994). The second section offers an in-depth description of Bey's explicitly Nietzschean reading of Chaos and how this functioned as the basis of Ontological Anarchism. The conclusion takes up the significance of citing Ontological Anarchism as the origin of Post-anarchism. Essentially, it will be argued that Bey's role in the formation of Post-anarchism obliges scholars to recognize why he, and others, perceived natural affinities between anarchism and esotericism. Finally, brief mention is made of a slightly earlier syncretism of Chaos ontology, Nietzschean philosophy, esotericism, and anarchism termed Discordianism, which heavily influenced Bey's formulation of Ontological Anarchism.[6] It will be argued that the inclusion of Discordianism in the early historiography of Post-anarchism will lead scholars to recognize how the origins of Post-anarchism in an occult milieu is not simply an oddity or an aberration, but representative of a grossly underappreciated historical alliance between anarchism and esotericism beginning from the late 1950s onward.

---

[6] Just as scholars of Post-anarchism have neglected to explore the sources anthologized within *TAZ*, so too have scholars of Discordianism failed to examine its origins in the zine scene. Carole Cusack's work on Discordianism exemplifies this unfortunate trend. See Cusack, 2010 and ibid, 2011.

DISCURSIVE TRANSFERS "BENEATH THE UNDERGROUND"

In olden days I was a Prophet, today I am a rabble-rouser.

Joel Biroco, "Renegade"

Today, it is no secret that Wilson and Bey are the same individual. However, when Bey's *Chaos* and the AOA communiqués were printed in the mid-1980s zine network, this secret was closely guarded.[7] Similarly, while the AOA's greatest asset was the forceful eloquence of the provocations issued by its only public representative, Bey, the mystery concerning its size and militancy lent it an undeniable mystique. In hindsight, Bey seems to have been its only official member; yet, as mentioned he too was a mystery at that time. The most plausible explanation as to why Wilson adopted his pseudonym after his return from Iran following the 1979 revolution, was so that he could safeguard the respectability of his academic work which he continued to be publish under the name Wilson. As Bey, Wilson's writings were unapologetically radical in both style and content. Understanding the difference between the once-separate identities of Wilson and Bey is the key to understanding how Ontological Anarchism was formed. While Wilson was an independent, Traditionalist scholar of Islam and Persian poetry, Bey, the prolific anarcho-mystic and man-boy-love propagandist, was a prime mover in a vibrant, "sub-underground" known as the "zine scene" that flourished in North America and the UK from the mid-1970s to the early 1990s.[8] This milieu can most accurately be described as a network of political, sexual, and spiritual non-conformists, all of whom communicated through small-circulation hand-made magazines called fanzines, abbreviated to zines, as well as taped letters, self-recorded music, mail-art, and "comix" sent through the mail. Named after the company that allowed for the cheap production of these publications, xerography established itself as the central pivot of this outsider milieu. Aside from a general, but by no means totalizing acceptance of anti-authoritarianism and the rejection of censor-

---

[7] This is exemplified in the video recording of Joseph Matheny's "T.A.Z." event that featured Robert Anton Wilson and Hakim Bey as speakers. Whereas Robert Anton Wilson's part was filmed with only minimal distortion effects, Wilson, performing as Bey, is blurred out almost entirely with the use of psychedelic colors and patterns in the video (Matheny, 1993).

[8] For a detailed overview of the Traditionalist context where Wilson began his academic writing career see Sedgwick, 2004: 147–160, and Versluis, 2010.

ship, those who participated in this network were anything but homogeneous in taste, opinion, and areas of interest (Black, 1994: 4). As an embedded authority, Bob Black described the milieu stating: "abhorrent topics, from space colonization to Holocaust Revisionism, are taken in stride" and it was not uncommon to have ads for Situationist or queer zines in magick publications and vice versa (Black, 1994: 6).

Both thematically and aesthetically, labels like punk, queer, anarchist, and magick do more to misrepresent the material within the zines than categorize them, as each of these elements were routinely reconfigured in any number of ways throughout the network. This is clearly true for Chaos Magick publications like *Salvation Army* and *Kaos*, both of which were embraced by both anarcho-queer individuals disenfranchised with what they saw as the commodification and banalization of homosexuality as a fixed identity, and anarchists whose esoteric worldviews ran afoul of their atheist materialist comrades.[9] Certainly, the zine scene was an exceptionally fecund network in regards to the cross-pollination of radical politics, illegal sexualities, and esotericism, and as such stands as "an undiscovered continent" of primary source materials for scholars of contemporary anarchism, cultural studies, and esotericism (Wobensmith, 2012).

The Acknowledgments page of *TAZ* indicates the extent to which vastly different discourses overlapped in the rhizomatic zine network, which inspired and disseminated the writings that would be collected as *Communiqués of Ontological Anarchism*. The list of publications on the Acknowledgments page reads as a who's who of the most influential zines in the network. Of particular note is Joel Biroco's *Kaos*, Mike Gunderloy's *Factsheet Five*, R.U. Sirius' *Mondo 2000*, and *Popular Reality*. These titles bare mention because aspects of each (magick, cyberpunk, alternative sexuality, etc.) are essential components in Bey's Ontological Anarchism and characterize the major themes within the zine network more generally.[10]

---

[9] As leading lights in Chaos Magick, the alternative sexualities of Aleister Crowley and William S. Burroughs are cited by numerous Chaos magicians as evidence that sexual nonconformity is magical by nature: See Hine, 2003. The Church of the Subgenius and Discordianism are two religious groups whose reworking of anarchism through religious language, humor, and esoteric symbolism effectively excludes them from consideration as part of contemporary anarchism.

[10] Scholars looking to reconstruct the most notable individuals and publications within the zine network could scarcely find a better resource

As space constraints prohibit a broader analysis of Ontological Anarchism's development across a number of zines, focus shall here be on one zine, Joel Biroco's *Kaos,* as it not only served as the most influential platform for non-sectarian discussions on Chaos Magick, but also because it printed much of what later became the *Communiqués of Ontological Anarchism.*[11] Before linking the contents of *Kaos* to the development of Ontological Anarchism, though, a few descriptive issues regarding *Kaos* and Chaos Magick merit addressing. As to the latter, providing a brief outline of an entire magical discourse is difficult enough, and this especially so for one oriented in the postmodern project of destabilizing essentialist positions so as to align the magician with the Chaos thought to undergird reality. Suffice it to say that Chaos Magick is a largely existentialist worldview initiated in the late 1970s by two British magicians, Peter Carroll and Ray Sherwin, that is based largely on Nietzsche's "theory of magical science" concerning the will to power, Crowley's religious teachings, and the English mage A.O. Spare's sigilization technique (Rocket, 1988: 18).[12] Essential to Chaos Magick is the meta-belief that belief and identity are tools, indeed "magickal force[s]", that can be used to manipulate reality according to one's will (Caroll, 1987: 39–41). As for the zine, issues of *Kaos* open with incendiary editorial introductions by Biroco, which are followed in no particular order by letters-to-the-editor, longer essays, pirated and original art, book reviews, and a mail-order listing of other zines. Based on both the belief that letters-to-the-editor retained a vitality lost in other modes of writing and Biroco's policy of printing everything, *Kaos* had an exceptionally long and patently polemic letters-to-the-editor section. The result was that passionate discus-

---

than *TAZ*'s acknowledgment page and back-cover. These pages link the most influential agents in the zine sub-underground to the aging cultural icons who paved the way for them, including Burroughs, Leary, and Ginsberg, all of whom have blurbs on the back cover.

[11] *Kaos* changed it name from *Chaos* in issue 7 to distinguish itself from another Chaos Magick zine, *Chaos International.*

[12] Two articles in *Kaos* 11 illustrate the way in which Crowley's influence in Chaos Magick is denigrated to the point of being lamentable, whereas Nietzsche's is elevated to the highest possible rank. Ramsey Duke's claim that, "Nietzsche [XXX] was my prophet: I preach the Superman, and the Death of God" encapsulates the latter, while Yael Ruth Dragwyla's statement "Crowley was . . . a young and soul-crippled child" articulates the former. Nearly every account of Chaos Magick cites A.O. Spare its first and the most significant theorist. Duke, 1988: 26; Dragwyla, 1988: 20.

sions and vitriolic diatribes alike often extend over a number of issues, and as a primary contributor, Bey's work was both constantly referenced, celebrated, and disparaged.

As *Kaos* operated under a print-everything standard, its international audience encompassed a wide-spectrum of the "lunatic fringe" and topics were often revisited from a number of perspectives. *Kaos* 6 illustrates this point well, as it features an anarchist analysis of language by post-left anarchism luminary Bob Black that responded to an earlier piece by the zine's editor, Biroco, about the language of magick, which was then referenced later in issue 6 by Stephen Sennitt, the creator of the influential zine *NOX,* in an article about the interface between esotericism and linguistic psychology and physics. However, for all of the variety within each issue, opinions concerning the nature of Chaos and in particular the means by which it was to be used magically were central in every issue. While it would be impossible to prove Bey's formulation of Chaos was the most influential of those presented therein, it can be said that Ontological Anarchism was amongst the most discussed approaches in the zine; accordingly, the origins of the formal Post-anarchist discourse cannot be understood outside of the competition between leading schools within the Chaos Magick discourse, and thus informed by Ontological Anarchism's competitors, namely, Thelema, and Genesis P. Orridge's Thee Temple ov Psychick Youth.[13]

If we are to read Ontological Anarchism against competing influences within the Chaos Magick discourse, it is necessary to first characterize their common assumptions. Basically, they all shared the belief that the experience of "gnosis" through magical techniques, rituals, and psychedelics, revealed the anarchic, yet malleable, interplay of the forces that structure reality. Additionally, it was believed that the structure of reality was actively obscured by the "barrage of psychic propaganda" frequently identified in Situationist language as the "Spectacle" (Alistair, 1986; Jackson, 1986). The difference between the competing interpretations of Chaos Magick was in the course of action suggested by the gnostic experiences of Chaos.[14] Far from undisputed, Bey's

---

[13] Arguments over these approaches to Chaos Magick are commonplace in *Kaos;* see Paul B., 1986: 15; Rocket, 1988: 18; Biroco, 1986: 35 and 1988: 35.

[14] While it has been suggested that the term Gnosticism be abandoned altogether, debate over the correct ways in which the term gnostic can be used remains heated. The best introduction to the dispute is Williams, 1999. It is set with scare-marks to indicate its emic use in *Kaos.*

conclusions concerning these experiences—which appeared many times within a number of issues—were attacked for being everything from the ramblings of a post-psychedelic airhead to the fearful poses of an intellectual dilettante (Bey, 1988: 9). The majority of critiques directed towards Bey stemmed from his insistence on reading Chaos as a primarily generative force wherein "the Way & the Great Work", or the path of the Chaos magician, was to manifest his imagination in such a way that encompassed the desire of others and in so doing transcend the forces of "thanatos" which in his estimation belong exclusively to the Spectacle (Bey, 1986; 1987a; 1987b; 1978c; 1988).

As mentioned, Ontological Anarchism was a heated topic within the pages of *Kaos*. Bey's strident optimism was in the minority amongst contributors who reveled in pessimistic nihilism, and specifically the exaltation of murder, torture, and the end of the world (Bey, 2003; Biroco, 1988). As evidenced in a text that later became communiqué #4 in *TAZ* (but was entitled "The End of the World" in *Kaos* 6), as well as the text that would become communiqué #5, "Intellectual S / M Is the Fascism of the Eighties—The Avant-Garde Eats Shit and Likes It", it was pure revulsion that spurred Bey, and by extension the AOA, to the position summarized in the line: "Ours is no art of mutilation but of excess, superabundance, amazement" (Bey, 2003: 37). In defining himself against those who were "queer for death" insofar as they celebrated not conviviality but "thanatosis" and *Schadenfreude*, Bey increasingly altered his theorizing in the mirror of the other authors published in *Kaos* (Bey, 2003: 38). The tension between these two camps—with Bey's "self-realization, beauty, and adventure" approach to Chaos set against the "gnostic fascism" of Rabbi Rabinowitz and Stephen Sennitt (to name only two representatives)—came to a head across four issues on the topic of using the image of the murderer, and specifically Marquis de Sade, in black magick practice and Chaos Magick in general. The numerous responses from Bey contained in each issue reflected the development of Ontological Anarchism over and against those enticed by the power of the darker aspects of Chaos Magick. Considering that Bey's responses, many of which underwent no editing from the original form they possessed in *Kaos*, were collected years later as the *Communiqués of Ontological Anarchism* and inserted as the middle section of *TAZ*, it is not an overstatement to claim that in neglecting their original context, historians cannot understand what Ontological Anarchism is or to what it was responding.

The dispute over de Sade was by no means an isolated incident. As Ontological Anarchism, like Bey's concept of Chaos, was routinely foregrounded in the pages of *Kaos,* so too were the critiques of it. To clarify what Chaos actually meant to Bey, and in turn shed light on Post-anarchism's origin, the next section shall outline how Bey defined this concept and the implications he saw therein for realizing autonomy through esoteric spirituality.

ONTOLOGICAL ANARCHISM

> *This is not just a matter of spiritual dandyism, but also of existential commitment to an underlying spontaneity, to a philosophical "tao." For all its waste of energy, in its very formlessness, anarchism alone of all the ISMs approaches that one type of form which alone can interest us today, that strange attractor, the shape of chaos—which (one last quote [from Nietzsche]) one must have within oneself, if one is to give birth to a dancing star.*
>
> Hakim Bey, "Post-Anarchism Anarchy"

Ontological Anarchism is Bey's formulation of a more authentically anarchist anarchism, one which reflects the ontological state of being, which he identifies as the boundless vitality of Chaos. Harking back to A.O. Spare, whom Sherwin and Carroll recognized as the father of the Chaos Magick discourse, Hakim Bey describes Chaos as synonymous with the Dao of the *Daodejing* and *Zhuangzi.*[15] Further, utilizing the palimpsestic approach that characterizes much of his work, Bey additionally references the Babylonian Goddess Tiamat, fractals, and Hesiod's *Theogony* as illustrating variant aspects of Chaos, which, he argues, exceeds the capacity of any rendering or conceptualization. In essence, Chaos, the primordial and infinite, "inert & spontaneous," and "original undifferentiated oneness-of-being" is the indestructible, unmitigated potentiality that simultaneously vivifies and is all that exists: in his words, "chaos is life" (Bey, 2001: 1; 2003: 3).

---

[15] The decontextualization and appropriation of the Dao in the Chaos Magick discourse follows a trend that runs through much of 20th and 19th century esotericism. Nearly a century before figures like Biroco, Bey, and Sherwin adopted the Dao as a synonym for their conception of Chaos, Crowley incorporated an idiosyncratic interpretation of Daoism into his religious system known as Thelema. Space constraints limit any discussion of the notable influence of Crowley's idiosyncratic conception of Daoism in the Chaos Magick milieu, however, it nonetheless remains a topic ripe for research. For an extended discussion of Crowley's engagement with Daoism see Nillson, 2013: 118–124.

Characteristic of the Chaos Magick milieu, Nietzsche's philosophy also plays a major role in Bey's work and his conceptualization of Ontological Anarchism is no exception. Reminiscent of the opening passage of the *Daodejing*, Bey makes clear that Chaos cannot be defined; however, it can be described, and he does so in explicitly Nietzschean terms as being "based on nothing" and as a consequence, inherently "for Life" (Bey, 2001: 1). Described as explicitly against what Bey saw as the fashionable nihilism and pessimism of the time, he argued that Chaos' basis in nothingness and expression as sheer potentiality meant that nothing, be it natural law or god, obstructed the expression of will; in fact, the chaotic nothingness afforded the will absolute power to create. Chaos is, for him, a limitless existential affirmation of all creation and possibilities, an overtly generative and gratuitously generous force that allows humanity to create the values that best serve the fulfillment of its desires. Articulating what Lewis Call would later term Nietzsche's "affirmative anarchism of becoming" (Lewis, 2001: 50), Bey describes Chaos by stating:

> If I wanted to be fancy I could call this *nothing* the Abyss . . . or even god, if only to confuse the issue. My pet term is "ontological anarchy"—meaning that being itself is in a state of chaos, & that life is free to generate its own spontaneous orders. . . . *the generosity of being IS becoming.* (Bey, [undated]: 8)

At the heart of Ontological Anarchism is the knowledge that Chaos, conceived of not as a single entity, but as the undetermined, creative potential that underwrites being, defines reality, and this potential allows humanity, to paraphrase Nietzsche, to give birth to a dancing star.

As eminent Sinologists A.C. Graham and Arthur Waley noted of the Dao, ontological Chaos effectively undermines the legitimacy of all hegemons and abrogates all laws—be they laws of nature, church, or the state (Graham, 1989: 299-305; Waley, 1939: 70-75) More than simply nullifying them, recognizing Chaos as the ontological state of existence renders law an impossibility according to Bey.[16] Condensed into the slogan "Chaos never

---

[16] The claim that the ontological state of reality invalidates even the possibility of law or governmemnt is commonly attributed to Zhuangzi in Discordian and to a lesser extent Chaos Magick texts; however, no such matter of fact claim is made is present in the text attributed to him. See Wilson, 1998: 304; Shea, 1975: 1.

died", Bey argues that every form of law is a perverse impossibility because the cosmos is an ever-changing flux of potentiality, which makes the imposition of order a spurious illusion only made true by coercion. In Bey's words: "Ontological Anarchy however replies that no 'state' can 'exist,' in chaos, that all ontological claims are spurious except the claim of chaos . . . and therefore that governance of any sort is impossible" (Bey, 2001: 2). That is, the propagation of law, as well as its apparent existence, is illusory in the sense that it is the product of someone's imagination which has gained general acceptance over and against every other possible alternative. Bey is careful to point out that ontological Chaos means everything is equally real, even illusions, and what is more, they can serve deadly ends (Bey, 2001: 2). From this conclusion, Bey asserts that insurrectionary action against the forces that impinge on one's autonomy is less important than overcoming the insidious self-alienation that occurs when one internalizes the illusions of "Babylon or the Spectacle, Capital or Empire, [or the] Society of Simulation" (Bey, 2003: 84). In this vein, it is important to note Bey's recurrent advocacy of violence against *ideas* in the form of "poetic terrorism" and "art sabotage," which supersede the futility of battling the police and potentially martyring oneself for some abstract cause. While one cannot hope to defeat the police state, according to Bey, one can overcome the *idea* of police and achieve an even more meaningful form of liberation since physically battling the police serves to dignify the illusions they represent and perpetuate—like law, order, state control—which may in turn lead to them being internalized. Adopting the illusions of the state, or any hegemon, destroys the possibility of any substantive attempt at autonomy, for it is only from the unmitigated freedom of Chaos that true autonomy, that is, self-ownership free from what Nietzsche termed resentment, can arise (Bey, 2003: 64–71; 2001:1).

Bey believes that Chaos, which is to say existence itself, is defined by its propensity for creativity and abundance, and by virtue of being inextricably embedded in it, humans too are fundamentally endowed with the ability to be ever more imaginative in regards to affirming the chaotic nature of reality. However, the normative status and acceptance of abstractions like work, history, and even the revolution occlude humanity's naturally cosmic magnanimity. Bey argues that through the faculty of the imagination and use of the will, as well as magical techniques and the administration of sacraments ("The AOA sacraments are hemp, wine, coffee, tea, meat & brandy . . . & of course psychedelics"

(Bey, 1987c: 20)), reality can be directly experienced for what it is, Chaos, and in so doing one learns to fashion it according to one's desires as opposed to those of the Spectacle. While we will return to Bey's description of this fashioning as sorcery, it is important to note that he likens breaching the false simulacra of life perpetuated by advertisers and the entertainment industry with a gnostic experience of the marvelous, and that the manner in which Bey describes the act of breaching the *images* of life so as to access it in its actuality represents an innovative synthesis of the occult philosophy of William S. Burroughs and Raoul Vaneigem's concept of the revolution of everyday life.

Lest autonomy or the Dao become mere images of themselves, Bey insists that they be understood as "identical" insofar as they only exist in the unmediated enjoyment of the tangible benefits of such things as "[f]ood, money, sex, sleep, sun, sand, & sinsemilla" (Bey, 2003: 10, 79–83). Following groups like Ranters, Diggers, and Hassan-i Sabbah's mythical Assassin,[17] whom he claims as spiritual anarchist forbearers, Bey's assertion concerning humanity's innate potential and rejection of mediation lead him to proclaim: "[t]here is no becoming, no revolution, no struggle, no path; already you're the monarch of your own skin—your inviolate freedom waits to be completed only by the love of other monarchs" (Bey, 2003: 4). These conclusions concerning the anarchist revolution should be read in the antinomian tradition, that is, with the understanding that humanity already possesses whatever benefit would be conferred upon them by some holy event, be it the Second Coming or The Revolution. In addition to affirming the universal presence of Chaos, the previous quote also illuminates another integral tenet of Ontological Anarchism: the elusive dream of the anarchist utopia is now possible in the form of an intersubjective union with other ontological anarchists, a state which reflects the natural, non-dual order of the cosmos.

---

[17] Through his personal relationship to Brion Gysin and William Burroughs, both of which made the legend of Hassan-i Sabbah a central feature in their fictional works, Wilson would come to adopt the figure as his own. When writing as Bey, the mythic qualities Hassan-i Sabbah and his Assassins would be referenced to demonstrate the "still unimagined liberties" to be gained through Ontological Anarchism, yet, when writing as Wilson, the historical aspects of the legend would be brought to the fore. Much remains to be written about the cultural reception of Sabbah both in and outside of the interface between esotericism and anarchism. See Burroughs, 1994; Murphy, 1997; Bey, 2003: 13–14; Wilson, 1999.

Described in terms of the Surrealist concept of Amour Fou, Bey identifies love as the key factor in the synthesis of Individualist Anarchism, esotericism, and Daoist non-dualism which produced Ontological Anarchism. This love is neither romantic nor fraternal, but akin to an exalted state of transcendental, interpersonal union; indeed, it is the incarnation of Eros that holds within it supreme enlightenment. Paraphrasing Hesiod's *Theogony*, he writes: "After Chaos comes Eros—the principle of order implicit in the nothingness of the unqualified One" (Bey, 2003: 21). As a non-ordinary state of consciousness, the experience of erotic union is, like other gnostic experiences, equated with directly knowing Chaos itself: through Eros the "Other completes the Self—the Other gives us the key to the perception of oneness-of-being" (Bey 2003: 69). Thus, by breaching the abstractions and images of civilization, one comes closer to the source of being, Chaos; and its primary means of expression, Eros, functions as the precondition and substance of autonomy, the natural state of cosmos and humanity. As part of an inspired response to the de Sade debate in *Kaos*, Bey defined this mystical form of intersubjective autonomy as vital to Ontological Anarchism:

> Ontological Anarchy defines itself according to the monist principle that the self involves the Other, is identifiable with the Other; that the self's freedom depends on the Other's freedom in some degree . . . a politique of eros not thanatos. (Bey, 1987c: 20)

Breaching the world of mediation, whether through Eros, magic, or psychedelics, stands as the goal of Ontological Anarchism. As such, Bey devoted a large part of his career to this end by researching the history of and theory behind what he termed Temporary Autonomous Zones, or T.A.Z.—areas of geography where the imagination was as liberated as the soil.[18] It bears repeating here that his most celebrated piece, the long essay entitled *TAZ*, was developed from ideas already present in his zine *Chaos* and the communiqués, and that the book in which the essay appears is a collection of these three works, despite being referred to in the singular as *TAZ*. Most of the research on Bey and Wilson (of

---

[18] Though Wilson would, in a lecture in 1999, claim: "the book is old enough to read itself and it really should as there is a lot of outdated nonsense in that book," it remains an important aspect of his corpus and a necessary link to his current work on the intersection between Luddism, radical environmentalism, and hermeticism. See Wilson, 1999; 2007.

which there is little to begin with) revolves around the "temporary autonomous zone" and thus I will only state that he explained it as the matrix for the emergence of a Sorelian myth of "Uprising" and a "pre-echo of the Insurrection . . . a necessary step towards the Revolution that will realize utopia" (See Grindon, 2004; Moore, 2004; Matheny, 1993).

Ontological Anarchism is based on the claim that Chaos defines reality, and whether through Eros or psychedelics, a direct experience of it constitutes an altered state of consciousness that holds vast power. One outlet for this power is sorcery; as Bey claims, "the goals of ontological anarchism appear in its flowering" (Bey, 2003: 23). In other words, the widening of perception necessary for harmonizing with Chaos will inherently lead the individual to understand the ways in which consciousness and the will represent real forces and how the products of the imagination can be made tangible when one understand how they function. Bey illustrates this point in *Kaos* 8 when, mediating between two opposing magicians, he recommends "[saving] our bile for the shits who really deserve it, the really successful evil magicians, the bankers, advertisers, weapons-salesmen, educators & self-appointed rulers" (Bey, 1987a: 12). The reality of banks, ads, guns, and law-men exemplifies the way in which these "evil magicians" have manifested the contents of their imaginations to the point where they are taken as really existing. Against these evil magicians, Bey advocates breaking the "Spook world's" monopoly of control with a counter-magic, sorcery in fact, which in the process of materializing the individual's true desires banishes the illusions of the social order (Matheny, 1993). He explains: "[s]orcery breaks no law of nature because there is no Natural Law, only the spontaneity of natura naturans, the tao" (Bey 2003: 23). Thus, insofar as the impossibility of law derives from the world being inherently chaotic, it would not be incorrect to claim that Bey's investment in this counter-magick is more fundamental than his opposition to the law as such.

With titles like "Black Magic as Revolutionary Action", the communiqués published in the Chaos Magick milieu testify to the complimentary nature of anarchism and esotericism as Bey construed them.[19] Further, as the communiqués represent the longest

---

[19] As mentioned, the communiqués were published in a number of zines and Bey estimates the number being possibly in the hundreds; however, if one can gauge appreciation in terms of both influence and polemics, then it seems reasonable to suggest that the Chaos Magick milieu remained among the most committed audience for Bey's work as he

section in *TAZ*, one cannot but read the book's popularity as a sign of the underground appeal of anti-authoritarian texts engaged with esotericism. Insofar as Ontological Anarchism cannot be divorced from the magical milieu in which it matured, one must ask how developments from it, like Post-anarchism, rest on thoroughly esoteric conceptions of consciousness, the will, and Chaos, perhaps unknowingly. For historians of Post-anarchism, Bey's *Chaos* zine and the communiqués of the AOA represent founding documents, and the job of reconciling their esoteric worldview to Post-anarchism remains unfinished.

CONCLUSION

In the AOA, Ontological Anarchism possessed a body, both in the sense of an institutional framework (however imaginary) and one composed of flesh and bones, namely, Wilson's.[20] Always written in the third person, the communiqués of the AOA presented themselves as representing the post-Situationist avant-garde of the anarchist movement, which, it is important to note, used as its primary channel the most popular underground magickal movement of the 1980s, i.e., Chaos Magick. Ontological Anarchism distinguished itself as the premiere form of both occultism and anarchism through its denunciations of Leftist anarchism, New Age religion, and rival "Death freak" occultism. Its stirring provo-

---

developed Ontological Anarchism. Also, it bears noting that Bey's work, numbering *well over* a hundred texts of various lengths, would be nearly impossible to catalogue, as a result of (with a few significant exceptions) the tragic lack of interest in organizing zines and underground publications. This is to say nothing of accounting for the disorganized collections of low quality and in some cases clandestinely recorded lectures, Naropa classes, and Moorish Orthodox Crusade radio dispersed across the web.

[20] While Bey admits to initiating a number of hoaxes, it would be incorrect to categorize the AOA as such on account of its single person membership. For all intents and purposes, the AOA represented a serious contribution to the Chaos Magick and anarchist discourse and thus does not deserve to be disregarded as a hoax. This is not to say that hoaxes cannot make serious contributions to any given discourse; they can and do, as may be the case with the text attributed to Zhuangzi and is certainly the case with Discordianism. See Ziporyn, 2009: xv.n.8. It remains to be said that Bey's most notable hoax remains his participation in Ong's Hat (see Kinsella, 2011). In terms of related hoaxes, see also the forged Italian language Hakim Bey book *A Ruota Libera,* and what looks like a second forgery, *Il Giardino dei Cannibali,* although I have yet to confirm this personally (Anonymous, 1996; 2011).

cations for radical action through black magick, ubiquitous pane-
gyrics for queer spirituality, and ludic revolt are noteworthy in
themselves; furthermore, its inflammatory position papers, the
most relevant of which is "Post-anarchism Anarchy" is where the
formal Post-anarchism discourse is said to have originated. It is
interesting to wonder if Bey's Ontological Anarchism would have
been credited as founding Post-anarchism if he had not written
this piece and in the process coined the term "Post-Anarchism".
Surely, Ontological Anarchism would be just as noteworthy an
innovation regarding the anarchist tradition without the text. Yet,
would his thorough investment in esotericism, or any of his other
unpopular preoccupations, have kept him from being cited as the
originator of the Post-anarchism discourse?[21] If any serious arguments can be raised that insist on excluding him on the basis of
their spiritual or sexual inclinations, one must question a great
deal more than the insistence on the negation of identity that is
so often promoted as integral to defining Post-anarchism.

In lieu of pursuing the above question any further (and a definitive answer is, in any case, impossible) attention should be
focused on Bey's "Post-Anarchism Anarchy" text, as it is singled
out as particularly significant in the history of Post-anarchism.
Without detracting from the originality of Bey's work, what
emerges after close analysis of this text is that much of the AOA's
9-point program for a Post-Anarchism is derived from a pre-
existing anarcho-esoteric group, the Discordian Society, which
Bey mentions in his communiqués (Bey, 2003: 60). Indubitably,
convenience is a major factor in the convention to cite the "Post-
Anarchism Anarchy" communiqué as the birth of formal Post-
anarchism discourse for the very good reason that Bey coined the

---

[21] This article opened by citing an anecdote from Knight's biography of
Wilson. It bears mentioning that Knight's text is far from authoritative or
even fully reliable. Half way through the text Knight claims to have
become suddenly aware that Wilson promoted and espoused man-boy-
love as a viable sexuality and immediately lost interest in recording his
subject's life. Knight then proceeded to finish the text with
autobiographical writings intermingled with fictitious episodes of an
Islamic superhero. His description of realizing Wilson's sexuality,
though, rings particularly bogus on account of the fact that Wilson is
quite open about his sexuality, even to the point of devoting numerous
texts to intergenerational relationships. It seems certain that Knight
would have been well aware of Wilson's sexuality long before starting to
write his biography, and simply used it as an excuse to present his own
work as superseding that of his former guru. See Knight, 2012. For a
sample of Wilson's writings on man-boy love see Bey, 1980; Bey, 1993.

term; however, historically, Discordianism provides an even better site for the birth of the cluster of discourses that compose contemporary Post-anarchism. It not only predates Ontological Anarchism (it was formed in 1958), but presaged Ontological Anarchism in a number of important ways: it heralded Nietzsche as the necessary component in the synthesis of Daoism and anarchism, it promoted the worship of Eris, the Greek goddess of Chaos, and it operated through the mail-order home-made publication network that would eventually develop into the zine network which popularized Ontological Anarchy (and of which Bey calls for the further development in point 4 of his Post-anarchy Anarchism "program" (Bey, 2003: 62)).[22] As a religious formulation of anarchism based upon a Nietzschean reading of Daoism and occultism, Discordianism laid the groundwork for Chaos Magick, and Ontological Anarchism in particular. It did this by shifting the ontological foundations of anarchism to an esoteric reading of Chaos, whereupon liberation could no longer be conceived of in terms of material gains won from the oppressor class, but in the freedom to (re)create reality. Before Bey called for a revitalized anarchism based upon mystical experience, figures like Kerry Thornley and Robert Anton Wilson (both of whom were close friends of Bey) had already published their most popular Discordian works, based on a revitalized spiritual anarchism informed by esoteric systems including the Kabbalah and the work of Aleister Crowley. Thornley's *Zenarchy* and Wilson's *Illuminatus!* trilogy (co-authored with anarchist zinester Robert Shea) stand out as particularly influential texts which combine anarchism with spiritual principles along the lines Bey suggests in "Post-Anarchism Anarchy." The indistinguishability between Discordianism and Bey's Ontological Anarchism has led many within the Chaos Magic milieu to anachronistically label Discordianism a form of Ontological Anarchism and by extension Chaos Magick; this may not be too far off the mark, as the original Dis-

---

[22] A notable parallel between Discordianism and Ontological Anarchism concerns the misreading of their primary sources by various scholars. Like *Chaos*, the primary text of Discordinanism, *The Principia Discordia*, originated as a copylefted zine, which circulated for years within the zine network before eventually being published as a book. In the years it circulated, it was altered significantly as a result of the sub-culture that embraced it. Scholars who read the *Principia* and *TAZ* as monolithic texts fail to understand both how the texts came about and the issues that inspired them. See Cusack, 2010: 8–52; Urban, 2006: 233–239. No assessment of Discordianism has been written that takes zines into consideration.

cordians themselves embraced Bey's work as a form of Discordian scripture (Thornely, 2009: 18).

While designating Bey's Ontological Anarchism as the birth of a formal Post-anarchism discourse has been helpful as a historical sign-post for scholars looking to date Post-anarchism, scholars must recognize that this designation is somewhat arbitrarily applied to Bey's work as he was the first to use the term. In truth, Ontological Anarchism was largely a generalization of the conspiratorial anarcho-occultism first theorized in Discordianism and, as such, it would be much more accurate to state that formal Post-anarchism discourse began with Discordianism. However, the question remains: how do scholars benefit from shifting the origin of Post-anarchism to Discordianism? The answer concerns both historical accuracy and the advantages of adopting an anti-essentialist understanding of identity and origin. Whereas scholars once recognized Ontological Anarchism as the progenitor of Post-anarchism, now that Bey's work has been set within its occultist context, they are obliged to take into consideration Chaos Magick, Discordianism, and a host of alternative magickal systems that continue to shape Post-anarchism discourse. Far from being dead weight, the esoteric discourses integral to Ontological Anarchism offer scholars of Post-anarchism entirely new regions of theoretical terrain as well as a range of unexpected alliances that have gone without notice for decades. The integration of these overlooked esoteric antecedents into Post-anarchism will create a fuller historical picture, and in so doing will reveal it to be a rich hybrid of a number of diverse discourses.

Indeed, Post-anarchism did not begin with any single author or group; its origins are hybrid and stem from a multiplicity of discourses: post-structural criticism, the fiction of William Burroughs, Chaos Magick, Discordianism, Nietzsche, Stirner, etc.; the list could go on indefinitely. However, historical texts can act as a prism through which topics like post-anarchism can be understood more clearly. In this vein, the loose anarcho-queer-magickal zine network beginning with the Discordian Society stands as a prime example of the sociality that post-anarchism would claim to herald decades later. The mailing of home-made zines, mail-art, and xerography exemplified the mutual connectedness of polycentric, volunteer association networks composed of self-organizing systems that many postanarchists hold as the structure of postanarchist politics. In this sense, Joel Biroco, speaking for the anarcho-queer-magickal milieu, may have been right when he wrote: 'I am the early representative of a future crowd'

(Biroco 1988: 5). As the cross-pollination of magick, anarchism, and queer sexualities within the zine network, and then in the pages of *TAZ*, helped create the next generation of cultural radicals, scholars must be prepared to adjust their scholarly instruments to meet new sources and new conceptions of anarchism as well as its history.

Christian Greer is currently writing his PhD at the University of Amsterdam. His academic interests include the interface between anti-authoritarianism and esotericism, the "Beat generation," Type-3 & Post-Anarchism, and underground publishing. His non-academic life is devoted to the free skool movement (particularly Corvid College), nature (*natura naturans*), zine making, and "the ludic."

REFERENCES

Alistair. "The Future is Ours," *Kaos* 6: 32–34.

Anonymous [Hakim Bey forgery]. 1996. *A Ruota Libera: Miseria del Lettore di TAZ: Autocritica dell'ideologia Underground*. Rome: Castelvecchi.

Anonymous [Hakim Bey forgery]. 2011. *Il Giardino dei Cannibali. I Viaggi Filosofici*. Milan: ShaKe.

B., Paul. 1986. "Here to Do Shamanism," *Kaos* 6: 14–15.

Bamford, Christopher, Pir Zia Inayat Khan, Kevin Townley, & Peter Lamborn Wilson. 2007. *Green Hermeticism: Alchemy and Ecology*. Aurora, Colorado: Lindisfarne Press.

Bey, Hakim. undated. "Fuse for a Few Sparks," *Kwatz!* [no publishing data].

_____. 1980. *Loving Boys: Semiotext(e) Special*. New York: Semiotext(e).

_____. 1986. "The End of the World," *Chaos* 6: 18.

_____. 1987a. "Gnostic Fascism," *Kaos* 8: 11–12.

_____. 1987b. "Hierarchy in Chaos," *Kaos* 9: 6–8.

_____. 1987c. "Marquis de Sade," *Kaos* 9: 20–21.

_____. 1988. "Reality of Metaphor," *Kaos* 11: 9–11.

_____ (trans.). 1993. *O Tribe That Loves Boys: The Poetry of Abu Nuwas*. Amsterdam: Entimos Press.

_____. 2001. *Immediatism: Essays by Hakim Bey*. San Francisco/Edinburgh: AK Press.

_____. 2003. *T.A.Z.: The Temporary Autonomous Zone, Ontological Anarchy, Poetic Terrorism*. Brooklyn: Autonomedia.

Biroco, Joel. 1986. "Epilogue," *Kaos* 6: 34–35.

_____. 1988. "Epilogue," *Kaos* 11: 35.

_____. 1988. "Renegade," *Kaos* 11: 2–5.

Bogdan, Henrick & Martin R. Starr (Eds.) 2012. *Aleister Crowley and Western Esotericism.* Cambridge: Cambridge University Press.

Burroughs, William S. 1994. *The Ticket That Exploded.* New York: Grove Press.

Black, Bob. 1994. *Beneath the Underground.* Portland: Feral House.

Call, Lewis. 2010. "Editorial—Post-anarchism Today." *Anarchist Developments in Cultural Studies* 1: 9–15.

_____. 2001. "Toward an Anarchy of Becoming: Postmodern Anarchism in Nietzschean Philosophy." *Journal of Nietzsche Studies* 21: 48–76.

Caroll, Peter. 1987. *Liber Null & Psychonaut: An Introduction to Chaos Magic.* York Beach: Weiser Books.

Crowley, Aleister. 1992. *Magick in Theory and Practice.* Secaucus: Castle Books.

Cusack, Carole M. 2010. *Invented Religions, Imagination, Fiction, Faith.* Burlington: Ashgate Publishing Company.

_____. 2011. "Discordian Magic: Paganism, The Chaos Paradigm and the Power of the Imagination." *International Journal for the Study of New Religions* 2.1: 125–145.

Dragwyla, Yael Ruth. 1988. "The Demon Aiwass." *Kaos* 11: 18–20.

Duke, Ramsey. 1988. "The Antichrist." *Kaos* 11: 22–27.

Graham, A.C. 1989. *Disputers of the Tao: Philosophical Argument in Ancient China.* Chicago: Open Court Press.

Grindon, Gavin. 2004. "Carnival Against Capital: A Comparison of Bakhtin, Vaneigem and Bey." *Anarchist Studies* 12.2: 147–161.

Hanegraaff, Wouter J., Jean-Pierre Brach, Antoine Faivre, and Roelof van den Broek (Eds.). 2005. *Dictionary of Gnosis and Western Esotericism.* Leiden: Brill.

Hanegraaff, Wouter J. 2012. *Esotericism and the Academy: Rejected Knowledge in Western Culture.* Cambridge: Cambridge University Press.

Hine, Phil. 1991. "Breeding Devils in Chaos: Homosexuality & the Occult," *www.philhine.org.uk*: http://www.philhine.org.uk/writings/flsh_breeding.html.

Kinsella, Michael. 2011. *Legend-Tripping Online: Supernatural Folklore and the Search for Ong's Hat.* Jackson: University Press of Mississippi.

Knight, Michael Muhammad. 2012. *William S. Burroughs Vs. the Qur'an.* Berkeley: Soft Skull Press.

Matheny, Joseph (Producer). 1993. *TAZ: Temporary Autonomous Zone,* VHS. San Francisco: Sound Photosynthesis.

Moore, John. 2004. "Lived Poetry: Stirner, Anarchy, Subjectivity and the Art of Living." In *Changing Anarchism: Anarchist Theory and*

Practice in a Global Age (Purkis, Jonathan and James Bowen, Eds.). Manchester: Manchester University Press. 55–72.

Murphy, Timothy S. 1997. *Wising Up the Marks: The Amodern William Burroughs.* Berkeley: University of California Press.

Newman, Saul. 2010. *The Politics of Postanarchism.* Edinburgh: Edinburgh University Press.

Nillson, Johan. 2013. "Defending Paper Gods Aleister Crowley and the Reception of Daoism in Early Twentieth Century Esotericism." *Correspondences* 1.1: 103–127.

Pasi, Marco. 2012. "Occultism." *The Brill Dictionary of Religion* (Kocku von Stuckrad, Ed.). *Brill Online*: http://www.encquran. brill.nl/entries/brill-dictionary-of-religion/occultism-COM_00321.

Rocket, Jimi. 1988. "Essentials of Thelema." *Kaos* 11: 18.

Sedgwick, Markl. 2004. *Against the Modern World: Traditionalism and the Secret Intellectual History of the Twentieth Century.* Oxford: Oxford University Press.

Sellars, Simon. 2010. "Hakim Bey: Repopulating the Temporary Autonomous Zone." *Journal for the Study of Radicalism* 2: 83–108.

Shea, Robert. 1975. *No Governor* 1.1: 1.

Thornely, Kerry. "Introduction (i)." In *Principia Discordia*, 5th edn. Lilburn: IllumiNet Press. 11–39.

Versluis, Arthur and Peter Lamborn Wilson. "A Conversation with Peter Lamborn Wilson." *Journal for the Study of Radicalism* 4.2: 139–165.

Williams, Leonard. 2010. "Hakim Bey and Ontological Anarchism." *Journal for the Study of Radicalism* 4.2: 109–138.

Williams, Michael Allen. 1999. *Rethinking "Gnosticism": An Argument for Dismantling a Dubious Category.* Princeton: Princeton University Press.

Wilson, Peter Lamborn. 1999. "Peter Lamborn Wilson Lecture: Assassins," *Naropa Poetics Audio Archives*: http://archive.org/details/ Peter_Lamborn_Wilson_lecture__June__99P053.

Wilson, Robert Anton. [1981] 1998. *Schrodinger's Cat Trilogy.* New York: Dell.

Wobensmith, Matthew. Personal Communication, April 15, 2012.

Anarchist Developments in Cultural Studies
ISSN: 1923-5615
2013.2: Ontological Anarché: Beyond Materialism and Idealism

Anarchism and the Question of Practice Ontology in the Chinese Anarchist Movement, 1919–1927

Tom Marling

ABSTRACT

Ontology has been an under-realised aspect of historical analyses of the final years of anarchist organisation in China. However, in the latter stages of the movement a number of anarchist voices would emerge, which indicated the formulation of a new ontological direction in Chinese anarchism at a time when classical anarchist approaches were becoming practically divorced from local reality. In particular, a subjective, structuralist and localised application of anarchist theory was placed at the forefront of an emergent debate between two anarchist factions, namely an old guard of leftist classicalists and a younger group of divergent, conceptually malleable quasi-iconoclasts. This article sets out to establish this group of younger anarchists within the movement as theoretical antecedents of post-leftist anarchism, in particular with regards to their emphasis on pragmatism, locatedness and de-centered analyses of power and revolution. I theorise that this group was deeply influenced by the New Culture movement in China, and that the intellectual atmosphere the time, in synthesis with anarchism, allowed for the ideological space to act on the theoretical boundaries of anarchism itself for the first time.

KEYWORDS

de-essentialized ontology, post-leftist, subjectivity, evolutionism

> *If we can offer the masses something better, so much the better; but to stick one's hand up one's sleeve and engage in opposition from the sidelines, while perfectly all right for bourgeois scholars, is no less than a crime for revolutionaries. It is acceptable for an individualist to say, 'if it is not complete, it is better not to have it', but a*

revolutionary cannot say such a thing, because that is not what the masses demand. (Dirlik, 1993: pp. 258–9)
Ba Jin, "Anarchism and the Question of Practice," 1927

In 1907, when Li Shizeng predicted that the anarchist revolution was to be "one without end," it is unlikely that he or his early anarchist contemporaries in China could have foreseen the high-water mark of pragmatism the sentiment would represent for the movement (Li Shizeng, 1907).[1] Had Li been available for comment by the time of Ba Jin's above statement some 20 years later, he is more likely to have observed that the anarchist revolution had become "one without change," as essentialist mantras had become entrenched in a movement whose standard operating procedure was better suited to a China in which the country's post-Imperial societal revolutions had yet to begin.

For the vast majority of the period between Li and Ba's statements, the Chinese anarchists embodied classical anarchism to the point of self-abnegation; often not just on the sidelines but in the bleachers, with their hands firmly up their sleeves.[2] By the 1920s however, there emerged internal dissatisfaction with the prospects for an anarchist project built on these dissociative foundations. Ontology became the unspoken watchword for a generation of anarchists looking to re-involve the movement in the wider processes of the time. This was the case for the afore-mentioned Ba Jin, who in 1927 was openly forwarding an analysis which reflected both impatience with, and self-assurance toward, the doctrine of anarchism itself. The prioritisation of locality and practicality ahead of doctrinal essentialism in the application of anarchism to China, as well as the focus on the interests of the

---

[1] Pusey (1983: p. 371) has suggested that Li was influenced by newly emerging social-Darwinist theories is China when he stated that "there is no affair of thing that does not progress . . . Revolution is nothing but the cleansing away of obstacles to progress."

[2] A great deal of attention (Krebs, 1998), (Dirlik, 1993) has been paid to espousers of classical anarchism in China, most notably Liu Sifu (the "soul" of Chinese anarchism), the Tokyo and Paris anarchist groups, and the "Six No's Society" founded by Cai Yuanpei. However, each of these factions succeeded in occupying a space more theoretical than functional—the Tokyo and Paris anarchist groups literally existed outside of the fetters of a Chinese setting as theoreticians rather than revolutionaries, whereas Cai Yuanpei and Liu Sifu and his followers' near-total non-involvement in anything from sedan-chairs to even the most equanimous organisational structures led them to a position of equal abstraction, even as they operated within China itself.

populis ahead of abstracted vanguardism, would both be recurrent themes of the time. So too was his choice to demure from the previously archetypal notion of the anarchist individualist, in Ba's case by referring to himself—invoking an appellative whose significance we will return to—simply as a "revolutionary."[3]

This assessment of the pertinent issues facing the Chinese anarchist movement during its final years was not an isolated one, as the mid-1920s find anarchist writings increasingly peppered with statements which belie more than a minor degree of ontological purposefulness. Yet although this development and its importance have been lost behind the broader narrative of the movement's material decline occupying the historical foreground, these were interrelated phenomena. This assertiveness found its roots in emergent and pressing divergences between theory and practice which were undermining the classical theoretical foundations which had informed the movement in China throughout its lifetime.[4] As the validity and relevance of classical anarchist essentialism was brought into question, the anarchists faced the question of how to adapt anarchism for the first time. We will consider how one group of younger anarchists looked to act adaptively through anti-ideological, situationalist and evolutionary approaches to anarchist doctrine—in effect proto-anarché. These anarchists' direct contact with the intellectual atmosphere of New Culture liberalism—including pragmatism, experimentalism, localism and evolutionism—will be nominated as a crucial factor in both the innovation and legitimation of a participatory, de-essentialized anarchist ontology.

The final generation of anarchists in China were the first to fully engage with enlightenment influences, situated as they were—ideologically, temporally and spatially—at the putative apex of early intellectual modernisation in China.[5] During the May Fourth and New Culture movements of the 1920s, urbanised

---

[3] The changing meaning of individualism (个人主义) during the May Fourth period, covered in detail by Lydia Liu (1996, pp. 77–102), is relevant to this discussion.

[4] Anarchist opposition to the state, nationalism, and hierarchical organisation structures were all coming under strain by the 1920s as the material pressures of the time began to be drawn into discussions of idealised activity.

[5] Various specialised approaches to Chinese modernity have placed the epicentre of modernity in some combination of, or variation on—the 1920s, modernising cities (in particular treaty ports), and radical youth, some examples are Esherick (2000), Wenxin Ye (2000), Yue Dong and Goldstein eds. (2006), Kai-wing Chow (2008), and Mitter (2004).

anarchist organisations would swell significantly, primarily with radical youth who came of age in the intellectual shadow of Dewey, Darwin, Hegel, and Bertrand Russell. However, the traditional understanding of the anarchists' relationship with the contemporary intellectual atmosphere of the New Culture movement has been one of mutual dislocation. Arif Dirlik has discussed in detail anarchism's (explicitly indirect) influence on the movement, yet the collective scholarship of Chinese anarchism has appeared unwilling to allow for any genuine reciprocity in this regard (Dirlik, 1993: p. 162). The resultant characterisation has at worst been that of a collective permeating antimodernism, at best a movement merely persistently subject to what Scalapino and Yu (1961, p. 33) referred to as a "political pendulum," which "could always swing back under certain conditions, causing them to revert to orthodoxy."[6]

The Chinese anarchists certainly had an ambiguous relationship with the intellectual modernity of which they were a part, often falling back on the kind of scepticism which presumably informed the above analyses from Dirlik and Scalapino and Yu. Yet in spite of this, the intellectual trends of the New Culture movement were not universally disregarded, and in the case of many of the younger anarchists, they were contingently internalised as the kind of theoretically productive jump start which was required in a time of crisis.

Jesse Cohn (2006: p. 15) has noted that anarchism's doctrinal essentialism requires every generation of anarchists to identify themselves "(diachronically) with the historical movement as well as (synchronically) with their living cohort." In the case of the younger anarchists their diachronic duties to classical anarchism came into conflict with a growing sense of modern dynamism, resulting in a pervasive frustration with classical anarchism's habitual reliance on dogma. Their response was not to abandon anarchism, but to direct themselves at dismantling inherited and idealistic notions of "correct" applications of anarchist doctrine for the first time, and to turn towards the task of forming a dynamic, adaptive and de-essentialized ontology for anarchism in China. With this is in mind it is worth noting that although reductive, Scalapino and Yu's political pendulum raises the critical concept that this inquiry is predicated upon, that of "orthodoxy" itself. Their explicit assessment—that orthodoxy was derived

---

[6] Peter Zarrow's (1990) preoccupation with rooting anarchism in a Daoist tradition seems to have prefigured against a role for modernity in his narrative of Chinese anarchism.

from devotion to the strictures of anarchism and to be orthodox was to revert to a Westernised mean—represents an implicit assumption in much of the scholarship of Chinese anarchism. We will consider an alternative orthodoxy, in which the contingent adoption and application of New Culture liberal reformism impinged upon the linearity of the presumptive relationship between orthodoxy and piety. That the younger, more "modern" group of anarchists would come to define orthodoxy through the lens of a de-essentialized anarchist ontology afforded them the agency to act, not within or without, but upon doctrinal boundaries; as subjects rather than objects of classical anarchism.

THE NEW CULTURE MOVEMENT AND ANARCHISM IN CHINA

Subject-object relationships between doctrine and its adherents marked the discursive epicentre of the political wing of the New Culture movement during the 1920s. At this time, a new generation of intellectual leaders came forward to criticise their forebears' over-reliance on doctrine as "a death sentence to the cause of improving Chinese society" (Bishop, 1985: p. 369).[7] Under the rubric of New Culture liberalism the multiplicity of political doctrines which had emerged in modernising China were no longer to be understood as a panacea, and instead genuine applicability was sought through investigation into their relevance to practical issues (Chow Tse-tsung, 1967: p. 218).

In arguing that the spirit of New Thought was a "critical attitude" which undertook to "oppose blind obedience," this aspect of the New Culture Movement owed an intellectual debt to the combined influence of John Dewey's notion of pragmatism (Hu Shi, 1924).[8] New Thought's distrust of determinism and conviction that political theories be studied in the light of evolution also shared fundamentally Dewey-esque principles. In this vein, a "genetic method" was made integral to a revolution which was understood to be achieved through "drop-by-drop reconstruction."[9]

In historical approaches to Chinese anarchism, the traditional understanding of the anarchists' relationship with these aspects of the New Culture and beyond has been one of comparative dis-

---

[7] Furth (1972: pp. 59–69) offers a further discussion on this topic.

[8] For further discussion, see Min-chih Chou (1984), Lei Yi (2006: pp. 33–50), Manicas,(1982: pp. 133–158) and Grieder (1970).

[9] A "genetic method" was first broached by Hu Shi in 1920 (1920: pp. 15–25).

location. Dirlik (1993, p. 164) has discussed in detail anarchism's (explicitly indirect) influence on the New Culture movement, yet the collective scholarship of the Chinese anarchist movement has appeared unwilling to allow for any genuine reciprocity in this regard. However, many facets of New Culture liberalism and anarchism correlate; and the two ideologies occupied political spaces in China that were prone to overlap.[10]

Among the intellectual pioneers of New Culture liberalism, Hu Shi's dedication to non-political reform—advocating "no talking politics for twenty years; no political activity for twenty years"—was a position which was shared with the anarchists.[11] Chow Tse-tsung (1967; p. 223) has also pointed out that "people who advocated keeping remote from the politics of the time . . . included at least three groups: certain scholars and intellectuals such as Hu Shih and Chang Tung-sun; merchant groups . . . and the anarchists."[12] Many younger anarchists also occupied a physical space which overlapped with that of the New Culture Movement, both in their ties to the Hu Shi and Chen Duxiu-edited journal, *Xin Qingnian*, in which anarchist articles often appeared; and in Dewey's base at Peking University (Bishop, 1985: p. 369). University President (before Hu Shi himself took over) Cai Yuanpei was a quasi-anarchist, and the campus was a hotbed of anarchist activity.[13] Many prominent anarchists were based at Peking University during New Culture, including Liu Shipei and Li

---

[10] Dewey himself professed a strongly anti-authoritarian streak; Sidney Hook (1939: p. 18) even characterised him as "a cross between a philosophical anarchist and Robert Louis Stevenson," which despite being made in passing, only mildly exaggerates some more systemic comparisons. For further discussions please see Manicas (2003), Lothstein (1978), and D'Urso (1980).

[11] This was a vow he would break repeatedly, of course, but the ideal remains ideologically consistent with the wider atmosphere toward anarchism at the time.

[12] See also Sor-Hoon Tan (2004: pp. 44–64).

[13] "During this period, anarchist thought and writings penetrated deeply into student circles at Peking University and elsewhere. Student journals such as *Chin-hua* (Evolution), *Hsin ch'ao* (New Currents), and *Kuo-min* (The Citizen), carried the mixture of Anarchist, Socialist, and democratic ideas that were now flowing into China" (Scalapino and Yu, 1961). One of the ways in which New Culture intellectuals and the older anarchists like Wu Zhihui were likely brought together is through the work-study organisations. In particular the Beijing Work-Study Corps could claim Hu Shi and Chen Duxiu as members alongside many young anarchists discussed in (Weston, 2004: p. 195).

Shizeng; as well as numerous anarchist journals, including *Ziyou Lu* (Freedom Record);[14] *Jinhua Zazhi* (Evolution);[15] *Xin Ch'ao* (New Currents), *Guomin* (The Citizen) and *Fendou* (Struggle);[16] and the *Peking University Students' Weekly*, edited by vocal anarchist Huang Lingshuang.[17]

A new understanding of the anarchist relationship with New Culture liberalism will undergird this discussion. That the final generation of anarchists were able to approach anarchism *through* New Culture, as the epistemologies coalesced with no implicit exclusivity between the two. This does not imply that these new approaches were taken up universally however. In fact, a localised version of the wider "leftist-liberal" divide which had emerged in the May Fourth community also materialised amongst the anarchists during the mid-1920s.[18] While the "post-leftist" anarchists, as we will refer to them, appear to have selectively incorporated liberal ideals into an emergent assertive approach to anarchist doctrine, the "leftist" anarchists professed the classical

---

[14] *Freedom Record* was a product of the "Truth Society" (Shishe) at Peking University, a group of primarily Guangzhou anarchists studying at the university, there was only one issue (Weston, 2004: p. 194).

15 *Evolution* was a publication of the Evolution Society, an umbrella organisation which incorporated three smaller anarchist groups at Peking University, it lasted three issues (Weston, 2004: p. 164).

[16] *Fendou* was founded by Yi Junzuo, Zhu Qianzhi and Guo Chuliang (Weston, 2004: p. 191).

[17] The physical links here deserve further investigation (Zarrow, 1990: p. 222, Weston, 2004: p. 191). It is worth at this point noting some of the titles of these journals as indicative of some of the new approaches to anarchism that we will be discussing, in particular "Evolution" and "Struggle." The Peking University anarchists were evidently preoccupied questions of "struggle" and "evolution," which as we will come to see, were separate aspects of a wider pragmatic liberal turn for a younger generation of anarchists germinating in an environment steeped in these ideals.

[18] The schism between Shen Zhongjiu and the younger anarchists fits into another wider discussion which was occurring at the time, namely the "debate between science and metaphysics," which began in 1923. The defenders of science in this discussion again read as a relative who's who of the ideological core of Liberal Reformism amongst the older May Fourth radicals, including Wu Zhihui. The wider resonance of the debate is well understood; Zarrow (1990: p. 179) considers it to be a debate over "not so much science versus metaphysics but how to define roles for the scientific and the spiritual or intuitive; not so much West versus East but how to selectively adapt; not so much determinism versus free will but how to balance inner and outer freedom."

anarchist distrust of reformism and experimentation.[19] While the 1923 debate between Wu Zhihui and Shen Zhongjiu marks the ostensible core of this division within the movement, this article focus on a group of younger "post-leftist" anarchists who were developing in a more radically subjective and ontological direction. The primary source material for these anarchists will be a symposium entitled 'Anarchism and the Question of Practice,' which was also printed in *Ziyou Ren*. Although some of Ba Jin's comments from the symposium have been referenced before, the other participants, Wei Huilin and Wu Kegang, and its broader overarching post-leftist / ontological implications have been previously been overlooked.

A LOCALISED, EXPERIMENTAL APPROACH TO ANARCHISM

The first aspect of the post-leftist position to be considered is a developing subjectivity toward the inherited doctrinal pillars of anarchism itself, and a reemphasising of presence and locality when it came to the application of this doctrine to the Chinese setting. A sense of subjectivity also informed the prevalent attitude of "ceaseless experimentation" toward inherited ideologies which had emerged during the New Culture movement. This pragmatism borrowed from post-Kantian subjectivism in its "spirit of *fansi* (reflection), *pipan* (critique) and (*zijue*) self-consciousness" (Fung, 2010, p. 10). During the 1920s, "to rethink values, to bring them to the level of consciousness, and to ask whether they [were] still suitable to the needs of the day was defined as the true meaning of new thought."[20] These qualities formed the basis

---

[19] It would be tempting to characterise Shen Zhongjiu as a staunch traditionalist. In fact Shen occupied more common ideological ground with his opponents in the debate than with any of the Shifu and He Zhen-associated "old guard." He was a supporter of anarchist youth and labour organisations, as both a founding member of the Federation of Shanghai Syndicates and as editor of one of the prominent Zhejiang anarchist journal *Tides in Education*, and later as editor of Geming Zhoubao, both of which often provided platforms for some of the more radical voices in the movement. It might be more accurate to characterise him as the rhetorical standard-bearer of countermodernity in the anarchist movement.

[20] Localism was another of the underpinnings of the New Culture pragmatic doctrine, as Hu Shi believed that intellectuals must always be aware of the setting in which the doctrine that they were appropriating was formulated, and should compare this to the material realities of the

of a fundamental ontological shift during New Culture—the broadening of orthodoxy beyond piety and the growing sense that transgression *was* orthodox when it looked to make doctrine more effective in application.

The discursive intellectual space of the 1920s was character-ised by prevalent synthesis and cross-applicability between sci-ence and wider societal issues. The massive expansion in inter-disciplinary journals between philosophy, politics and science included two titles, *Eastern Miscellany* and *New Youth*, in which anarchist articles were frequently published (Wang Hui, 2006: p. 86).[21] In their engagement with the contrasting requirements of doctrinal piety and localised practicality, and parallel questions over the universality of anarchist doctrine, the post-leftist anar-chists would share more than a discursive arena with the broader New Culture community, they would also face the same implicit dilemmas. Their pursuit of a more subjective relationship with anarchist doctrine in response to this certainly bears the hall-marks of New Thought pragmatism, as this group looked toward an anarchism which was not functionally dislocated and "un-touchable," but a malleable entity which required adaptation to remain relevant.

In Wei Huilin's section of "Anarchism and the Question of Practice" for instance, he offers a post-leftist understanding of doctrine which closely corresponds to the ontological underpin-nings which we have already identified, in which the past is min-imised and the present is placed in the centre of a discussion on practicality.

An anarchist is not an exceptional person or a scholar who just plays with words. It is a person that has been freed from the old social system and morals, making efforts to develop himself fully. The anarchist movement is about 'people' but not about pious people who harbour simple beliefs . . . Although anarchism has become systematic and detailed through the efforts of several smart antecedents, it is not yet absolutely right or rigid. We should think it over through the truths we have experienced and the problems

---

setting in which it is applied (Bishop, 1985: p. 369); See also Schwarcz (1986: p. 122).

[21] That both *New Youth* and *Eastern Miscellany* were key sources of anar-chist writings, is indicative of just how close to the epicentre of these scientific ideals—and Chinese intellectual modernity itself—they stood.

of our time. The anarchism I refer to here is closely connected to the practical problems of our time.

The reason why our past movements ended in failure
is that they failed to take action based on practical situations. It is completely incorrect to think that the anarchist
movement merely an ethical one. (Huilin, 1927)[22]

The dilemma of needing to selectively adapt anarchism whilst
remaining *anarchist* lay at the heart of the post-leftist incorporation of New Culture pragmatism. Consider what Wei distances
himself from here, inherited universal standards and the presumptive reliance on piety and morality ahead of practicality and
locality, but not anarchism itself. By equating the younger anarchists' focus on practical problems with the desire for a less ca-
nonical and more practical relationship with doctrine, Wei arrives
at what is ultimately a situationalist and utilitarian, rather than
openly iconoclastic, approach to forging a new anarchist ontology. In reiterating that *duty* to anarchism was inclusive of questioning, refining and ultimately adapting anarchism, a construc-
tivist quality—indicative of the influence of New Culture's sense
of experimentalism—informed much of these discussions.[23] In
fact, when one unnamed anarchist ("A.D.," 1924) stated that, "I
hope we youth will not become followers of such doctrines, but
will act as critics of such doctrines," he could have been channel-
ing Hu Shi himself.

The influence of the New Culture critique of intellectual piety
toward doctrine is equally evident in Wu Kegang's parallel evalu-
ation of anarchist utopian individualism. In support of the claim
that anarchism in China was "underdeveloped," Wu focuses in
particular on the abstracted dislocation that the movement had
come to embody in China, associated with an overreliance on
classical anarchist dogma. By establishing that the failings of his
forebears in China were rooted in this ideological piety and slo-
ganeering, and by disavowing "doctrine, theory and principles"
(主义, 理论, 学说), he makes the kind of statement of pragmatic and
localised agency which once again bears the hallmarks of the
wider culture of localism of which it was a part:

---

[22] All quotations are author's own translation unless otherwise indicated.
[23] Bishop (1985: p. 369) paraphrases Hu Shi's thought in this regard as
such, "Hu Shih did not really oppose the study of isms. Isms were worthy
of study as long as they are regarded as theories, hypothesis or
instrumentalities."

> The reason why anarchism is underdeveloped is that we
> have paid too much attention to doctrine, theory and prin-
> ciples, but neglected reality and action.
> This is a common fault of the anarchist party in the
> world, and China is no exception. However, we should try
> to control it. Anarchism is a civilian movement, but Chi-
> nese anarchism is totally unrelated to civilians. Phrases
> like 'splendid individualism,' 'we should put our hopes in
> the great past or ideal future,' and 'escape from the de-
> pressing reality and into utopia' should not have been ut-
> tered by anarchists. (Wu Kegang, 1927)[24]

New Culture's notion of scientific subjectively was of particular
importance to the anarchist movement (as opposed to say Marxism) because it did not subject itself to the kind of pure/impure
binaries which undergird classical anarchism. As this subjectivity
took hold among the younger anarchists, the dialectical nature of
classical anarchist tropes, here referred to as anarchism's "idealism," became a common point of departure, as doctrine's practical
dislocation from the modern Chinese reality came under fire.
Although anarchism was never directly stated to be impractical,
the repeated criticism of the doctrinal intransigence and mono-
theism of the previous generations of anarchists functioned as a
byword for this realisation. In the place of this outmoded idealism, as Ba Jin indicates below, facts could determine the future
direction of an anarchism of which the post-leftist anarchists had
taken rhetorical ownership.

> Although we can not deny that some articles in the publi-
> cations of Chinese anarchists have neglected the facts and
> just deduced everything from one principle, it does not
> represent all the comrades of anarchism. That is what I
> want to declare.
> The reason Kropotkin could systematize anarchism is
> not because he was an extraordinary thinker but because
> he was born in the time that capitalism was broken and
> the proletariat was active. Kropotkin has never said that
> any part of anarchism was created by him, so we certainly
> can not take his principles as something sacred. (Ba Jin,
> 1927)

---

[24] It seems possible that the reference to "escape from the depressing
reality and into utopia" is a transliteration of classical anarchist slogan
"another world is possible."

As a manifesto of constructive transgression in response to this awareness; these statements embody the kind of "call and response" between an anarchist legacy and an anarchist necessity in which a unique approach was forged by the post-leftists. When Kuli (1925) suggested that "anarchism's attitude towards other parties has two aspects, theory and fact (无政府主义者对他党之态度有理论与事实两方面)" it appears that he too was fully aware of this divergence. In fact, in all of the above statements the authors appear acutely aware of the boundaries of classical Western anarchism, and critically appraise their *relevance* to a Chinese situ. This was an appraisal which was bolstered through the adoption of the ideals, and even in many cases the terminology, of New Culture liberalism. When the younger anarchists talked of "practical problems," "neglecting facts," and "relying on principles," they were not simply aping these aspects of New Culture but utilising them to 'modify the discursive field' of Chinese anarchism, to establish a space for their ontology.

The conviction borne of these appraisals stands in relatively stark contrast with the leftist anarchists, as evidenced in Shen Zhongjiu's response to Wu Zhihui in 1924. The leftist response relies on oppositional binaries, reducing the dualities of the time to a value judgement informed solely by the perpetuated theoretical strictures of classical anarchism.

> 'Presence' and 'absence' are always opposites. Presence of government and absence of government; Presence of private property and absence of private property; which are obviously adverse. I am not smart enough to understand how a person holds two opposite opinions and goes in for two adverse movements. I would guess even those with scientific minds can not find out the reason for this absurdity.
>
> Those who are linked through doctrine can be called partisans, while those who are just linked via feelings can only be called friends. Friendship is friendship and doctrine is doctrine, and we cannot change our doctrine because of friendship. It is strange that Mr Wu [Zhihui] advocates the combination of doctrine and following personal considerations at the same time. (Xin Ai, 1924)

By juxtaposing Wu Zhihui's actions as a contradiction between "personal considerations" and a conversant piety to doctrine, Shen is speaking to the fundamental contradictions which we have established. His is a judgement made from within the dialectical boundaries of classical anarchism, reducing ideological transgression to the typical (and oft-perpetuated) narrative of ethical subordination.[25]

Although pragmatism functioned as part of an affective re-conceptualisation of anarchism and ultimately a re-situation of the place of power, through its constructivism rarely did the post-leftist position openly reject the epistemological foundations of anarchism. The focus on practical problems which the anarchists made central to their discussions was in fact a pursuit of complexity, a refusal to frame the diversity of the contemporary Chinese environment through delimiting dialectics of opposition. New Culture's reinforcing of the importance of locatedness also provided a framework by which the younger anarchists could prioritise action over inaction and, much like Bakunin, "throw themselves into the whirlpool" of the times:

> What I have said does not mean that there is something wrong with the principle of anarchism, rather to express that a principle is not everlasting and almighty. Furthermore, anarchism is the product of practical mass movements, so it can not go without reality. Practically speaking, anarchism is not a kind of fancy that can *transcend time.*
>
> If we want to be true revolutionaries, we should throw ourselves into the whirlpool like Bakunin, and lead the tide of revolution into the ocean of anarchism. (Ba Jin, 1927)

Ba Jin's above statement speaks to a crucial new development in the anarchist conceptualisation of anarchism, formed in the atmosphere of the New Culture. This was the supra-historical nature of classical anarchism, that in existing outside of the fetters of setting and practical necessity it was able to "transcend the times" (超时代) of which it was a part. Unwilling to perpetuate this pedestal, the post-leftist approach endeavoured to draw anarchism into the practical and the complex. The quotidian questions of practice and scientific methodology which had infiltrated to

---

[25] Fascinatingly he may even by alluding to the fundamental presence-absence dialectic which defines structuralism in opposition to post-structuralism, suggestive of an greater degree of epistemological awareness pertaining the modern thought; although this is an avenue deserving of further study.

discursive arena in China were utilised by the younger anarchists as means by which to develop a "limit attitude" and to disregard the more essentialist notions of anarchism which had ensured that the anarchist movement had remained so unvarying in China. For the post-leftist anarchists, the classical binaries had resulted in a rigid and outmoded anarchist movement in China, a future was required in which action became prioritised over inaction and malleable, contingently divergent understandings of orthodox anarchist activity were brought to the fore.

REVOLUTION AND REFORM

The intellectual atmosphere of the New Culture period was not only characterised by the subjective critique of doctrine, but also by a coeval collective faith in evolutionism (Popp, 2007). The valorising of the political and social relevance of *jinhua* (evolution, 进化)—a rhetorical conflation of the new evolutionary concepts of Darwin and Spencer with evolutionary determinism—was both a popular trope of the period and a further factor in the developing ontology of the post-leftist anarchists.[26] The oppositional counterpart of *jinhua—bianhua* (change, 变化)—better describes the classical anarchist preoccupation with singular and total revolution however; in which progress and development eventually lead to a point which requires the totalising change and immediacy of revolution.[27] Zarrow (1990: p. 99) summarises the attitudes of the previous generation's leaders along these lines when he notes that "Liu [Sifu] fundamentally saw nothing inevitable about progress . . . Liu and He Zhen did not believe in incremental improvement. They believed in revolution."

The influence of *jinhua* however would subvert this immediacy and totality, allowing for the forging of a new conception of anarchist revolution which was closely intertwined with, and

---

[26] This was comparable to a Hegelian anthropomorphic notion of development in which "collective human experience in time appears to undergo the same stages of growth as human life" (Tang, 1996: p. 230). In fact Li Shicen, editor of the anarchist journal People's Bell (Possibly Li Shizeng, although he was not the editor), associated himself with the evolutionary abstract ideals of Henri Bergson, stating that, "His [Darwin's] so-called origin is nothing less than the vital impulse of life, and this impulse is hidden in our consciousness to stimulate and encourage ourselves to incline toward creative paths constantly . . . Bergson, however, considers fitting to be no more than illustrating the tortuous and unsteady path of evolution;" (Tang, 1996: p. 118).

[27] Tang (1996: p. 117); see also Schwartz (1964: p. 46).

furthered the justification of, approaching anarchism through staged diachronic tactics. This evolutionary form of revolution was forwarded with particular directness by Zhu Qianzhi in his 1925 article "Prophecy of Universal Revolution" (宇宙革命地预言), in which these new evolutionary understandings were set up as the antithesis of both dialectics and the classical anarchist growth-revolution-growth dynamic, a migration which Zhu disregards as a form of nihilism (虚无主义).[28]

> Nihilism is based on dialectics, thinking that the evolution of the universe is a kind of *migration* that turns nothing to existing, and existing to nothing. Universal revolution is a kind of evolutionary progress. What's more, evolution is always heading for the true, the good, and the beautiful. The range of revolution will expand wider and wider as snowball runs. From middle class revolution to the fourth class revolution; from political revolution to anarchic revolution, the climate of revolution never stops. Universal revolution meets the needs of the true, the good, the beautiful, so it simply fits the theory of evolution. (Zhu Qianzhi, 1925)

The characterising of revolution as an 'ever-widening snowball' (滚雪球一般, 越滚越大) marks a crucial development, which established a parallel aspect, alongside pragmatism, of the new ontological approaches which were being fostered. By introducing the possibility that the anarchist revolution was neither a linear, nor a totalizing, project, goals both outside of a purist anarchist understanding and even those that seemed to initially work *against* an anarchist future were increasingly justifiable, as quantitative changes become prioritised ahead of qualitative ones.[29] The disavowal of dialectics—a recurrent theme of evolutionary approaches to anarchism—is symptomatic of the influence of both *jinhua*

---

[28] Presumably this was a response to the leftist faith in dialectical materialism during the New Culture—Qu Qiubai for instance was the "first teacher of dialectical materialism" in China after his return to China in 1923 (Bo Mou, 2008: pp. 520–521).

[29] In terms of ascertaining the physical links with New Culture on statements such as this, it is worth noting that Zhu was—to return to our point on the physical proximity of pragmatism and anarchism—one of the editors of the Beijing University-based journal *Fendou* (Struggle), and was a student in the law division during the New Culture heyday (Weston, 2004: p. 191).

and experimentalism, as once again essentialist responses were put aside in favour of an embracing of complexity.

In the atmosphere of New Culture, many anarchists began to prominently utilise terms such as struggle, development, and adaptation, without associated stigma. Even older totemic anarchists like Wu Zhihui were unafraid to approach evolutionary concepts with heretofore absent commitment, as in this statement from 1924.

> Today we are in the transitional stage of republicanism and anarchism. From dawn to dusk, will it take a hundred years? A thousand? No one can yet say, for we only know it will take a long time. But if we acknowledge the infinitude of the universe, then the number of years it will take is just from dawn to dusk. (Zarrow, 1990: p. 82)

By 1928, Li Shizeng (1928) too would justify both his membership in the GMD, and his contentious interpretation of Sun Yat-Sen's Three People's Principles, through a progressive conceptualisation of revolution. As Dirlik (1993: p. 271) has noted, "he [Li] now explained that 'present-day revolution' meant nothing more than 'present-day progress.' Revolution, as progress, signified the evolution of mankind from bad to good, simple to complex." Whilst Zarrow (1990: p. 220) too has noted that "Wu [Zhihui]'s emphasis shifted from fast and easy solutions to long and complex struggles," neither has chosen to tie these developments into a reformist dynamic, even though Wu and Li had emerged as the custodians of these ideals within the movement.

Turning to the younger post-leftist generation of anarchists—who were steeped in this temporal awareness—it becomes clear that this evolutionary perspective had taken on a broader purchase. As with Zhu Qianzhi, once again the evolution-revolution-evolution teleology was rejected, in the case of the younger anarchists to be replaced with the repeated *conflation* of evolution and revolution. Take Ba Jin, who explicitly states that evolution was not just the maker of revolution but that they are essentially one and the same—a conclusion justified once again through the situationalist necessities of a specifically Chinese setting:

> Revolution doesn't collide with evolution. Shao Keli has said: 'Evolution and revolution are successive activities of the same phenomenon; evolution comes before revolution, and then evolves into revolution.' The realization of anar-

chism can not be achieved in a short time, but will be achieved after constant revolutions and constructions. In the present environment of China, it is impossible for us to realize the ideal of anarchism immediately . . .

Although the result of the Russian Revolution is far away from the expectations of the former revolutionaries, we have to confess that Russia is much better than Czarist Russia. If you studied revolutions in history, you would find that the result of each revolution was far from its expectation. In the French Revolution, the brave masses, even women, took up arms to fight against their oppressors. But what was the result? Did they just want to set up a capitalist government? 'Liberté, Égalité, Fraternité' were their slogans. How much has been realized between the Napoleonic Government and now? Maybe you will be angry because French Revolution was just a half-measure since you know that there are still monarchical parties in France, but what kind of time would we be in if there had not been the French Revolution? (Ba Jin, 1927)

Although the allusion to diachronic approaches is not as explicit as in Zhu Qianzhi's article, the above statement is nonetheless telling in its more conciliatory and less essentialist juxtaposition of failure and success, which relies more on the space between essentialist responses. The discursive capacity which we have begun to establish, to look at both abstract examples such as these and at the material realities of applying anarchism to China from outside of classical binaries, was heavily dependent on this evolutionary conceptualisation of time and revolution. For when the notion of building the unique conditions required for an immediate anarchist revolution was removed, a constructive future for anarchism potentially emerges from any number of parallel and previously "unorthodox" activities.

Wei Huilin's contribution to the same symposium echoes Ba in its favouring of contingent approaches and progressive non-linear development ahead of waiting for a totalising revolution.

We can not say like a determinist that some social system is an inevitable journey before the realization of anarchism, which will delay the arrival of our aim. This claim will just prolong the old system that ensures antagonism between the dominator and the dominated. What we should do is to realise our ideals based on the present truth and the tendency of our time. We all know that the progress of the human being comes from the efforts people take gradually. We don't plan to build an anarchist society suddenly, but we can try to get as much freedom and happiness as possible as we do so. (Wei Huilin, 1927)

That the classical anarchist conviction that only certain situations are legitimate precursors to anarchist revolution could be brushed aside as "determinism" (定命论) is indicative of the assertiveness which was manifesting itself among the younger anarchists. The influence of the New Culture movement is once again tangible in this regard, as the use of determinism (in particular as a pejorative) had emerged as part of the critique ideological piety in only the preceding five or ten years. Perhaps even more interestingly Wei speaks more explicitly to the classical anarchist preoccupation with dialectical power structures when he states that "the old system" ensures "antagonism between the dominator and dominated." To disavow antagonism between dominator and dominated—a bold contradiction of a fundamental tenet of anarchist theory—is a perfect example of the agency wrought by evolutionism. Much as with Zhu above, the dialectical overturning of power that was the anarchist revolution failed to suit a Chinese reality. In place of this old system, Wei returns to our repeated New Thought pattern of approaching doctrine pragmatically and prioritising localised and necessitated responses ahead of inherited approaches.

The converse faith in a spontaneous and total anarchist revolution would however remain a persistent identifier within leftist groups, whom pursued the fervent belief that the conditions for a total anarchist revolution were imminent and that revolution could be achieved through commitment and purity of ideals alone. Shen Zhongjiu saw progression as a linear act toward anarchism, in which divergence was characterised as "regression" (退步):

It is progress to develop from the Nationalist Party to anarchism, which surely deserves praise. However, if we change from anarchists to nationalists, we can only say that it is a kind of regression. (Xin Ai, 1924)

It is clear that the perpetuation of the ethical pedestal of singular revolution remained a key aspect of Shen's understanding of "true anarchism," characterising evolutionary and adaptive ideals

merely as a means to justify ideological capitulation and oppor-
tunism. For example, Shen wrote:

> In my opinion, we should know the difference between
> revolution and reformation if we want to understand revo-
> lution. First, they both seek for evolution and alteration,
> but revolution seeks for complete and fierce change while
> reformation seeks for partial and slow alteration. The evo-
> lution from revolution is always more fierce than that
> from reformation, which can last for hundreds of years.
> Reformation changes the old state and old power gradually
> while revolution overturns them fundamentally. Secondly,
> they adopt different methods. Reformers often compro-
> mise with the old society in a moderate way . . . Third, the
> reformers often mix themselves with the targets to be re-
> formed, and sometimes they cooperate; Revolutionaries
> adopt adverse attitude to their targets. Reformers just
> want to get personal improvement, but revolutionaries
> want to overturn some class. Revolution always changes
> with the times. (Xin Ai, 1924)

Much of Shen's analysis is rooted in classically dialectical approaches to reformism—that a revolutionary self-defines by relying on oppositional binaries (表示敌对的行动), and that reformism
always acts as a veiled cover for ethical dalliance. This approach
has at various junctures been retrospectively associated with a
kind of ideological and moral purity of purpose by anarchist historians.[30] Yet, as Todd May (1994: p. 54) has noted, "the mistake
that is made in contrasting revolution and reform lies in the assumption that the former involves a qualitative change in society,
while the latter involves only a quantitative change." This is an
analysis which adeptly characterises the binary approaches to
revolution and evolution amongst this group.

For the post-leftist anarchists, their diachronic understanding
of an anarchist hereafter became one that was less utopian, even

---

[30] Take for instance the following assessment—"Anarchists demand our
attention, not for who they were or what they accomplished, but because
against a revolutionary strategy that presupposed a necessary compromise of revolutionary goals in order to confront the demands of immediate political necessity, they reaffirmed a revolutionary consciousness
that provides an indispensable critical perspective from the Left" (Dirlik,
1993: p. 198) I would also like to note this does not say "not *only* for who
they were," although this would seem far more reasonable.

less singular; there was no longer the typically precise anarchist programme for action but more of a collective and continuous negotiation and refinement. The political field would have to be seen without the "hope of a final emancipation," as the anarchist revolution was decentered via the notion of evolutionary development. This sense that unitary understandings of revolution were becoming an anachronism is evident in Wu Kegang's open refusal of the singular essential tactic, associating it with a time of more ideological certainty and less practicality within the movement:

> "Better none than imperfect. A 'pure' anarchist movement should not take part in any movements unrelated with anarchism."
>
> I had the same thoughts as above three years ago, but now I have the courage to confess that I was wrong. I did not know revolution at all then. Any revolution can never be purely of anarchism. I assert that we don't need to talk about revolution any more if we wait until there is anarchist revolution . . . There has never been and will never be a revolution which is controlled only by one ideality. (Wu Kegang, 1927)[31]

Throughout this period, evolutionary approaches are associated with the decentering of power relationships, of dominator and dominated, in the post-leftist understanding of revolution. The twin notions of reformism and decentered power structures are often closely intertwined in anarchist theory as it faces modernity, and it is worth noting the chronological equivalence in China.[32] Newman has noted that the

> notion of dispersed power renders the idea of revolution as the final, dialectical overturning of power an anachronism . . . once the strategic picture of concentric circles or hier-

---

[31] Wu Kegang, "Wuzhengfu zhuyi yu shiji wenti" in *WZFZYSX*, 826–49; It is potentially illuminating that Wu cites 1923—the year of the "Debate Between Science and Metaphysics" and Wu Zhihui and Shen Zhonjiu's defining debate as the turning point in which he began to look at anarchism from outside of the boundaries of the pure and impure divide (Schwartz, 1986: p. 433).

[32] For a discussion on the decentering of power in Early-Modern China see Fitzgerald (1996: pp. 70–80), Rankin (2000) and Bodenhorn (2002) among many others in an expanding field.

archies is dropped, so is the idea that revolutionary change can be distinguished qualitatively from reformist change. (Newman, 2001: p. 79)

It is clear that for the post-leftist anarchists even distinguishing revolution from evolution had become a misnomer, they believed them to be one and the same.

As the temporal boundaries of revolution were made more malleable, divergent acts could be justified as part of a long-term continuum, broadening the boundaries of orthodoxy considerably. It is in the combining of these two elements, the focus on the practical and the local, and temporal decentering of the anarchist revolution, that we find the root of my contention that these anarchists were early adopters of the "tactical" aspects of post anarchism. May (1994, p. 10) has noted that,

> One of the central characteristics which binds various strategic political philosophies together, and which distinguishes them from tactical political philosophy, is that a strategic political philosophy involves a unitary analysis that aims toward a single goal. It is engaged in a project that it considers the center of the political universe.

The incorporation of evolutionary approaches pushed the post-leftist analysis in China beyond a mere focus on pragmatic application, and into the realm of the undermining of the unitary analysis of power and revolution.

FORMING ORTHODOXY FROM HETERODOXY—NEW CULTURE AS A MEANS OF EXTERNAL LEGITIMATION

Beyond providing the framework around which the post-leftist anarchists structured their new approach to anarchist doctrine there remains a secondary aspect to the importance of New Culture ideology and terminology to post-leftist anarchism. The epistemological framework offered by the New Culture functioned as an alternative source of legitimacy for the younger anarchists as they distanced themselves from their more conservative counterparts and adopted a heterodox position toward anarchism. As the essentialism at the heart of the movement was reducing divergent approaches to ethical subordination, New Culture provided the kind of externally-legitimated structure and identity which was required if this heterodoxy were to become orthodoxy.

That both the leftists and post-leftists looked to the terms "revolution" and "revolutionary" as territorial spaces to be claimed on behalf of their understandings of anarchism was reflective of their mutual desires to determine the direction of anarchism in China. Take for instance Shen Zongjiu's characterisation of a platonic revolutionary:

> Revolutionaries always try to build up a brand new power to fight against the old society. Before the revolution succeeds, the old society usually frustrates the new power in many ways, but revolutionaries *never compromise* with the old society. (Xin Ai, 1924)

And compare with that of Wu Kegang's:

> I believe that China is truly in the midst of revolution. This revolution seems to have no direct relation with anarchism, it is not a pure revolution from anarchism's perspective. However, are there no other revolutions besides a purely anarchist revolution? Now China is in the time of revolution, so the anarchist party *should take part in it* if they are revolutionaries. (Wu Kegang, 1927)

Although revolution marks the apex of these passages, both are imprecated within a more resonant question—"what is an anarchist?" This was not a discussion of whether either group were anarchists *or not* so much as an appraisal of their role *as* anarchists. For the leftists, to be a revolutionary was to embody purity of conception and dedication, the revolutionary as antithesis of the reformer. The post-leftist anarchists' revolutionary self-conceptualisation however was scaffolded by the broader ideas which were drawn from New Culture. Their revolution was reliant on involvement in a "revolutionary moment" rather than standing on an ideological pedestal, the antithesis of the revolutionary ideologue. As they repeatedly asserted a more participatory role for themselves in the application of anarchism, the post-leftist anarchists were looking at reconceiving the role of anarchism itself in China, rooted in a more participatory anarchist paradigm which no longer spent so much time on the sidelines. By participating in a long-term project, the revolutionary reformer understood the flaws in the notion of revolution and perhaps had, much like Bey's ontological anarchist, given up wanting the idealised anarchist revolution at all.

Shen Zhongjiu's attempts to reduce divergence to ethical subordination are indicative of a desire to rhetorically set the boundaries of anarchism; but the younger anarchists too, with this structure in place, were able to be assertive. New Thought pragmatism played a significant role in allowing the post-leftist anarchists to form a comprehensive anarchist identity which was not predicated on reaction or contrarianism but on a complete and yet divergent understanding of what it meant to be an anarchist. Once again, poststructural anarchism represents an analogous response to an analogous question. When May (1994, p. 61) asked, "are the struggles, and the vision which motivates that struggle reducible to a single strategic goal, or instead are anarchism's tactical moments its proper articulation?" he was referring to the very same grand question of theory and praxis that the decline phase anarchists wrestled with some sixty years before. The two groups' differing material attempts to rhetorically establish and justify their approaches are ancillary, what is important is that each side sought to *legitimate* their approaches. This is indicative of our key assumption, that neither side was reactionary or short-termist, that instead they harboured fundamentally divorced visions for anarchism in China, both of which were epistemologically complex conceptualisations, fully-rounded and yet existing at the relative extremes of a holistic anarchist nomenclature.

CONCLUSION: THE SYSTEMATISATION OF ANARCHISM

> Most of the anarchists of China do not come from civilians, so we don't know the life, feelings, needs and wishes of civilians. Our anarchism is out of translated Western books, so our enterprise is just something theoretical. We don't know civilians, and they don't know us. (Ba Jin, 1927)

When the post-leftist generation of anarchists referred to anarchism as an "abstract theory" translated from Western books, this was indicative of a collective *dialogue* being established for the first time between the synchronic requirements of the anarchist movement in China and the diachronic doctrine of anarchism which we established at the outset.[33] This dialogue was mediated

---

[33] Take one of the most well-known quotations of Wu Zhihui on Guomindang collaboration: "Burned to ash, I am a Guomindang party member, and at the same time one who believes in anarchism." Wu's statement is a statement of diachronic and synchronic duality, both a

by pragmatism and evolutionism and is worth noting in the long-run chronology of global anarchism and anarchist ontologies.

The result of this dialogue was that even as the classical anarchist binaries fell apart during the movement's decline, this younger generation neither clung to their continued relevance, nor did they abandon anarchism (as some anarchists had for the CCP over the previous seven years). With the declining relevance of classical anarchism a flourishing of possibilities took place, implicit in which was the opportunity to recalibrate anarchism in a manner which would make it more effective without leaving it behind. This resultant attempt to pursue early forms of non-foundational, post-structuralist ontology was referred to internally as "systematisation" (无政府主义系统化), as in Wei Hulin's statement here:

> We must have our own organization to fight against our enemies, which should have two functions: One is to set up the basis of the future society; the other is to cope with some of the problems of the particular period. Now our primary problem is the systematisation of anarchism, which is the practical problem of all anarchist movements. (Wei Huilin, 1927)

As a choice of wording alone, systematisation reflects two conclusions we have drawn regarding the post-leftist anarchists. First, that their divergent approaches were part of a *rational* attempt to overcome the deficiencies of the existing culture, rather than a reactionary aberrance. Second, this ontological approach was understood as a refinement of anarchism, a duty to make anarchism better, rather than a tacit abandonment. New Culture provided a diachronic source of reason for this process, just as the wider intellectual community was looking to "imaginatively transcend its one-dimensionality," the systematisation of anarchism served as a more localised but comparably emancipatory sense of reconstructive completion for the anarchist movement.

The post-leftist anarchists directed themselves toward achieving a position of objective analysis and subjective action, much like Hakim Bey or Reiner Schürmann. In this manner they were

---

question of what Wu believed (he 'believes' in anarchism) and what he deemed to be necessitated (he is a 'member' of the GMD). Yet with the question of identity in mind it is interesting to note what has never been transposed or discussed, the closing phrase of Wu's very next sentence—"I am on the verge of depersonalisation" (我才是人格破产).

able to decenter the place of power in the anarchist paradigm, away from classical anarchism which, in application to China, had "lurched toward rigid polarities and flat totalisations" (Berman, 1987: p. 24). Had the movement's precipitous decline not stood as the logical endgame of these changing processes it is entirely plausible to assume that the post-leftists could have established a more codified version of these loose progressive ideas and eventually a fully-formed pragmatic programme for action. R.W. Sleeper (1986: p. 1) has argued that the Deweyan pragmatism which so informed New Culture, "seems to be teaching us how to transform the culture that is decaying around us, rather than just how to 'cope' with its collapse." The existing narrative of the anarchists has been one of them merely coping with collapse during the decline phase; our narrative has looked to establish the post-leftists as a group with the agency to actively transform anarchism in line with the doctrines they idealised. With this in mind, it is worth noting Wu Kegang's (1927) arresting commentary, that "reasons produce results, and results turn into reasons, which move in endless circles" (许多多因 产生一个果 果又变为因 循环不已 永不停止) in which he embodies the most lasting prognostication of modernity—that not only is it transitory, fleeting and a "ruthless centrifuge of change," but that to embrace it opens up transformative possibilities.

Tom Marling is a first-year Ph.D. candidate at Hong Kong Baptist University. His research focuses on non-Western appropriations of Western doctrine, with a specific focus on the Chinese anarchist movement. Contact address: tommarling22@gmail.com.

ABBREVIATION

WZFZYSX 1 / 2: Ge Maochun et al., (1984) *Wuzhengfu Zhuyi Sixiang Ziliao Xuan* [无政府主义思想资料选]. Beijing: Beijing Daxue Chubanshe.

PRIMARY REFERENCES

A.D., (1924) 'Weishenme fandui Buerxueweike' in *Wuzhengfuzhuyi zai Zhongguo* [无政府主义在中国] (Gao Jun et al., Ed.). pp. 386–393.

Huang Yibo, (1926) "Wuzhengfu zhuyi zhe zai Guangzhou gao gonghui huodong huiyi" [无政府主义者在广州搞工会活动会议], *Guangdong Wenshi Ziliao*, 5, 1962, pp. 1–4.

Huilin (Wei Huilin), Feigan (Ba Jin), Wu Kegang, (1927) Contributions to symposium, "Wuzhengfuzhuyi yu shiji wenti" [无政府主义与实际问题], in *WZFZYSX* 2, pp. 826–49.

Kuli, (1925) "Zhongguo wuzhengfutuan gangling caoan" [中国无政府团纲领草案], *Minzhong*, No. 13, reprinted in *WZFZYSX* 2, pp. 712–716.

Li Shizeng, (1928) "Fenzhi Hezuo Wenti" [分之合作问题], *Geming*, pp. 31–32, 36.

Li Shizeng, (1928) "Xianjin Gemingzhi Yiyi" [现今革命之意义].

Mao Yibo, (1927) "Geming zhongzhi zhishi jieji yu wuchan jieji" [革命种植知识阶级与物产阶级]" *Minfeng* 2, no.1.

Xin Ai (Shen Zhongjiu), (1924) 'Wuzhengfuzhuyizhe keyi jiaru Guomindang ma?' [无政府主义者可以加入国民党吗?], *Ziyou Ren (Free People)*, no. 5.

Zhu Qianzhi, (1925) "Yuzhou geming de yuyan" [宇宙革命的语言], *Revolutionary Philosophy* (Gémìng Zhéxué, 革命哲学), reprinted in *WZFZYSX* 2:, p. 477.

SECONDARY REFERENCES

Berman, Marshall (1987). *All That is Solid Melts Into Air: The Experience of Modernity*. Durham: Duke University Press.

Bey, Hakim (1985). *The Temporary Autonomous Zone, Ontological Anarchy, Poetic Terrorism*. New York: Autonomedia.

Bishop, Donald H. (1985). *Chinese Thought: An Introduction*. Delhi: Motilal Banarsidass.

Bo Mou (2008). *History of Chinese Philosophy*. London: Routledge.

Bodenhorn, Terry Dwight (2002). *Defining Modernity: Guomindang Rhetorics of a New China, 1920–1970*. Ann Arbor: University of Michigan Press.

Chow Tse-tsung (1967). *The May Fourth Movement: Intellectual Revolution in Modern China*. Stanford: Stanford University Press.

Cohn, Jesse S. (2006). *Anarchism and the Crisis of Representation: Hermeneutics, Aesthetics, Politics*. Selinsgrove: Susquehanna University Press.

D'Urso, Salvatore (1980). "Can Dewey be Marx's Educational-Philosophical Representative?" *Educational Philosophy and Theory* 12: 21–35.

Esherick, Joseph (2000). *Remaking the Chinese City; Modernity and National Identity, 1900–1950*. Honolulu: University of Hawai`i Press.

Fitzgerald, John (1996). *Awakening China: Politics, Culture, and Class in the Nationalist Revolution*. Stanford: Stanford University Press.

Fung, Edmund S. K. (2010). *The Intellectual Foundations of Chinese Modernity: Cultural and Political Thought in the Republican Era*. New York: Cambridge University Press.

Furth, Charlotte (1972). "May Fourth in History." In *Reflections on the May Fourth Movement: A Symposium* (Schwartz, Benjamin I., Ed.). Cambridge: Harvard University Press. 59–69.

Grieder, Jerome B. (1970). *Hu Shih and the Chinese Renaissance: Liberalism in the Chinese Revolution, 1917–1937.* Cambridge: Harvard University Press.

Hook, Sidney (1939). *John Dewey: An Intellectual Portrait.* Westport: Greenwood Press.

Kai-wing Chow (2008). *Beyond the May Fourth Paradigm: in Search of Chinese Modernity.* Lanham: Lexington Books.

Krebs, Edward S. (1988). *Shifu: Soul of Chinese Anarchism.* Lanham: Rowman and Littlefield.

Lei Yi (2006). "On the Differences and Similarities in the Thought of Hu Shi and Ding Wenjiang." *Chinese Studies in History* 39.3 (Spring 2006): 33–50.

Liu, Lydia (1995). *Translingual Practice: Literature, National Culture, and Translated Modernity-China, 1900–1937.* Stanford: Stanford University Press.

Lothstein, Arthur (1978). "Salving from the Dross: John Dewey's Anarcho-Communism." *The Philosophic Forum* 10 (Autumn 1978): 55–110.

Manicas, Peter T. (1982). "John Dewey, Anarchism and the Political State." *Transactions of the Charles S. Peirce Society* 18.2 (Spring 1982): 133–158.

Manicas, Peter (2003). "John Dewey: Anarchism and the Political State." In *Rescuing Dewey: Essays in Pragmatic Naturalism* (Mancias Peter T., Ed.). Carbondale: Southern Illinois University Press.

May, Todd (1994). *The Political Philosophy of Poststructuralist Anarchism.* University Park: Penn State University Press.

McGowan, John (1991). *Postmodernism and its Critics.* Ithaca: Cornell University Press.

Min-chih Chou (1984). *Hu Shih and Intellectual Choice in Modern China.* Ann Arbor: University of Michigan Press

Mitter, Rana (2004). *A Bitter Revolution: China's Struggle with the Modern World.* New York: Oxford University Press.

Newman, Saul (2001). *From Bakunin to Lacan: Anti-Authoritarianism and the Dislocation of Power.* Lanham: Lexington Books.

Popp, Jerome A. (2007). *Evolution's First Philosopher: John Dewey and the Continuity of Nature.* New York: State University of New York Press.

Pusey, James (1983). *China and Charles Darwin.* Cambridge: Harvard University Press.

Rankin, Mary Backus (2000). "State and Society in Early Republican Politics, 1912–18." In *Reappraising Republican China* (Frederic E. Wakeman and Richard L. Edmonds, Eds.). Oxford: Oxford University Press. 6–27.

Scalapino, Robert A. and George T. Yu (1961). *The Chinese Anarchist Movement.* Berkley: University of California Press.

Schwarcz, Vera (1986). *The Chinese Enlightenment: Intellectuals and the Legacy of the May Fourth Movement of 1919.* Berkeley: University of California Press.

Schwartz, Benjamin (1964). *In Search of Wealth and Power: Yen Fu and the West.* Cambridge: Harvard University Press.

Schwartz, Benjamin (1986). "Themes in Intellectual History, May Fourth and After." In *The Cambridge History of Modern China: Republican China 1912–1949*, Vol. 12. (Fairbank, John K. Ed.). Cambridge: Cambridge University Press. 97–141.

Sleeper, R.W. (1986). *The Necessity of Pragmatism: John Dewey's Conception of Philosophy.* New Haven: Yale University Press.

Wang Hui (2006). "Discursive Community and the Genealogy of Scientific Categories." In *Everyday Modernity in China* (Madeleine Yue Dong and Joshua L. Goldstein, Eds.). Seattle: University Washington Press. 80–120.

Wen Hsin-Yeh (1996). *Provincial Passages: Culture, Space, and the Origins of Chinese Communism.* Berkeley: University of California Press.

Wenxin Ye (2000). *Becoming Chinese: Passages to Modernity and Beyond.* Berkeley: University of California Press.

Weston, Timothy B. (2004). *The Power of Position: Beijing University, Intellectuals, and Chinese Political Culture*, 1898–1929. Berkeley: University of California Press.

Xiaobing Tang (1996). *Global Space and the Nationalist Discourse of Modernity: The Historical Thinking of Liang Qichao.* Stanford: Stanford University Press.

Yue Dong, Madeleine and Joshua Goldstein, eds. (2006). *Everyday Modernity in China.* Seattle: University Washington Press.

Zarrow, Peter (1990). *Anarchism and Chinese Political Culture.* New York: Columbia University Press.

Anarchist Developments in Cultural Studies
ISSN: 1923-5615
2013.2: Ontological Anarché: Beyond Materialism and Idealism

Jurisprudence of the Damned
Deleuze's Masochian Humour and Anarchist Neo-Monadology

Gregory Kalyniuk

ABSTRACT

In this essay, I argue that Gilles Deleuze's presentation of the micropolitics in Leopold von Sacher-Masoch's novels develops themes that might inform some aspects of an anarchist philosophy, particularly Daniel Colson's anarchist neo-monadology. Rather than institutionalising anarchy as the final way of doing away with laws, as the Marquis de Sade had ironically envisioned, Masoch subverts the law through a humourous proliferation of successive contracts, aiming for a transmutation of the sense of guilt. Between Deleuze's readings of Masoch and G. W. Leibniz, a common point can be found in the replacement of the absolute Good with a relative Best as the foundation of the law, according to which the determination of its principles must be grounded in a consideration of its consequences. While Leibniz positions God as the determinant of the Best in order to ensure the moral consequence of the greatest diversity in the world, in God's absence the horizon of morality is displaced by the contingency of historical becoming, and guilt can no longer be said to have any sufficient reason within the system of pre-established harmony. What would the appeal to the Best be like in a world where incompossibles co-exist, and what role might Masoch's humour play in relation to this?

KEYWORDS
bêtise, desire, thought, law, humour

What, if any, is the relation of Gilles Deleuze's philosophy to anarchism? Deleuze claimed that both he and Félix Guattari had remained Marxists, however each in their own way (Deleuze, 1995: 171). In Deleuze's work, anarchy appears under the guises of the Marquis de Sade's institutions of perpetual motion and Antonin Artaud's crowned anarchy. Taking this darker tone, whereby the assumption of a natural goodness innate to human nature is abandoned, any possible link to anarchism as a political philosophy must be carefully negotiated. In this essay, I will argue that Deleuze's presentation of the micropolitics in Leopold von Sacher-Masoch's novels offers a clue as to how this negotiation might be done.

Deleuze claims that Masoch's work has great anthropological and clinical value for showing how a specific type of perverse eroticism could reflect an attempt to come to terms with the vicious excesses of human history, while also encompassing a political philosophy that parodies the law on the basis of the contract. Whereas Deleuze presents Sade's subversion of institutional power as operating according to an art of irony, Masoch's subversion of the contractual relationship is likened to an art of humour, exemplified in such dispositions as mocking by submission and working to rule.[1] A common point between Deleuze's reading of Masoch and G. W. Leibniz is the replacement of the absolute Good with a relative Best as the foundation of the law, according to which the determination of its principles must be grounded in a consideration of its consequences. The man who obeys the law then no longer becomes righteous but guilty in advance, like the debtor who inherits a debt that can never be repaid. While Leibniz positions God as the determinant of the Best to ensure the moral consequence of the greatest diversity in the world, in God's absence the horizon of morality is displaced by the contingency of historical becoming, and guilt can no longer be said to have any sufficient reason within the system of pre-established harmony. What would the appeal to the Best be like in a world where incompossibles[2] co-exist, and what role might the subversive force of Masoch's humour play in relation to this?

---

[1] "Working to rule" is an action whereby workers, in lieu of a strike or a lockout, undertake to decrease the efficiency of their labour by following the rules and regulations stipulated under their contracts to the letter.

[2] According to Leibniz, the best possible world was chosen to pass into existence by God, because out of an infinity of possible worlds, it met the criteria of being the most diverse while retaining the maximum of continuity between its diverse elements. Compossibility is this relation of continuity, whereby the diverse elements are able to converge upon the same world. Incompossibility, on the other hand, is the relation of discontinuity whereby Adam the sinner and Adam the non-sinner, for instance, cannot converge upon the same world. Adam the sinner cannot include the world in which Adam has not sinned, while Adam the non-

Inspired by Pierre-Joseph Proudhon and Deleuze, Daniel Colson has appropriated some elements from Leibniz's monadology in his writings on anarchism for the purpose of laying out its ontological foundation, as well as describing some of its proposed economic arrangements. But there is a way of implicating Deleuze and Masoch (as well as Artaud and Nietzsche) in this undertaking that would broaden the scope of Colson's project beyond its syndicalist orientation. The following discussion is focused on exploring what the aforementioned thinkers may have to contribute towards understanding some of the existential ambivalences surrounding anarchy and revolution, with particular regard to questions pertaining to animality, stupidity, desire, thought, law, and, of course, humour.

ANARCHIST NEO-MONADOLOGY

Colson finds the all-inclusive nature of each monad's point of view to be one of the main features that makes monadological thought agreeable for anarchists. As simple spiritual substances, monads are each defined by a unique point of view upon the world which is contained within them, and which becomes the object of their consciousness according to individual appetite or desire. "Apperception" is the name that Leibniz gives to this form of consciousness, which takes minute perceptions already contained within the monad as its object. Leibniz's strange insistence that monads are windowless and that they only apperceive perceptions from within themselves can be understood as the consequence of rejecting relations of direct causality between them. Besides this, it is also the consequence of their relative freedom in determining what is apperceived of their internal perceptions. But without the pre-established harmony overseen by a calculating God who determines the compossibility of the world, or the coherence between the multiplicity of monadic points of view that converge upon it, what is there to prevent the diversity of the world from degenerating into contradiction? Without God, the natural state of the world is not one of compossibility, but incompossibility: the monads are left free to desire beyond the artificial limits of what was formerly thought to be pre-established, and

---

sinner cannot include the world in which Adam has sinned. See Deleuze (1993), *The Fold*, pp. 59–61. I claim that Masoch's subversion of the relative Best involves the co-existence of incompossibles, insofar as the transmutation of the sense of guilt allows Adam to be both sinner and non-sinner simultaneously.

the world multiplies into as many variations of itself as there are desires willing them into existence. But the Death of God also brings with it the birth of the human sciences and the emergent techniques of biopower and subject formation, which from modernity onwards have put windows on the monad and replaced the mythical calculations of divine providence. The foldings interior to the monad, no longer the sole object of an analytic rationality that would account for their uniqueness according to the *a priori* sufficient reason of an individual concept that subsumes them, now become the object of synthetic rationalities *a posteriori*, which construct the subjectivity of the human soul at the same time that they claim to illuminate its objective being. For contemporary anarchist politics, this technocratic appropriation of desire clearly forms the more urgent object of possible subversion, as opposed to the old theological dogmas. For Colson, the incompossible multiplicity of monadic points of view expresses a "strange unity" capable of driving this subversion, and of fulfilling an experiment in the creation of new arrangements and associations amongst beings.

Beyond subjective predispositions and prejudices, and beyond the social institutions that produce subjectivity through an exercise of power guided by various historically contingent forms of knowledge, what is left of our point of view over the world that could still be said to be our own, and not simply the product of these disciplinary, normalising mechanisms? When freed of the social imperatives to which it is subordinated, is the human subject left with the volition to create values independently? Or was it always nothing more than an assemblage of reactive forces which devolves into animality in the absence of discipline? Or could a volition towards higher values, such as those affirmed by the will to power for Nietzsche, or which Proudhon would have called Justice, somehow be implicit to this animality peculiar to thought? Colson traces the source of such a volition to the ancient Greek notion of *apeiron*, whose paradoxical meaning encompasses both ignorance and infinity. In *A Short Philosophical Dictionary of Anarchist Philosophy From Proudhon to Deleuze*, Colson describes it as "the indefinite and unspecified foundation from which the infinity of things is unceasingly born" (Colson, 2001: 138).[3] The pure difference of *apeiron* accounts for the sufficient reason of each monad's singularity and qualifies the pri-

---

[3] I would like to thank Jesse Cohn for sharing his unpublished translation of Colson's *Petit lexique philosophique de l'anarchisme de Proudhon à Deleuze*, which was an invaluable reference for this essay.

mordial fullness of desire against the oppressive mechanisms that would dictate its lack and make it into the enforcer of its own subjugation. But when Colson considers the complementarity of good sense and common sense, he says nothing about *apeiron*. Instead, he tries to save common sense from the "mixture of clichés and received ideas" (Colson, 2001: 297–98) that form good sense. It is here where he falls short of seeing his critique of representation through to its end by overlooking the insights of Artaud, arguably the most important anarchist in Deleuze's canon.

In *Difference and Repetition*, Deleuze credits Artaud for having inaugurated a transcendental empiricism that opposes the *genitality* of a fractured thought to the assumed innateness of a common sense incapable of escaping its subjective or implicit presuppositions (Deleuze, 1994: 147).[4] For Artaud, "innateness" does not consist of common sense and its presuppositions, but of a genitality that violently forces thought to think its own central collapse, and discover that its natural "powerlessness" is indistinguishable from its greatest power. Before it is possible to begin thinking, one must first be liberated from all that *everybody knows* and *no one can deny*, or the postulates of the system of non-philosophical knowledge that constitute what Deleuze calls the dogmatic Image of thought. In stripping the moral variant of this Image of its prephilosophical pretensions, Nietzsche had discovered its authentic repetition in a thought without Image, which he allied with paradox in a war against representation and common sense (Deleuze, 1994: 134). Meanwhile, for Colson it is common sense itself which affirms creation in the "interstices of the authorised discourses" (Colson, 2001: 298) belonging to the dogmatic Image. But how can the "strange unity" grounding anarchist thought be accessed through these interstices without becoming perverted by the authorised discourses? For Artaud, the work of managing to think something at all is a painful and difficult process requiring a violent encounter that will force it to confront the conditions of a previously unknown problem. In *The Theatre and its Double*, for instance, he envisioned the possibility of bringing about a revelation that would finally exteriorise the "latent undercurrent of cruelty through which all the perversity of which the mind is capable, whether in a person or a nation, becomes localised" (Artaud, 1999: 19). This revelation would take place through the medium of theatre:

---

[4] See Kalyniuk (2014), "Crowned Anarchies, Substantial Attributes, and the Transcendental Problem of Stupidity," p. 196, where I discuss this theme at greater depth.

theatre ought to pursue a re-examination not only of all aspects of an objective, descriptive outside world, but also all aspects of an inner world, that is to say man viewed metaphysically, by every means at its disposal. We believe that only in this way will we be able to talk about imagination's rights in the theatre once more. Neither Humour, Poetry, or Imagination mean anything unless they re-examine man organically through anarchic destruction, his ideas on reality and his poetic position in reality. (Artaud, 1999: 70)

Artaud's decadence and self-destructive character may make him seem like the prototype of what has been derisively described as "lifestyle anarchism," or the nihilistic posturing that abandons the imperative of social transformation while retaining anarchy as a mere fashion statement. But the affective immediacy that bypasses the constraints of representational thinking in his theatre of cruelty, which had the clear aim of liberating all of social reality from spiritual degeneration, is something that common sense simply cannot duplicate.

To truly affirm the mode of speculative thinking demanded by anarchism, common sense is not enough. Common sense fails to grasp what stupidity [*bêtise*] is in relation to the individual who thinks, the ground of their thought, and the process of individuation through which the thinking individual and the ground are linked by virtue of the question of stupidity (Deleuze, 1994: 151–52).[5] Against the notion that error, understood as the failure of good sense within the form of an intact common sense, comprises the sole "negative" of thought, Deleuze claims that stupidity, malevolence, and madness must be understood as properly transcendental problems in their own right, the distinctness of which makes them irreducible to error (Deleuze, 1994: 148–151).[6] Colson's insistence upon the legitimacy of common sense in the absence of good sense would be akin to Deleuze's definition of error itself. For Deleuze, error is an act of misrecognition in relation to

---

[5] The French term *bêtise* means both stupidity and animality. For Deleuze, transcendental stupidity or groundlessness is the animality peculiar to thought, without being animality *per se*. It is thought in its genitality, or the natural "powerlessness" that is indistinguishable from its greatest power. See Deleuze (1994), *Difference and Repetition*, pp. 275, 150.

[6] I discuss this further in Kalyniuk (2014), p. 197.

a positive model of recognition or common sense that assumes the honesty of the one who is mistaken, while stupidity is all the more mysterious for not presupposing any such positive model or honesty (Deleuze, 1994: 148–49). When workers spontaneously converge to take over factories and form new associations, for instance, what leads them to stop short of questioning the positive model of their form of work, or of "work" itself? Colson is fond of Peter Arshinov's slogan, which was addressed to the Makhnovists: "Proletarians of the world, look into the depths of your own beings, seek out the truth and realise it yourselves: you will find it nowhere else" (Arshinov, 1987: 261). Would the proletarians have encountered the limits of thought in the depths of their beings, only to be forced to think new thoughts like Artaud? When stupidity and cruelty are channeled through individuation, the ground of thought is raised to the surface without being given any recognisable form (Deleuze, 1994: 152–53). Deleuze is still optimistic, however, that the constitution of the highest element of a transcendent sensibility will still be possible once the individual reaches the point of intolerance for stupidity and cruelty, a turning point at which a revolutionary consciousness of limits informs the creation of new values. The ignorance and infinity encompassed by *apeiron* must for this reason be given priority over common sense and be confronted with the force of an existential imperative, or else anarchism may be fated to repeat the very stupidity that it rightfully holds in contempt for appropriating human progress, not to mention the emancipation of life that is as irreducible to discourses of progress as stupidity is irreducible to error.

Amid the ruins of the Platonic Good and the supposed neurosis of human Reason during the Baroque crisis, Deleuze explains how Leibniz, acting as God's attorney, had to rebuild the same world on another stage according to a universal Jurisprudence (Deleuze, 1993: 67–68). Instead of asking what object corresponded to a given luminous principle, he asked what hidden principle or concept could be invented for this or that perplexing case or singularity. Through a multiplication and proliferation of such principles, he aimed to neutralise his enemies and make them incompossible with the world as he had rebuilt it. Already anticipating the Death of God, Leibniz undertook this method in an attempt to defend God's cause and prevent the world from descending into contradiction. This involved his infamous justification for evil as the unavoidable consequence of pre-established harmony, according to which God chose the least quantity of conceptual complexity for the set of ideas determining the greatest quantity of diversity amongst monads converging upon the best of all possible worlds. A less perfect world, according to Leibniz, would be both less diverse and more evil: more evil because the complexity of the set of ideas determining it would be greater, and therefore more arbitrary. In all possible worlds, the damned are the victims of evil. They are incapable of forming ideas any clearer than their simple hatred of God, and in this sense function like automata incapable of actual thinking (*ibid.*, 71). Like the men of resentment and slave morality whom Nietzsche would later condemn in the *Genealogy of Morals* (Nietzsche, 1989), Leibniz saw them as finding their only purpose in being dominated by those of a stronger will. As Deleuze mysteriously claims, they are the only souls to whose detriment happier and more capable souls are able to make any progress (Deleuze, 1993: 74). Would this be because their stupidity illuminates the ground that rises to the surface, or the natural powerlessness of thought that is indistinguishable from its greatest power? Or would it be for the more straightforward reason that they produce the inescapable condition of domination that animates the world? With a twisted sense of optimism, Leibniz positioned the infinity of the damned as the foundation of the best possible world, in that *they liberate an infinite quantity of possible progress in the service of other monads* (*ibid.*). In a world that has liberated a greater quantity of possible progress than any previous era of human civilisation, the social forms of capitalism are often touted as reproducing the laws of nature itself.

Does pre-established harmony obscure a more fundamental distinction between the social and the proprietary, or does the distinction between the social and the proprietary obscure a more fundamental pre-established harmony? According to Georges Gurvitch, Leibniz's preoccupation with the metaphysical doctrine of pre-established harmony prevented him from pursuing the antinomies he had uncovered between the juridical frameworks of society and State, and between the *jus societatis*, or right of society, and the *jus proprietatis*, or right of property, to their full conclusion (Gurvitch, 1947: 65). First opposing the identification between society and State, Leibniz claimed that because all laws (including natural laws) were essentially contingent and arose from "truths in fact," their origins had to be sought in the smallest groups making up society (*ibid.*, 65). The autonomous social laws engendered and possessed by these groups and the power derived from them presupposed both a harmony between equivalents and integration into the whole. The common life of the group there-fore enjoyed a social law of peace. But opposed to this was an inter-individual law of war, which resulted from the enslavement of the common life of the group to the law of individual property (*ibid.*, 64–65). Leibniz maintained that the subordination of social power to the right of property originated out of relations of uni-lateral possession between men and animals being transposed into the common life of the group, where the law of domination eventually succeeded in dominating men themselves through the intermediary of animals and things (*ibid.*, 65). This account of the origin of social domination is dramatised in what Deleuze and Guattari call the becoming-animal of masochism, according to which instinctive forces are rendered immanently thinkable by undergoing the senseless cruelty of domestication to which ani-mals are subjected (Deleuze and Guattari, 1987: 155–56, 259–60). The purpose of this child-like exercise is to tame stupidity, or the animality innate to the power of thinking, by reliving the history of social domination in relation to the domination of animals that lies at its origin. But the crisis of property provoking this exercise is first and foremost reflected in Leibniz's theory of appurtenance itself: the organic body is a self-contained world full of little ani-mals that are inseparable from its fluid parts and which are also worthy of life, despite the body being the property of a thinking monad (Deleuze, 1993: 109). Animal monads are perpetually re-shuffled between bodies, and insofar as they are damned, liberate an infinite quantity of possible progress for the world. In re-sponse to this crisis, Gabriel Tarde was led to re-conceive all so-cial relations in terms of mutualised and universalised possession and reduce being to the terms of *having* (Tarde, 2012: 51–52), while Peter Kropotkin, in responding to the related crisis of Social Darwinism, speculated that facts of unconscious mutual aid would someday be discovered in the life of micro-organisms (Kropotkin, 2006: 8). The right of society and the right of property become virtually indistinguishable once relations between men and animals are problematised on the microcosmic scale internal to the organism, since the organism is both a society of parts as well as the property of a monad. This would mean that the food chain is a fundamentally ecological instance of pre-established harmony, and that the smallest groups making up society exist on a sub-molecular level. Echoing Proudhon's infamous proclama-tion that *property is theft*, for Alfred North Whitehead this would mean that *life is robbery*, since the organism, as a living society, may or may not be a higher type of organism than the food that it

JURISPRUDENCE OF THE DAMNED | 225

ingests, therefore requiring a moral justification for the robber as much as for life itself (Whitehead, 1978: 105).

But did Proudhon grasp the ultimate implications of the Baroque crisis? In *What is Property?*, he likened the right of property to a moral quality infused into things, laid claim to by a proprietor who exhibited the power-of-attorney over the Creator (Proudhon, 1994: 125). In more practical terms, he defined property as the right to enjoy and dispose of the fruits of another's industry and labour while lying idle and not working (*ibid.*, 129). But since production is proportional to labour and not to property, property must be impossible *quid juris*, or insofar as it is considered a question of right; since it demands something for nothing, the law of increase must be impossible in principle. As a principle, it has no reason for existing aside from legitimating the power of invasion that makes possession into a fact. For Proudhon, the extension of the natural fact of original possession into the arbitrary laws set consistently with the right of property defies jurisprudence, according to which a fact, such as the universal recognition of the right of property, cannot produce or legitimate the right of property itself (*ibid.*, 64). If it could, then the right of property would be capable of objectifying concrete relations of having according to abstract terms of being, putting the proprietor into an element of calm in relation to his property as if this relation could be established once and for all (Deleuze, 1993: 110).[7] According to Gurvitch, Proudhon's response to Leibniz's irreducible antinomies was to emphasise the importance of the law as a principle that regulated their unstable equilibrium, and to idealise the economic law of society against the political law of the State (Gurvitch, 1947: 70–71). While opposing Leibniz's preestablished harmony for its neglectful elimination of the irreducible antinomies, Proudhon attempted to free the economic laws from their subordination to the right of property by tracing their origin to non-statist society. But despite his early claim that property is theft, in his mature phase he would admit that freedom is not possible without property, and that property is the greatest revolutionary force in existence.[8] As we have already

---

[7] For Deleuze and ostensibly Proudhon, relations of having are by their very nature impermanent.

[8] Ironically, Proudhon's claim that property is the most revolutionary force in existence is especially true in light of Deleuze and Guattari's claim in *Anti-Oedipus* that desire is revolutionary in its own right, without "wanting" revolution *per se* (Deleuze and Guattari, 1983: 116). While a person who wants personal freedom may take out a mortgage

seen, property, like monadic appurtenance, is immanent to the very constitution of organic bodies. Without taking property into account, economic law (as a law of peace) could only be distinguished from political law (as a law of war) by also transcending the concrete multiplicity of groupings making up social life, to which property is essential. As Proudhon became increasingly aware of the falsity of idealising the economics of society against State politics, he re-conceived the order of law engendered by the various groups making up non-statist society to be larger than the framework of economic law itself, since each of these groups would be the source of its own specific legal framework (Gurvitch, 1947: 70–71). In place of the political power of the State, the economic forces immanent to society, expressed through small-scale property ownership, would be organised into an agricultural-industrial federation based on democratic and mutualist principles. But would this new system have been able to adequately safeguard against the abuse of property to dominate and exploit the work of others, let alone the natural world itself? And despite his insistence upon immanence in his later work, did Proudhon's analysis sufficiently address how the immanent system of capitalism was capable of constantly overcoming its limitations, only to come up against them once again in a broader form (Deleuze, 1995: 171)?[9] The crisis of property that Deleuze sees as linking capitalism to the Baroque not only appeared with the growth of new machines in the social field, but with the discovery of new living beings in the organism as well (Deleuze, 1993: 110). The contemporary spread of genetically modified organisms in the agricultural industry and elsewhere, for instance, and the right of property established through the patenting of DNA and the human genome itself, signal the urgency of this latter appearance of the crisis now more than ever. But despite Proudhon's acceptance that the living man was a group whose organs formed secondary groups, he was unable to see how the crisis of property could conceivably extend to the fluid parts of the organic body, instead preferring to idealise the

---

on a house, for instance, the desire that transcends their subjective wants and needs may not, in fact, "want" freedom at all. As we will see, Masoch's attempt to restore property to its cruel physical immediacy in his novels entails a selective thought whose aim is to clarify the distinction between salvation and servitude, which all too often becomes obscured by virtue of the revolutionary nature of desire.

[9] Deleuze and Guattari maintain their allegiance to an ahistoricist interpretation of Marxism on the basis of this essential criterion.

transcendent existence in the sensible, intelligent and moral man (Proudhon: 2009: 23–24). Would he have then been prepared to face the full implications of the moral dilemma posed by Whitehead, that life is robbery, or did progress for him entail a foreclosure of the problem of domination outside the context of human groups, so that the proprietor of the human organism, understood in terms of the natural fact of original possession, could be put into an element of calm in relation to his property?

Voltaire and Proudhon reacted strongly against Leibniz's attempt to defend God and the existence of evil. While Voltaire made a mockery of Leibniz's optimism in his satirical novella *Candide*, Proudhon renounced all providential theism and proclaimed, "God is *the* evil" (Quoted in Löwith, 1949: 63). In an attack against the religious interpretation of history based on divine providence that Leibniz had upheld, Proudhon aimed to show how the illusion of God as its fatal determinant was the creation of man himself. Rather than associating human progress with God and the best possible world, his alternative was a Promethean, humanitarian atheism, which he identified with the figure of Satan. But while he may have fought against God and divine providence for the sake of human progress, he did not abandon the monadological thought of Leibniz altogether. In *Justice in the Revolution and in the Church*, Proudhon reoriented the *quid juris*, or question of right in Leibniz's monadology, as a *quid facti*, or question of fact, in order to find a proof for liberty in the reality of its function within a system of nature where the linkage of parts was only thought to be determined by God (Proudhon, 1868: 206–7).[10] Would his monadology have then operated according to a universal jurisprudence, in which the rights of rational beings are assumed to be substantiated by facts while the damned are sacrificed for the greater good, or according to what we are calling a singular jurisprudence or a *jurisprudence of the damned*, which calls hegemonic rationalities into question on behalf of the automata that liberate an infinite quantity of possible progress for the world?[11] Instead of posing the problem in

---

[10] Jesse Cohn's translations of passages from *De la Justice dans la Révolution et dans l'Église*, which are referenced in this essay, are available at collectivereason.org, 2009.

[11] Deleuze's understanding of universal jurisprudence seems to be quite different from the axiomatisation of "wise charity" that Leibniz had envisioned leading to the invention of a *calculus ratiocinator*, but it is debatable to what ends Deleuze may intend to appropriate universal jurisprudence as his own concept. While the reflective use of invented

these terms, Proudhon asked whether the things in which power appears are simply the vehicles of the infinite power as they were for Spinoza, or whether they possess within themselves the force with which they are endowed, as they did for Leibniz. Rejecting Spinoza's determinism, Proudhon ultimately showed a preference for Leibniz, but with considerable revision of the theocratic presuppositions of monadological thought. In place of a collective absolute that would act as a determinant rather than as a resultant, for Proudhon liberty emerges from the collective synthesis of human faculties as the power to be freed from fatality (Proudhon, 1868: 208–10). Its immanent function is constituted between the heights of a determinable ideal and the depths of a determining chaos: instead of creating ideas or things, liberty, as a power of appropriation, takes them for material and makes them different. Proudhon named the instinct for sociability preceding liberty Justice, and in opposition to its idealisation as God's immutable will, oriented Satan as the free cause animating the world. Without Satan, he claimed, Justice would have remained an instinct. But how will Satan be able to take the created ideas and things of industrial capitalism and make them different enough to render its structures of domination and exploitation incompossible with the conditions of a new world? The answer, we will argue, is by means of a special kind of humour, which enacts the subversion of both stupidity and common sense alike.

DELEUZE'S MASOCHIAN HUMOUR

Humour, as Deleuze understands it, is one of two known ways, along with irony, of overturning the moral law (Deleuze, 1994: 5). However, irony and humour also share an important relation to the classical conception of the law: not in a sense that threatens to subvert morality, but in a sense that upholds it and makes political philosophy itself possible (Deleuze, 1991: 81). While irony

principles may have the conceptualisation of singularities as its object, its rationalist and anthropocentric presuppositions cast some doubts over the extent to which the universality of jurisprudence could truly be capable of repeating the event in its singularity. For this reason we have opted to distinguish a singular jurisprudence, whose object is the singularisation of the universal from the point of view of the damned according to becomings-animal, rather than the universalisation of the singular from the point of view of an attorney who speaks on behalf of God. If God is dead, then what sense does it make to continue speaking of universal jurisprudence outside of the specific historical context in which Leibniz was writing?

seeks to trace the laws back to an absolute Good as their necessary principle, Deleuze argues that humour attempts to reduce the laws to a relative Best in order to persuade our obedience to them (*ibid.*, 82). Whereas Leibniz had been content to believe that the relativity of the Best resulted from God's determination of a world with the greatest quantity of diversity, and that man needed to learn to see beyond its apparent injustices since they could have been all the worse if God had been less charitable, Deleuze conceives of Masoch's approach to the Best more subversively. Instead of a proliferation of principles, each of which would express the sufficient reason of this or that perplexing case in the absence of an absolute Good, Masoch dramatised the perplexity of the case through a proliferation of contracts that would parody the law for the sake of drawing out its unseen consequences. In contrast to Leibniz's defence of the Best as the ultimate and most compossible consequence of all principles, in Masoch the relativity of the Best is revealed through consequences that are profoundly incompossible with one another. By descending to the consequences of following the law with too-perfect attention to detail, it is possible to dramatise the absurdity of the injustices that the morality of guilt compels the acceptance of. The law can then be derailed from the application that its legislators had intended for it, provoking the very disorder that they had sought to prevent. This method can be likened to a kind of jurisprudence, since it brings to light the perplexing case which cannot be subsumed under any existing laws. In the case of Masochian humour, the descent towards consequences takes place by means of what Deleuze describes as a "double suspension": on the one hand, the subject suspends his awareness of the world as legislated under the father's law, while on the other he clings to the feminine ideal incarnated in his fetishistic object of desire (*ibid.*, 33).[12] Suspended between the external law and his own desires, the Masochian

---

[12] Masoch's idealisation of women provides an interesting point of contrast to Proudhon's own intolerant misogyny in his prophetically titled diatribe *On Pornocracy*. While Proudhon's position on the subject of women's emancipation could not be more antithetical to Masoch's in this infamous, posthumously published work, what they do share in common is an obsession with woman's ability to seduce: either through a desexualising of desire that moves in the direction of higher ideals, or through a desacralising of love that moves in the direction of lower animal instincts. Where they most significantly differ is over the implycations of woman's seductive power for the oppressive uses of the right of property.

hero vacillates as if caught between incompossible worlds.[13]

The contract is central to Deleuze's understanding of Masoch's humourous subversion of the law. Rather than institutionalising anarchy with the establishment of mechanisms of perpetual motion as the final way of doing away with laws, as Sade had ironically envisioned, Masoch's method involved a humourous proliferation of successive contracts, the terms of which would become increasingly strict in order to prepare the way for a utopian law that would eventually override them (Deleuze, 1991: 92–93). In contrast to Rousseau's social contract, according to which freedom could only be attained under the constraint of submitting oneself to the abstract principles of the general will, both Proudhon and Masoch understood the contract in more concrete terms, and preferred for there to be many different contracts tailored to the desires of particular individuals. But while Proudhon saw the contract as the only moral bond that free and equal beings could accept (Proudhon, 2003: 171), for Masoch freedom could only come after the contract ran its limited course. For instance, in Masoch's novel *Venus in Furs*, Severin draws up an elaborate contract with a cruel mistress in which he gives away all of his rights and becomes her rightful property for a limited period (Sacher-Masoch, 1991). This use of the contract parodies the law (specifically the marriage contract) by making it more arbitrary and complex, while forcing desire to confront the stupidities that the law imposes over it in the most concrete terms.[14]

According to Leibniz, the arbitrariness and complexity of a law proves that it is not really a law, since it cannot be broken down into self-evident axioms. This arbitrariness and complexity is echoed in the guilt that Masoch would intensify through the contract, with the paradoxical aim of dissolving it with humour. Drawn up for the sole purpose of pushing the contracted party to annul its restrictive conditions, this parodying of the contract

---

[13] Jean-François Lyotard makes a similar connection between masochism and incompossibility in relation to the patient about whom Freud writes in his essay "A Child is Being Beaten." The patient is not certain whether the beaten child in her masturbatory fantasy is herself or someone else. Leaping from one version to another in a single instant, the fantasy presents a simultaneous occurrence of the incompossibles in the form of symptoms that ambiguously "phrase" more than one universe. See Lyotard (1988), *The Differend*, p. 83.

[14] Although Masoch had likened his contract to a pact with the devil, its relation to the liberation of desire seems to be completely at odds with the relation that Proudhon would have seen between Satan and human liberty.

brings attention to the law's power to enslave when taken for granted in its abstractness and put into the hands of the juridical elite. Through a humourous proliferation of contracts that would enact the punishment before the misdeed was committed, Masoch aimed to show how the intensification of guilt could result in the transmutation of its meaning, and inspire his readers to conceive of a utopian law of self-management modelled on the peasant communes that had emerged on the fringes of the Habsburg Empire during the mid nineteenth century.

In order to end his complicity with structures of patriarchal domination and be reborn a new Man, the Masochian hero submits himself to the imaginary law of an archaic, agrarian matriarchy by means of the contract, which comes to assume a ritualistic character for idealising hunting, agriculture, regeneration and rebirth in the image of femininity. While Masoch's idealisation of a matriarchal form of agrarian communism was probably a genuine reflection of his political beliefs, he also considered even more radical positions, such as those of the mystical sect of wanderers who once roamed the steppes of Galicia. Masoch gave voice to their beliefs in his short story "The Wanderer":

> "Nations and states are big people, and like the little ones, they are eager for plunder and thirsty for blood. It's true—whoever doesn't want to do harm to life—can't live. Nature has forced us all to rely on the death of others in order to live. But as soon as the right to exploit lower organisms is permitted by necessity, by the drive for self-preservation, it's not just restricted to man harnessing animals to the plough or killing them; it's the stronger exploiting the weaker, the more talented the less talented, the stronger white race the coloured races, the more capable, more educated, or, by virtue of a benevolent fate, more developed peoples the less developed" (Sacher-Masoch, 2003: 9).

If Severin's aim is to escape the father's law in order to be reborn a new Man, then the wanderer compounds this with aiming to also escape the mother's law, as embodied in Nature's cruelty. But rather than idealising an even earlier, pre-civilised or pre-agricultural form of society as an alternative, the wanderer is decidedly pessimistic about the prospects of humanity. While Proudhon exalted Satan as a Promethean figure of progress, for the wanderer it is Nature herself who is Satanic:

"I saw the truth," the old man cried, "and saw that happiness lies only in understanding, and saw that it would be better for this race of Cain to die out. I saw that it is better for a man to go to his ruin than to work, and I said: I will no longer spill the blood of my brothers and rob them, and I abandoned my house and my wife and took up the wanderer's staff. Satan rules the world, and so it is a sin to take part in a church or a religious service or the activities of the state. And marriage is also a mortal sin" (Sacher-Masoch, 2003: 11).

In response to the wanderer's disavowal of Cain's legacy, or love, property, the state, war, work, and death, Nature replies that she is beyond good and evil, and that it is childish to think that one could escape her cold and maternal severity by retreating into asceticism. Masoch's preference for agrarian communism could in this sense be understood as a middle position between syndicalist and primitivist strains of anarchism, albeit with a touch of decadent humour that fetishises the image of a gentle female despot under the guise of a cruel mistress, an agrarian matriarch, or Nature herself. The contractual pact with the devil, however, does not lead one to liberty on the basis of honouring its terms and conditions.[15]

DELEUZE, MASOCH, AND PSYCHOANALYSIS

The psychoanalytical understanding of masochism presents certain challenges to Deleuze, who wishes to validate Masoch against many of Freud's claims. According to Freud, the human organism is governed by two agencies of repetition: the life instincts and the death instincts. The normal tendency of these two agencies is to work together under the guidance of the pleasure principle, which renders the death instincts harmless to the organism by redirecting their aggressive force towards external objects, resulting in erotogenic sadism (Freud, 1984: 418). But a portion of the death instincts always escapes this outward transposition by the libido and is instead turned inward and dammed up within the organism, resulting in a primary, erotogenic maso-

---

[15] In a certain sense, Masoch's parodying of the law parallels some of the mechanisms that maintain the powerlessness of the chief in the Amazonian societies studied by Pierre Clastres, however in the guise of an idealised femininity rather than a pacified masculinity. See Pierre Clastres (1987), *Society Against the State*, pp. 27–47.

chism, which Freud took to be an innately human predisposition that made the unconscious sense of guilt possible (Freud, 1984: 418–21). "Defusion" was thought to occur when a flood of traumatic excitations would skewer the balance between outwardly transposed and inwardly dammed up death instincts, displacing and neutralising a quantity of cathectic energy and leading either the masochistic or the sadistic tendency to prevail. Freud called the compounding of the innate predisposition of erotogenic masochism with an introjection of erotogenic sadism "the economic problem of masochism," because he thought that in damming the flood of traumatic excitations, the life instincts were put in the service of the death instincts, resulting in the paradoxical striving for painful experiences, regression to childish or feminine behaviour, and an intensified sense of guilt manifested by an exceedingly severe superego. However, for Deleuze, Freud's attempt to explain secondary forms of masochism in this way presents the problem of rendering it reversible with sadism according to merely fluctuating combinations of life and death instincts, and of conflating the two perversions into a hybrid "sadomasochism." To the contrary, Deleuze argues that their perceived complementarity is only analogical and denies that they could be reversible or even operate within one and the same individual, claiming that a passage from sadism to masochism would have to entail a desexualisation and resexualisation of the libido in every hypothetical instance. The question would then be whether this is an actual, ongoing process, or a structural presupposition that would sever masochism from all communication with sadism (Deleuze, 1991: 107–10).

For Deleuze, there is only a kind of sadism that is the humourous outcome of masochism, and a kind masochism that is the ironic outcome of sadism (Deleuze, 1991: 39–40). Preferring the premise that sadism and masochism each presuppose desexualisation according to their own distinctive structural criteria, he claims that in sadism, desexualisation takes the form of an Idea of pure negation that constitutes thought in the superego, whereas in masochism, it takes the form of a fetishistic disavowal that founds the imagination in the ego (Deleuze, 1991: 127–28). In sadism, the superego expels its own ego and projects it upon victims whose destruction through a cumulative series of partial processes allows for a portion of libidinal energy to be neutralised and displaced (Deleuze, 1991: 126–27). This finally determines an egoideal that incarnates the death instinct as an Idea of pure negation. Thought becomes resexualised when the law is transcended in the direction of the Idea of Evil as the grounding principle for institutions of atheism, calumny, theft, prostitution, incest, sodomy, and murder. It assumes the ironic appearance of masochism in the sense that, despite all of the superego's apparent tyrannising in its ascent towards the Idea of Evil, tyranny cannot be equated with the principle itself, since it victimises all egos indiscriminately. But where sadism proceeds by way of speculative thinking and quantitative accumulation, masochism proceeds by way of mythical-dialectical thinking and qualitative suspense. In masochism, the ego disavows the paternally modelled superego and genital sexuality, allowing for the neutralisation and displacement of a portion of libidinal energy. But by entrusting the phallus to the mother-image, the threat of castration understood in the conventional psychoanalytical sense is avoided. The maternal phallus incarnates the death instinct as fetish out of the neutralised and displaced libido, and gives birth to the ideal ego of the "new Man devoid of sexual love" by suspending the passage of time in a frozen moment (Deleuze, 1991: 128). When the satisfaction (rebirth) of the punishable desire (incest) comes about as the ungrounded consequence of its very punishment (castration), however, the terms of the contract are transcended, and the imagination becomes resexualised. It assumes the humourous appearance of sadism in the sense that, despite the ego's disavowal of pleasure in its emulation of the ideal, the reborn ego assumes a narcissistic ideal of omnipotence and regains a sense of pleasure out of the superego's destruction.[16] Through this displacement of unconscious cathexes, the real father is excluded and the new Man becomes father of himself. In fact, the apparent absence of sexual love seems to only be a deception, since the new Man identifies sexual activity with incest and rebirth, and castration, as the symbolic condition for the success of this identification, simply stands for female control over the male genitalia (Deleuze, 1991: 93–94). With the displaced libidinal energy reinvested in the suspended reality, pleasure does not come about as the consequence of libidinally bound death instincts and erotogenic pain, but of repetition as the unconditioned condition of the pleasure principle, or desire in its pure and unmediated form,

---

[16] In this sense, Deleuze's understanding of humour stands in stark contrast to that of Freud, for whom the humourous attitude is brought about when cathectic energy is withdrawn from the ego and transposed on to the superego. The superego then assumes the role of consoling the ego and protecting it from the suffering that it was not able to cope with on its own. See Freud (1985), "Humour," pp. 427–433.

freed from pleasure as its determining constraint. In monadological terms, the amplitude of the animal monads would be increased through an *undamming of the damned* that, by way of a process of *vice-diction*, would decompose relations of domination and appurtenance within the organic body and suspend its relation of compossibility over an infinitesimal abyss.

To move beyond Freud's overly mechanistic conception of the life and death instincts, let us attempt to translate the economic problem of masochism into the Nietzschean language of forces. Whereas Sade derived a thought of pure negation from the perpetual movement of raging molecules using mechanically grounded quantitative techniques, Masoch's uninterrupted process of desire is rooted in a dimension of interiority that is irreducible to the vulgar materialist outlook. The qualitative relation of imagination that arises out of the dialectical interplay of disavowal and suspense in the masochistic ego is perhaps equivalent to the will to power, or the qualitative relation that corresponds to the difference in quantity between active and reactive forces (Deleuze, 1983: 37–44). While disavowal has the quality of a reactive force that separates the body from what it can do and establishes for it the consciousness of an ideal, suspense takes the quality of an active force that reaches out for power over what is reactive in the ideal (castration as the punishment for incest) and transforms it into something active (the pleasure of rebirth). The ideal ego of disavowal, like the perspectival falsification or will to truth that helps the body to preserve itself (Nietzsche, 2003: 50–51), ultimately comes to serve the will to power, or inner world of physical forces, which surfaces by way of the narcissistic reversal of the ideal in the suspended moment. By contrast, Sade's system, like some parts of Freud's speculative metapsychology, is limited to a mechanistic interpretation of forces that describes the process of desire on the basis of quantity alone. But whereas Freud designated the tendency in life to return to an earlier state of equilibrium as the morally ambiguous Nirvana principle, Sade attempted to cancel differences in quantity by reducing becoming to a terminal process that would find its *telos* in the Idea of Evil. For Sade, the qualitative interpretation of forces is limited to a thought of pure negation, which can only affirm the thought of eternal return mechanically by institutionalising a physically reversible system in which initial and final states are posited as identical (Deleuze, 1983: 46). Masoch's appropriation of the form of the contract, on the other hand, reverses slave morality by bringing about a reinterpretation of its corresponding qualities of force in the imagination, passing from a lower, reactive nature to the sentimental and self-conscious Nature that finally reveals itself to the wanderer (Deleuze, 1991: 76). Likened to a pact with the devil or "culturism" by Deleuze, it is similar to the special form of training that Nietzsche called "Culture" in opposition to the "Method" whose fault is to always presuppose the good will of the thinker and take the recognition of common sense as a given (Deleuze, 1983: 108). Masoch's contractual willing of the punishment before having committed the punishable misdeed affirms the eternal return as an ethical and selective thought, by way of a culturist training that aims to reinterpret the difference between salvation and servitude. The infinite debt from which the sense of guilt derives is absolved through the sacrificing of pleasure, yet pleasure returns as the consequence of the *nonsense* of guilt, once guilt has been freed from debt as its determining constraint. Guilt then becomes the humourous disguise from behind which desire, like Nietzsche's Zarathustra, is able to carry together into One what is fragment and riddle and dreadful accident, and recreate all *it was* into a *thus I willed it* (Nietzsche, 1954: 249–254). Unlike the moral masochism that is actually the ironic outcome of sadism and the Idea of Evil as the grounding principle of the law, Masochian humour, as will to power, paradoxically reveals Nature to be a force that acts beyond good and evil on the basis of its own perspectival falsifications and idealisations. The law of the eternal return, affirmed as the jurisprudence of the damned, suspends an infinite quantity of possible progress and brings about the universal ungrounding of the best possible world, rather than its foundation.

To the extent that there are latent political philosophies at work in the respective thinking of Sade and Masoch, how might discourses of progress and civilisation figure into them? Following Freud, Herbert Marcuse claimed that upholding sexuality as an end in itself posed the threat of allowing perversions such as sadism and masochism to reverse the process of civilisation that had turned the organism into an instrument of work (Marcuse, 1966: 50). But he left little room for the possibility that this reversal could escape reappropriation by the destructive dialectic of civilisation. Against the historically specific reality principle governing the origins and growth of civilisation by means of the repressive domination of instincts, perversions could enact a regression to the sadomasochistic phase of historical development, whose reactivation would release suppressed sexuality both within and beyond the domination of civilised institutions (Marcuse,

1966: 101, 202). But while Marcuse believed that the instinctual substance of perversions was distinct from their forms of cultural repression, he tended to see sadism and masochism as more often being complicit with war, genocide, forced labour, and more generally the reduction of thought to pre-established functions reflecting what was most common in a given historical period (Marcuse, 1966: 203; Marcuse, 1991: 177–78). Deleuze's refusal of the sadomasochistic binary, however, offers a way of understanding how the release of suppressed sexuality beyond the dominating constraints of civilisation might still maintain a revolutionary use that eschews both repression and civilisation itself. The conflict between reason and instinct that Marcuse would deny to be the strongest argument against the idea of a free civilisation (which for him would dispense with what he calls surplus-repression but not the necessity of repression as such) (Marcuse, 1966: 225–26), is perhaps indistinguishable from the conflict which instinct creates within itself according to the partial processes of destruction that determine the ego-ideal of sadism. The regressive sadomasochism referred to by Marcuse could in this sense simply be the historical instantiation of sadism's irony. To his credit, Sade saw anarchic institutions of perpetual motion as the final way of doing away with laws that would hypocritically valourise one type of murder while legitimating another.[17] But despite his hatred of tyranny, the final irony of Sade's vision of permanent revolution seems to have since been revealed through the historical legacies of Trotsky and Mao, who produced more tyrants and crowned anarchists in the Heliogabalic sense than crowned anarchies in the nomadic-noematic sense. It would therefore be futile to deny that instinct is beyond good and evil while still attempting to distinguish, as Marcuse had, necessary repression from surplus-repression (Marcuse, 1966: 226).

---

[17] With the French Revolution in mind, Sade posed the following questions in *Philosophy in the Bedroom*: "What study, what science, has greater need of murder's support than that which tends only to deceive, whose sole end is the expansion of one nation at another's expense? Are wars, the unique fruit of this political barbarism, anything but the means whereby a nation is nourished, whereby it is strengthened, whereby it is buttressed? And what is war if not the science of destruction? A strange blindness in man, who publicly teaches the art of killing, who rewards the most accomplished killer, and who punishes him who for some particular reason does away with his enemy! Is it not high time errors so savage be repaired?" See the Marquis de Sade (1990), *Philosophy in the Bedroom*, p. 332.

Instinct can only be beyond good and evil if repression is preceded by repetition as its transcendental condition, rather than *vice versa*. In contrast to Sade, Masoch's idealisation of the mother is closer to an attempt to recuperate something akin to the superid, or the pre-genital, prehistoric, pre-oedipal "pseudo-morality" that has not yet freed itself from the pleasure principle by virtue of maternal union. Marcuse believed this sensuous rationality to condition a natural self-restraint in Eros that would limit it from seeking absolute gratification (Marcuse, 1966: 228–29).[18] But whereas the superid is formed out of a secret alliance between the superego and the id against the ego and the external world, for Masoch it is the narcissistic ego that imagines the libidinal morality through a disavowal of the superego (the father's likeness) and the id (genital sexuality), and a suspension of the patriarchal reality principle. Insofar as it is understood to be the timeless ideal of pleasure, the frozen moment created by this suspension cannot be restrained by the superid, since as Nirvana it is the bond that binds Eros to the death instinct. Marcuse was led to deny the reality of a non-repressive existence on the basis of this bond, since the ego's subjection to the condition of time forced it to confront death and repress the promises of the superid (*ibid.*, 231). For Deleuze, on the other hand, the death instinct only appears with the desexualisation of Eros, and the formation of the neutral, displaceable energy whose reflux upon the ego makes it narcissistic while emptying time of its mnemic content (Deleuze, 1994: 110–14). Before it can serve as an ideal for pleasure, empty time is first and foremost the unconditioned condition for the genesis of thought. As the monstrous force of repetition, it lies beyond the pleasure principle *a priori*, allowing the innately genital new Man to bypass the repressive mechanisms of the Oedipal triangle and become father of himself, in both an oneiric and a worldly sense. His anti-oedipal humour only fetishises the pre-oedipal superid in order to stage the historical drama of becoming-animal, and affirm the eternal return of its innately active forces. It cannot therefore be the price of progress in civilisation, or have any complicity in maintaining the surplus-repression necessitated by social domination in Marcuse's theory.

When the genitality of thought is juxtaposed with anal eroticism, however, the desire to become father of oneself translates into the desire to accumulate money and have it breed with itself by accumulating interest, as Norman O. Brown had argued in *Life*

---

[18] Marcuse borrows the concept of the superid from psychoanalyst Charles Odier.

Against Death (Brown, 1985: 234–304). Building on psychoanalytical theories of infantile narcissism and anality, Brown argued that an unconscious equivalence between excrement, money, and time lies at the heart of the neurosis of modern capitalist society, in which it is manifested as the possession complex. Civilisation is driven by a repetition compulsion to regain a narcissistic ideal of omnipotence that is indistinguishable from the tensionless state of Nirvana, which only comes to assume the character of death when libidinal aggression fails to be cathected with external objects and is instead repressed. The tension produced by this repressed energy returns in sublimated form as guilt, and becomes the motivating force of the anal character's desire to accumulate money. Paralleling the economic problem of masochism, guilt is collectively expiated through the building up of an economic surplus, whose sublimated aim of escaping death finally turns life into a paradoxical death-in-life. Unlike Marcuse, Brown implicated the ambivalent relation to the mother no less than the reaction to the threatening father in the problem of guilt (Brown, 1985: 289–290). While the Masochian hero's guilt may have nothing to do, as Deleuze claims, with feeling that he has sinned against the father, his experience of it as the father's likeness within himself (Deleuze, 1991: 101) leaves the problem of how the sin will be atoned for in the social context of civilised life.[19] Despite the incorporation of guilt by the quantifying rationality of the money complex having a stronger affinity with the ironic pseudo-masochism of sadism, could the humourous pseudo-sadism of masochism, understood as the Dionysian force of affirmation that Brown believed could undo the social struc-

---

[19] In order to avoid any confusion when extrapolating upon Masochian humour beyond its original context, guilt should be understood in a metaphysical sense, capable of manifesting itself in many different ways that may not appear to have anything to do with experiencing the father's likeness within oneself. The father's likeness could simply be treated as the structural presupposition for any case in which obedience to existing social conventions may leave one feeling complicit with some form of injustice. For instance, neither mocking by submission nor working to rule would seem to have anything to do with experiencing the father's likeness within oneself, yet both are based around exaggerated acts of obedience whose aim is the destruction of the existing social conventions to which they are related. An interesting contemporary example of this might be FEMEN, the Ukrainian radical feminist group that stages topless protests against sex tourism, religion, international marriage agencies, and various other institutions that exploit and oppress women.

ture of guilt and its consequent death-in-life, conceivably save Masoch's fetishism of femininity and animality from being subsumed under commodity fetishism? In this worst of all possible worlds, what contribution is humour capable of making to the practice of a jurisprudence aiming to rescue the animal monads from their damnable fate as living currency that breeds with itself?[20]

MASOCHIAN FETISHISM AND COMMODITY FETISHISM

What, if any, is the relation between Masoch's fetishism and the mysterious fetishism of commodities? In *Capital*, Marx had shown how the social character of labour acquires an objective character that appropriates the social relation and makes it appear to emanate from the products of labour, rather than the act of labour itself (Marx, 1967: 76–87). When the products of labour are produced directly for exchange with other products rather than for their own utility, they cease to be valued according to the labour-time necessary for their production and acquire a uniform and apparently objective social status that is determined by their demand on the market. This mystification produces a false consciousness of the social character of labour that is akin to fetish-worship, as if the inanimate commodities and money itself could be imbued with the magical powers of the abstract, homogeneous human labour to which the products of concrete labour are reduced in their heterogeneity. The workers become alienated from the social products of their labour, while these products take on a life of their own as commodities: the object becomes more human and the human becomes more object. No longer simply

---

[20] The notion of a pestilential living currency that breeds with itself is a powerful image in the folklore of many pre-capitalist societies. In *The Devil and Commodity Fetishism in South America*, Michael T. Taussig (1980) examines the folkloric beliefs of Colombian peasants regarding the expropriation of their lands by surrounding sugar plantations, arguing that the peasants' understanding of wage labour in terms of devil contracts expresses a critical recognition of the dehumanising effects of capitalist production. For instance, the money earned through wage labour can only be spent on luxury commodities, and the wage labourer is destined to die an early and miserable death. Another belief involves the substitution of a hidden peso bill for a child at its baptism, after which the bill is imbued with the child's soul and becomes capable of robbing any cash register that it happens to end up in after its godparent has put it back into circulation, subsequently returning to its godparent with its spoils.

dominating things to produce products with a view to their use-value, the worker comes to be dominated by commodities whose exchange-value equalises the different kinds of labour that were necessary for their production. As a fetish, the commodity consummates the social relations that led to its production in its relationship to itself as an autonomous, monadic entity that internalises and objectifies these relations in an unrecognisable, thing-like form (Taussig, 1980: 35).[21] It reverses the relation of domination between worker and product by alienating the worker from his living labour and appropriating it as its own dehumanised, damnable appurtenance, as if the animal monads belonging to the body of the worker could be subsumed by the commodity as it exerts its mystical, fetishistic power over the thinking monad of the worker. In light of how it conceals the relations of domination and servitude that make capitalism possible, it is not difficult to see how commodity fetishism could be understood to relate to masochism in the conventional psychoanalytical sense. For instance, Marcuse or Brown might have understood the fetish to be an agent for the reappropriation of sadomasochistic impulses by the dialectic of civilisation. But Masoch is quite different from the psychoanalytical understanding of masochism. Rather than serving to disguise the oppressive abstractions of the law or capital, his uses of the contract and the fetish enact a micropolitics of concrete experience. Just as Rousseau's social contract constrains one to submit to the abstract principles of the general will in order to attain freedom, so Marx's commodity fetishism deceives the worker into falsifying his consciousness on behalf of an abstract humanity embodied in the exchange of goods. Masoch's contract, on the contrary, parodies the act of submission in the

---

[21] The Colombian peasants studied by Taussig (1980) seem to understand the commodity as a monadic entity. Rather than conceiving of the various individual terms involved in the capitalist market as atomistic corpuscles bound together by external relations, and thus conforming to the Newtonian paradigm of a self-regulating system, the peasants understand each term to embody the total set of relations in which it is bound up internally, as is apparent in the case of their magical beliefs regarding money. For Taussig, a critical understanding of commodity fetishism is only possible according to a philosophy of internal, as opposed to external relations, however he does not problematise this in terms of monadology. The significance of devil contracts to the problem of commodity fetishism strongly resonates with the connection that we are attempting to develop with the damned monads and Masoch's own contractual pact with the devil, however further elaboration upon this is beyond the scope of the present discussion.

most concrete terms in order to force new ways of thinking and desiring into existence. The suffering that the Masochian hero inflicts upon himself according to the terms of the contract have the aim of breaking the link between desire and pleasure (Deleuze, 1997: 53) and by extension the link between desire and need, in order to affirm desire as creation. Undergoing an infinite suspense that substitutes initiation rituals and becomings-animal for satisfaction, desire deliriously reinvests itself in different world-historical situations in order to relive the forgotten sacrifices that drove the progress of civilisation (Deleuze, 1997: 54). In doing so, it transcends the objectification of human labour that Marx saw as finding its sensuous expression in private property and the reduction of all physical and mental senses to the sense of *having* (Marx, 2007: 105–6), and paradoxically, it does this on the basis of the fetish.

According to Deleuze's understanding of Marx, fetishism is a transcendental illusion borne out of the conditions of common sense, for which it forms the natural object with regard to the recognition of value (Deleuze, 1994: 207–8). So long as the true problem of abstract labour casts its shadow over the cases of the concrete division of labour through which it is actualised, these cases will present a false consciousness of the problem in the guise of a fetishistic common sense. The true problem can only be grasped once it has been separated from the false problem lying in its shadow, along with the determination of the negative as the objective field of the false problem, and this is only possible if the transcendent exercise of the faculty of sociability can uncover its transcendent object in revolution (Deleuze, 1994: 208).[22] For Marx, the senses can only be emancipated from private property and the stupidity that it institutionalises by becoming rehumanised as theoreticians that reconceive of objects and utility in human terms (Marx, 2007: 106–107). However, by formulating the problem of private property in terms of the reduction of all physical and mental senses to the sense of having, Marx perhaps did not anticipate Tarde's Leibnizian insight that relations of having condition the senses from the very beginning, and are by their very nature impermanent. The illusion of private property instead

---

[22] Deleuze's transcendental empiricism is based on Kant's notion of the transcendent exercise of the faculties, according to which the experience of the sublime results from reason forcing the imagination beyond the limits of the sensible by denying it access to the rational Idea. Artaud is credited for duplicating this procedure when he opposes the genitality of thought to common sense. See Kalyniuk (2014), pp. 197–198.

arises from an objectification of concrete relations of having according to legally sanctioned terms of being. Masoch's subversion of the law takes this objectification as its point of departure, enacting its reversal by virtue of the temporary nature of the contract. Borrowing Marx's formulation of how the senses become theoreticians, Deleuze claims that Masoch aimed to represent the painful transmutation from animal to human through initiation rituals premised on the idealisation and objectification of women as works of art (Deleuze, 1991: 69).[23] For Masoch, the theoretical practice of the senses reveals the impossibility of property according to a doctrine of "supersensualism" that enacts the transcendent exercise of sociability by way of the fetish, however without recourse to the negative as its objective field, and in less exclusively human terms than it would for Marx. The role of desire as a creator of values is restored through a suspension of its sensuous object, which is then incarnated in fetishistic guise. But what could animal nature have to do with the objectification of social relations that results in commodity fetishism, and how could Masoch's fetishism of transmuted sensuality relate to the socialisation of the object that forms the theoretical undertaking of the senses for Marx? To the extent that the collective expiation of guilt through the building up of an economic surplus mirrors the economic problem of masochism, the social relation of guilt is objectified by the commodity as fetish, the consumption of which satisfies desire on the basis of its own punishment through the alienating conditions of labour, which are needed to reproduce the economic surplus of guilt. But whereas the fetishism of the commodity allows it to transcend the sensuous conditions of its manufacture, Masoch's supersensual fetishism allows desire to transcend its sensuous end in pleasure, while taking animality and femininity as its dual object. Closer to what Pierre Klossowski calls the economy of the eternal return than to the libidinal economy of masochism understood in the psychoanalytical sense, the becoming-animal of supersensualism enacts a re-willing of all one's experiences and acts, but not as *mine*; the meaning and goal of having and possession are liquidated by the pure intensity *without intention* of the eternal return (Klossowski, 1997: 68–70). Insofar as becoming-animal may lead one to relive the transcendental illusion that objectifies the social and lends an appearance of permanence to relations of having, it does this in

---

[23] This reference is discussed by Kazarian (2010) in "The Revolutionary Unconscious: Deleuze and Masoch," pp. 94–96.

order to force thought to grasp the true problem, rather than remain mystified by the false problem.

What ultimately distinguishes humanity from animality, and
of what use is becoming-animal for overcoming the illusions of
false consciousness and liberating the damned from their mystification? Colson claims that Marx's concept of species-being,
which distinguishes humanity on the basis of its opposition to
nature through labour, does not constitute any specifically human dimension according to libertarian thought, since it is a
characteristic that is shared by all animal species (Colson, 2001:
338).[24] The objectification of social relations would therefore
characterise the anthill or the beehive as much as it would the
industrial factory, however through the medium of instinct rather
than consciousness. But rather than finding its grounding in the
capacity to open itself up to nature and affirm labour as a part of
creation as it would on Colson's libertarian account (Colson,
2001: 338), human subjectivity for Masoch is distinguished from
animal nature on the basis of the culturism of its transmuted sensuality. This transmuted sensuality tames the stupidity that for
Deleuze would be the true species-being of humanity, by means
of becomings-animal that dramatise the history of social domination and the complementary reduction of having to the terms of
being. In contrast to the false consciousness of commodity fetishism that makes the worker into an appurtenance of the object, the
delirious consciousness of the Masochian hero is content to disavow its sensual appurtenances in material reality and wait in suspense for the moment of rebirth. In place of the commodity as

---

[24] While Colson may extend Marx's definition of species-being to all
animals, he rejects what he calls the "anti-speciesism" of animal
liberation movements, claiming that they unavoidably situate themselves
as representatives of the animal cause and should focus on unfolding
their own becomings-animal, instead of campaigning for rights on behalf
of animals. But this would be to overlook the extent to which becoming-
animal implies a kind of representation that transmits it through the
medium of culture, along with the variety of tactics utilised by animal
liberation activists to inspire becomings-animal in the general public.
Masoch's supersensualism could be understood in these terms as much
as the clandestine publication of video footage from slaughterhouses or
laboratories. Colson's account of anti-speciesism is ultimately disap-
pointing, not only for its oversimplification of animal liberation movements and the challenges that they pose to the law, but also for overlooking how becoming-animal reveals the secondary place taken by the
determination of species in relation to individuation (Colson, 2001: 33–
38).

fetish, the marble statue becomes exchangeable with the mistress, the mistress becomes exchangeable with the furs, and the furs become exchangeable with the mythical matriarchs of ancient history in an entirely imaginary and supersensual process of libidinal investment that renders desire incompossible with the structures of domination that it appropriates. Effectively, the power of thinking is reawakened by way of the concrete experience of the animal monads, or the stupidity that Deleuze calls the animality peculiar to thought, before any thinking monad can reclaim these animal monads as its own. But it is above all the type of humour that Deleuze finds in Masoch's novels and the way in which it is used to subvert the law that should be of interest to anarchists, rather than the particular objects of Masoch's fetishism. Unlike the black humour[25] that Deleuze and Guattari see as mystifying the contradictions of coexistence between paranoiac and miraculating machines in *Anti-Oedipus* (Deleuze and Guattari, 1983: 11), or, to return to Marx's conception of commodity fetishism, between the social character of labour and the objective character stamped upon it, Masochian humour has the aim of demystifying such contradictions by intensifying their experience to the breaking point.[26] As Severin proclaims at the end of *Venus in Furs*: "The treatment was cruel but radical, but the main thing is that I am cured" (Sacher-Masoch, 1991: 271).

CONCLUSION: JURISPRUDENCE OF THE DAMNED

Despite that neither of them were anarchists, both Leibniz and

---

[25] Brown would have perhaps conceived of this black humour in terms of the unconscious equivalence between excrement, money, and time.

[26] John Zerzan sees the schizo-politics of Deleuze and Guattari's *Anti-Oedipus* as coming close to the conviction that consumption constitutes a new form of resistance (Zerzan, 2012: 85). However, this would be to only consider one half of what is implied by the French term *consommation*, which means both consumption and consummation. Masoch can be implicated in both of these meanings, rightly and wrongly: wrongly in the mystified consumption of commodities that might parallel Marcuse's or Brown's understanding of the reappropriation of sadomasochistic impulses by the dialectic of civilisation, and rightly in the consummation of a new humanity that parallels Masochian rebirth. While Masoch may have idealised agrarian communism after having called the validity of existing reality into question, his humourous gesture of turning existing forms of domination against themselves, whether in the outside world or within the psyche, could just as easily describe the existential ambivalences that may lead others towards anarcho-primitivism.

Masoch[27] each have their own distinctive contributions to make towards an anarchist philosophy. While Colson finds Leibniz's notion of the world being composed out of self-contained points of view that are free to recompose it at will appealing in this regard, the monadological problem of domination remains unresolved so long as common sense is taken for granted. In our discussion, we have attempted to show how the humour that Deleuze finds in Masoch could take us some steps towards addressing this problem. In the absence of a positive model of common sense or recognition, Masoch, like Artaud and Nietzsche, seeks out the violent encounter that will force him to think and create new values. He turns his overbearing sense of guilt into a means by which to push desire to the point of delirium, and appropriates various world-historical situations in order to expose and transmute some of the relations underlying the psychology of domination and submission. Rather than resolving the perplexing cases of evil by prolonging their singularities over ordinary cases that are then taken to be their sufficient reason, as Leibniz had done in defence of God's calculation of compossibility for the relative Best, Masoch's humour reunites the singular with the universal on the basis of the contract, and by intensifying guilt to the point of parody, paradoxically succeeds in transmuting it. When guilt loses its meaning, the damned come a step closer to ending the fight for servitude that they are unwittingly implicated in. And if jurisprudence is to have any positive meaning for anarchism, it is perhaps in illuminating the ways in which desire can become complicit in its subjugation to interests that are not truly its own, and the extent to which those who are damned to this complicity, rather than being powerless before the abstract machinations of the law, have it within their power to recreate the law through their own concrete actions.

Gregory Kalyniuk is completing his Ph.D. in Cultural Studies at Trent University in Peterborough, Canada. He has a background in Continental Philosophy and Social and Cultural Anthropology, and a longstanding interest in anarchy and anarchism.

---

[27] While Masoch had apparently been influenced by Mikhail Bakunin and Panslavic libertarianism, his sarcastic ambivalence is apparent when he asks: "Will the Slavs achieve unity for Russia by getting rid of the Tsarist regime or should they aim for a strong State under the rule of a Tsarina of genius?" Quoted by Deleuze (1991) in *Coldness and Cruelty*, p. 93.

REFERENCES

Arshinov, Peter (1987). *History of the Makhnovist Movement (1918–1921)* (Lorraine and Fredy Perlman, Trans.). London: Freedom Press.

Artaud, Antonin (1999). *The Theatre and Its Double.* In *Collected Works, Vol. 4* (Victor Corti, Trans.). London: John Calder. 1–110.

Brown, Norman O. (1985). *Life Against Death: The Psychoanalytical Meaning of History.* Middletown: Wesleyan University Press.

Clastres, Pierre (1987). *Society Against the State.* (Robert Hurley in collaboration with Abe Stein, Trans.). New York: Zone Books.

Collectivereason.org (2009). "English translation of *De la Justice dans la Révolution et dans l'Église, Nouvelle édition, Tome troisième*": http://goo.gl/k4vzjR.

Colson, Daniel (2001). *Petit lexique philosophique de l'anarchisme de Proudhon à Deleuze.* Paris: Le Livre de Poche.

Deleuze, Gilles (1983). *Nietzsche and Philosophy* (Hugh Tomlinson, Trans.). New York: Columbia University Press.

Deleuze, Gilles (1991). *Coldness and Cruelty.* In Deleuze and Sacher-Masoch, *Masochism* (Jean McNeil, Trans.). New York: Zone Books. 7–138.

Deleuze, Gilles (1994). *Difference and Repetition* (Paul Patton, Trans.). New York: Columbia University Press.

Deleuze, Gilles (1993). *The Fold: Leibniz and the Baroque* (Tom Conley, Trans.). Minneapolis: University of Minnesota Press.

Deleuze, Gilles (1995). "Control and Becoming." [Conversation with Toni Negri, 1990]. In Deleuze, *Negotiations, 1972–1990* (Martin Joughin, Trans.). New York: Columbia University Press. 169–76.

Deleuze, Gilles (1997). "Re-presentation of Sacher-Masoch." In *Essays Critical and Clinical* (Daniel W. Smith and Michael A. Greco, Trans.). Minneapolis: University of Minnesota Press. 53–55.

Deleuze, Gilles, and Félix Guattari (1983). *Anti-Oedipus: Capitalism and Schizophrenia* (Robert Hurley, Mark Seem, and Helen R. Lane, Trans.). Minneapolis: University of Minnesota Press.

Deleuze, Gilles, and Félix Guattari (1987). *A Thousand Plateaus: Capitalism and Schizophrenia* (Brian Massumi, Trans.). Minneapolis: University of Minnesota Press.

Freud, Sigmund (1984). "The Economic Problem of Masochism." In *The Pelican Freud Library Volume 11: On Metapsychology: The Theory of Psychoanalysis* (James Strachey, Trans., James Strachey and Angela Richards, Eds.). London: Penguin Books. 411–26.

Freud, Sigmund (1985). "Humour." In *The Pelican Freud Library Volume 14: Art and Literature* (James Strachey, Trans., James Strachey and Albert Dickson, Eds.). London: Penguin Books. 426–33.

Gurvitch, Georges (1947). *Sociology of Law.* London: Routledge & Kegan Paul.

Kalyniuk, Gregory (2014). "Crowned Anarchies, Substantial Attributes, and the Transcendental Problem of Stupidity." In *Gilles Deleuze and Metaphysics* (Edward Kazarian, Alain Beaulieu, and Julia Sushytska, Eds.). Lanham: Lexington Books. 195–222.

Kazarian, Edward P. (2010). "The Revolutionary Unconscious: Deleuze and Masoch." *SubStance* 39.2: 91–106.

Klossowski, Pierre (1997). *Nietzsche and the Vicious Circle* (Daniel W. Smith, Trans.). Chicago: The University of Chicago Press.

Kropotkin, Peter (2006). *Mutual Aid: A Factor of Evolution*. Mineola: Dover Publications.

Löwith, Karl (1949). *Meaning in History: The Theological Implications of the Philosophy of History*. Chicago: University of Chicago Press.

Lyotard, Jean-François (1988). *The Differend: Phrases in Dispute* (Georges Van Den Abbeele, Trans.). Minneapolis: University of Minnesota Press.

Marcuse, Herbert (1966). *Eros and Civilization: A Philosophical Inquiry into Freud*. Boston: Beacon Press.

Marcuse, Herbert (1991). *One-Dimensional Man: Studies in the Ideology of Advanced Industrial Society*. Boston: Beacon Press.

Marx, Karl (2007). *Economic and Philosophic Manuscripts of 1844* (Martin Milligan, Trans. and Ed.). Mineola: Dover Publications, Inc.

Marx, Karl (1967). *Capital: A Critique of Political Economy, Volume I: The Process of Capitalist Production* (Samuel Moore and Edward Aveling. Trans. Frederick Engels, Ed.). New York: International Publishers.

Nietzsche, Friedrich (2003). *Writings from the Late Notebooks* (Rüdiger Bittner, Ed. Kate Sturge, Trans.). Cambridge: Cambridge University Press.

Nietzsche, Friedrich (1954). *Thus Spoke Zarathustra*. In *The Portable Nietzsche* (Walter Kaufmann, Trans. and Ed.). New York: Viking Press. 103–439.

Nietzsche, Friedrich (1989). *On The Genealogy of Morals*. In *On The Genealogy of Morals and Ecce Homo* (Walter Kaufmann, Trans. Ed.). New York: Vintage Books. 13–163.

Proudhon, Pierre-Joseph (1994). *What is Property?* (Donald R. Kelley and Bonnie G. Smith, Ed. and Trans.). Cambridge: Cambridge University Press.

Proudhon, Pierre-Joseph (2003). *General Idea of the Revolution in the Nineteenth Century* (John Beverley Robinson, Trans.). Mineola: Dover Publications, Inc.

Proudhon, Pierre-Joseph (2009). *The Philosophy of Progress* (Shawn Wilbur and Jesse Cohn, Trans.). LeftLiberty [pamphlet].

Proudhon, Pierre-Joseph (1868). *De la Justice dans la Révolution et dans l'Église, Nouvelle édition, Tome troisième*. Bruxelles: A. Lacroix, Verboeckhoven et Cie, Éditeurs.

Sacher-Masoch, Leopold von (2003). "The Wanderer." In *Love: The Legacy of Cain* (Michael O'Pecko, Trans.). Riverside: Ariadne Press. 1–15.

Sacher-Masoch, Leopold von (1991). *Venus in Furs*. In Deleuze and Sacher-Masoch, *Masochism* (Jean McNeil, Trans.). New York: Zone Books. 141–293.

Sade, Marquis de (1990). *Philosophy in the Bedroom*. In *Justine, Philosophy in the Bedroom, and Other Writings* (Richard Seaver and Austryn Wainhouse, Trans.). New York: Grove Press. 177–367.

Tarde, Gabriel (2012). *Monadology and Sociology* (Theo Lorenc, Ed. Trans.). Melbourne: re.press.

Taussig, Michael T. (1980). *The Devil and Commodity Fetishism in South America*. Chapel Hill: The University of North Carolina Press.

Whitehead, Alfred North (1978). *Process and Reality: An Essay in Cosmology* (David Ray Griffin and Donald W. Shelburne, Eds.). New York: The Free Press.

Zerzan, John (2012). *Future Primitive Revisited*. Port Townsend: Feral House.

Anarchist Developments in Cultural Studies
ISSN: 1923-5615
2013.2: Ontological Anarché: Beyond Materialism and Idealism

Review Essay

The Problem of an Anarchistic Civil Society

Shannon Brincat

Bamyeh, Mohammed A. (2010). *Anarchy as Order: The History and Future of Civic Humanity.* Lanham: Rowman & Littlefield.

This essay deals with a peculiar problem that has plagued anar-chist thought throughout its history: how to develop and main-tain an anarchistic civil society that at once ensures the freedom of all its members *and* overcomes all threats of domination within it but which is at the same time non-coercive. To be fair, this is not a question that perplexes just anarchism but the entirety of political philosophy since Hegel. In his recent volume, *Anarchy as Order: The History and Future of Civic Humanity*, Mohammed A. Bamyeh (2010) has grappled with this question, and his curious solution—a reliance on what he calls *civic humanity*—while of noble intention, suffers from an indelible weakness in balancing subjective freedom with the freedom of others in community. I do not here propose my own solution to this fundamental problem. Rather, my aim is to outline what is at stake in this debate and thereby highlight the urgent need for critical dialogue on this issue because the future of anarchism is, in no small measure, intimately bound with how we approach this question: whether we succumb to an individual voluntarism that is seemingly con-gruent with the spirit of anarchism but permissive of potentially dominating behaviour in civil society, *or*, whether we arrive (somehow) at a collective form capable of sustaining individual freedom *in* ethical life with others. While I am not satisfied in framing the question in this dualistic way, it is perhaps the most incisive method to focus on the key tensions involved.

Defining anarchy as the absence of domination and as pos-sessing a minimalist program of emancipation concerned more with the removal of restraints than in giving it positive content, Bamyeh's volume offers an account of his normative ideal of what *being human* should mean in anarchist society. Part rhetoric, part individualist libertarian, Bamyeh's aim is nothing less than the lofty goal of the "synthesis of both traditions"—the libertarian and the communitarian wings—of anarchism. The theme Bamyeh wishes to emphasise is the idea of "unimposed order" that he describes as the combination of communal self-determination and individual freedom (Bamyeh, 2010: 23, 22). Yet the problem is that the social dimensions of human life, and not least the socialist, collectivist, or mutualist, economic principles inherent to anarchist philosophy, recede almost to nothingness in his account. Stylistically Bamyeh does not detail the method or structure by which he hopes to achieve his aim. But far more problematic is his attempt to assert the primacy of civil society over the state without engaging the fundamental issue of how to reconcile in ethical community the competitiveness of subjective particularity in civil society that threatens to overwhelm his ideal of an 'unimposed order'. Just as Bamyeh invokes Foucault's notion of the inherent danger in ideas, I fear a denigration of the anarchist project in relying on Bamyeh's voluntarism as the ethical glue of a fluid, anarchistic, solidarity and the subordination of social life to market forces. In this regard, Bamyeh fails to meet the standards of his own radical critique—that is, pushing analysis to its logical conclusion no matter the outcome (Bamyeh, 2010: 9) because the reconciliation of self and society cannot be side-stepped by appealing to civil society alone, and Bamyeh's insistence on analysing civil society without examining economic or dialogical processes in community leads to an incurable analytic weakness. My critique revolves around this fundamental limitation.

Bamyeh focuses his attack on the state rather than economics or class. He asserts that the state, as a singular institution that claims to stand for the whole of society, inevitably leads to authoritarianism and domination and that such dangers would not exist "if the only arena of politics available . . . is that of civil society rather than the state" (Bamyeh, 2010: 7). Bamyeh is correct to observe the failures of Leftist thinking about the state as an historical problem that has led to the tragedies of vanguardism and unlimited power under the dictatorship of the proletariat. However, Bamyeh only defers this problem by relying solely on the social relations in civil society, which is an equally one-sided solution. This is because Bamyeh's voluntarist conception of the individual will remains unaware of, or fails to give any expression to, the dark side of civil society that Nietzsche captured in his depiction of this sphere as an "atomic mass of egoism" in which subjects crash into each other without any ability to derive collective aims (Nietzsche, 1954: VI, 336); or in Hegel's account of the dangers of unfettered subjective particularity in civil society through which agents would attempt to subordinate others to their own interests, thus making the wider forms of ethical life upon which anarchism is ultimately reliant, untenable. For Hegel, the rampant individualism unleashed in civil society was highly destructive of public connectivity and it arises precisely because civil society is premised on a necessary, but altogether insufficient, notion of subjective freedom in which the private concerns and ambitions of the self are paramount (Hegel, 1955: 115).[1] For this very reason, we should remain suspicious of any attempt to bind anarchism to the sphere of civil society because this ignores, downplays, or otherwise neglects, the wider human socialities necessary for the full expression of all the manifold aspects of human freedom. So aside from the relational contradictions of civil society that threatens the subjective freedom of one under the dominance of others, it is the fact that the market provides for only one dimension of freedom that it is unsatisfactory. The assumption that the paltriness of 'exchange and need satisfaction' exhausts the many facets of human freedom is the error common to all market ideologues.

Aside from these conceptual inadequacies, Bamyeh also fails to depict civil society in reality but instead renders it in an abstract and ideal sense—something that he elsewhere states he abhors—because his portrayal of civil society does not take into account how the civil society of today is saturated with bourgeois competitive egoism, nor does he explain how this existing state of civil society could be overcome so that we can safely arrive at an 'unimposed order' through it. As Honneth has recently shown, there have been considerable ruptures in the actualisation of freedom in civil society that have led to partial, if not wholesale, surrenders of its original achievements and potentiality. For example, hardly anything today recalls that the market once contained a promise of freedom, that of subjective freedom taken as mutually beneficial and of complementarity amongst agents. In actuality, however, it is today dominated by an egotism of interests that operates with ruthlessness towards other participants in

---

[1] Hegel sought to reconcile such objective and subjective will in an "untroubled whole" that is, of course, problematic, but which cannot be engaged here.

the market and thereby operates as a sphere of domination rather than freedom (Mayerhofer, 2012). It is for this reason that Bamyeh's critique falls to blatant idealism (he goes so far as to state that "the ideal is the real") (Bamyeh, 2010: 12) by assuming that through overcoming the state we can arrive at a cooperative, and yet at the same time radically particular, space of civil society and that this is somehow adequate for the diverse needs of human freedom.

It is the limited idea of freedom in civil society that ultimately requires sublation. Yet, the emphasis placed on the market and the tendency toward possessive individualism that colours Bamyeh's account threatens a unique form of social atomism and fragmentation.[2] What then of anarchist society that is inherently based in the life of the commons? For it is precisely the idea of the *commons* that has been rendered most vulnerable in modern civil society because of the dominance of capitalist exchange relations that have deformed this sphere in ways that largely preclude the formation of wider solidarities outside of the ability "to contract oneself out".[3] Hegel posited that the individual is the product of their society by virtue of how that individual participates—and is *enabled* to participate—in the public life of the community (Hegel, 2005: par. 150). The problem for the subject today is that we are *all* immersed within the relational webs of late global capitalism and remain 'porous' to the dominant behaviours within it; *we* inevitably become increasingly competitive, individuated, and exploitative. Civil society deforms to, at best, a place subjects can plunder in accordance to their particular wills; at worst, it is a realm of competitors whom one should guard against and exploit if possible. And it is for these reasons that Hegel feared the dissolution of the public sphere through an atomised form of individualism where the "self" is defined in total disregard for its existence as a social animal and subordinates questions of the common good to particular interests.[4] The question is how do we get out of this culturally patterned form of civil society that is dominated by capitalist relations, to the one Bam-

---

[2] On this see Macpherson (1979: 263ff).

[3] The expression is from Marx, "*sich zu verdingen*", and connoted a limited form of freedom, and for Marx, a perversion of its actual ideal (See Fetscher, 1965: 241).

[4] Of course, Hegel's own solution was highly problematic but that is not my concern here. For an example of attempts to subordinate the common good to particular interest, see G.W.F. Hegel, "On the English Reform Bill" (1831) (Hegel, 1999: 234ff).

yeh favourably depicts?

Bamyeh seems to recognise this problem, though he fails to engage with it, when he suggests that as anarchistic political life is clustered in civil society and divorced from state power there is an indeterminancy of outcome. Yet Bamyeh does not push this thought to its logical conclusion: he sees indeterminacy as natural and as the opposite of a singular will of a sovereign authority but, at the same time, wants to argue that this indeterminacy can account for and include common social goods (Bamyeh, 2010: 36.). He ultimately relies on a belief that in their exploration of the market, agents can—somehow—"identify certain goods as transcending in their public value any market price" (i.e., education, health, environment) and that subsequently *all* agents in civil society can come to a general agreement on these goods of public value (Bamyeh, 2010: 210). Yet indeterminacy of outcome cannot be asserted for one aspect of agency (i.e., the multiplicity of wills in civil society) but then be said to be determinative of others regarding why actors in civil society would choose basic common social goods. We are left with a form of pure voluntarism that Bamyeh attempts to overcome by insisting on a non-foundational notion of humanity; one that is not a *theory* of humanity, nor an account of its essential characteristics, but one based in the practice of constant enrichment, spiritual, ethical, and material, of "the drive toward self-knowledge, progress, emancipation, enhanced intellect, and sense of justice" (Bamyeh, 2010: 11–12). I don't think many anarchists would take issue with any of these qualities, but they cannot distract us from the *lack* in existent civil society of the conditions that would give rise to them, or to the nagging problem of agential determinacy given the pursuit of self-interest in the market.

Bamyeh cannot have it both ways because at some point the socialist and libertarian dimensions of anarchist thought, when pushed to their extremes, become antithetical. While Bamyeh is cognisant of some of the problems of the socialist extreme (i.e., vanguardism, dull uniformity, authoritarianism) he remains ignorant of the danger of the libertarian wing that he extols. This is highlighted in his inclusion of Stirner's egoistic anarchism and other pure individualist doctrines as somehow anarchist (that is, as somehow non-coercive). He goes so far as to include Ayn Rand and Robert Nozick—even Friedrich von Hayek's notion of "spontaneous order" (Bamyeh, 2010: 22–23)—as being anarchistic. Yet if we adopt Bamyeh's own definition of anarchy as *non-domination*, we cannot allow the subjective freedoms of individuals to determine those of others whether this occurs in the state *or* civil society. Yet it is precisely such outcomes that are heralded in Rand's notion of the "morality of rational self-interest" that determinatively privileges the interests of the gifted over those of others;[5] or in Nozick's non-negotiability of property rights that is placed over all other ends (see Nozick, 1974: 51ff, 167–174, 274–276). Even Hayek ultimately conceded that "In no [market] system that could be rationally defended would the state just do nothing" because rational choice theory is a zero-sum game for all members in civil society. The winners would dominate the losers in the market, making wider forms of social life unlivable (Hayek, 1994: 45).

Indeed, if Bamyeh is so sure that "[b]onds to large abstractions, such as the nation" are not organic and, following his favourable quotation of Nietzsche's that subjects are unable to feel the pain of distant others (Bamyeh, 2010: 29), then how can we rely on such a nebulous and expansive phenomena as civil society to achieve social harmony? If humans are only loosely bonded in states, nations, even local communities, then what accounts for the social cohesiveness of civil society on which Bamyeh's thesis is ultimately reliant? Bamyeh suggests that a "fluid solidarity" (Bamyeh, 2010: 38) is sufficient that acknowledges normal variety between persons and the changeable nature of solidarity itself in what he calls a negotiable arena of social action. Yet this gives no account of the interests and power that exist in civil society, those forces that can and will attempt to direct and hold civil society to its sway. In the absence of discursive and ethical practices, civil society will be reduced to a battleground of subjective wills. Yet because Bamyeh rejects the very notion of 'unity' as totalitarian fiction, this means the self-conscious choice of each subject could reject the ethical claims of others on the grounds of a 'fluid' concept of solidarity. This legitimates the imposition of subjective will over others which is merely the inversion of the "solid solidarity" he rejects; from one in which subjects follow social norms because they are programmed in their subconscious, to one in which subjects "imagine their society to be standing for

---

[5] The privileging of the ends of the gifted are most visible in John Galt's long speech in *Atlas Shrugged* that justifies the withdrawal of the accomplishments of society's most productive members away from the common good (Rand, 1992: 1000–1070). Similarly, the validation of egoism is played out fully as an instrumental calculation of self-interest most clearly in *The Virtue of Selfishness* (see Rand, 1964: 93–100, 162–169).

their own values and no others" (Bamyeh, 2010: 40). We are left then with little more than different tyrannies, either the tyranny of the state or the tyranny of a marketised civil society, the former in which we are ruled subconsciously, the latter through our imagination. Neither are rational, and hence, neither are freely chosen. By adopting this latter form, Bamyeh allows for the arbitrary whims of civil society to now direct human society.

Despite chapters and sections given to discussions related to human sociality (such as the common good, overcoming alienation, and so on), these are eventually overridden by Bamyeh's appeal to the market that rejects forms of democracy "based on mass society" to those "based on civil society" (Bamyeh, 2010: 206). Towards the end of the volume we see that a strong conception of the market is openly retained in Bamyeh's vision because for him anarchy "lives best with a market economy." In his footnote, he goes so far as to claim that the nineteenth-century anarchist focus on equality obscured its "fundamental concern" which he claims should be properly focused on opposition to any centralised political order (Bamyeh, 2010: 210n24). As his condemnation of centralised political order is based on its coercive form, if he explored further into the operative sphere of civil society rather than its abstraction, he would see that here too lingers the potential for domination. Moreover, this artificial prioritisation of anarchistic aims is not only simplistic but serves to bifurcate our social struggle as if opposition to inequality and opposition to dominating political forces were somehow separate. In late capitalist society—if not always—these forms of domination are inextricably tied to each other. As anarchists, our concern should be exposing and countering all forms of coercion, domination, and exploitation wherever they can emerge—and the state is only one site of such horrors, albeit a primary one.

In the end, while Bamyeh places moral caveats on the reach of this market, claiming that it should not be a central object of human freedom and that it should eschew monopolisation and exclusion (Bamyeh, 2010: 211), without any ethical controls, discursive relations, or democratic processes, it is hard to tell how these dark forces of an unbridled civil society are to be kept in check. The anarcho-capitalist vision of the 'good life' is exposed as nothing less than the forced mediation of all social relations through the so-called free-market, commodity exchange, the contract, and the "callous cash payment." Yet, they pursue this notion of freedom ideologically blind to the coercion that necessarily results if we render all things of value to a pricing mechanism. In its adoration of the myth of 'voluntary exchange,' anarcho-capitalism fails to see that the ability to sell one's labour is not the actualisation of freedom but its antithesis: the commodification of freedom to selling oneself out through wage-slavery. We are alienated from each other as competitors in the market; we alienate ourselves from our creative powers; and we dominate nature, all in the name of market freedom. The cracks in Bamyeh's thesis—common to all anarcho-capitalist ideologies—become most visible when he attempts to account for *who* structures such a market in the absence of such ethical controls, discursive relations, and democratic processes, across communities in civil society. In the absence of such processes, the swirling mass of egoism that is civil society will threaten to *dominate* some of its members under, and by, the interests of others. This is not order. It is not anarchy. It would be chaos, everyone against everyone.

Shannon Brincat is a University of Queensland Postdoctoral Research Fellow. He is editor of the 3-volume series *Communism in the 21st Century* (Praeger, 2013) and was a co-editor of *Critical Theory in International Relations and Security Studies: Interviews and Reflections* (Routledge, 2012). He is also to co-founder and co-editor of the journal *Global Discourse*. His current research focuses on recognition theory and cosmopolitanism in the context of debates surrounding climate change justice. He is also writing on dialectics, a topic for which he is editing a special issue of *Globalizations* called "Dialectics and World Politics" (2014). He has articles published in the *European Journal of International Relations* and *Review of International Studies* and *Constellations*, amongst others.

REFERENCES

Bamyeh, Mohammed A. (2010). *Anarchy as Order: The History and Future of Civic Humanity.* Lanham: Rowman & Littlefield.

Fetscher, Irving (1965). "Marx's Concretisation of the Concept of Freedom", in *Socialist Humanism: An International Symposium* (Fromm, E., Ed.). New York: Doubleday & Company.

Hayek, F.A. (1994). *The Road to Serfdom*, 50th Anniversary Edition. Chicago: University of Chicago Press.

Hegel, G.W.F. (1955). *Die Vernuft in der Geschichte*, (J. Hoffmeister Ed.). Hamburg: Meiner.

Hegel, G.W.F. (1999). "On the English Reform Bill" (1831). In *Hegel: Political Writings* (Dickey, L. and Nisbett, H.B., Eds., Nisbett, H.B., Trans.). Cambridge: Cambridge University Press.

Hegel, G.W.F. (2005). *Philosophy of Right* (Dyde, S.W., Trans.). New York: Dover Publications.

Macpherson, C.B. (1979). *The Political Theory of Possessive Individualism*. Oxford: Oxford University Press.

Mayerhofer, Bernd (2012). "Something of a Masterpiece—Axel Honneth's "Das Recht der Freiheit" (Uhlaner, J. Trans.). *Goethe Institut*: http://www.goethe.de/ges/phi/eth/en8636598.htm.

Nietzsche, Friedrich Wilhelm (1954). *The Portable Nietzsche* (Kaufmann, Walter, Ed. and Trans.). London: Penguin.

Nozick, Robert (1974). *Anarchy, State, and Utopia*. New York: Basic Books.

Rand, Ayn (1992). *Atlas Shrugged*, 1st edn. (reprint). New York: E. P. Dutton.

Rand, Ayn (1964). *The Virtue of Selfishness*. New York: New American Library.

Anarchist Developments in Cultural Studies
ISSN: 1923-5615
2013.2: Ontological Anarché: Beyond Materialism and Idealism

Response to Shannon Brincat

Mohammed A. Bamyeh

For a review essay about a book to be at least partially useful, it needs to give a reader a synopsis of what the book actually says, before it proceeds to evaluating it. Instead, Shannon Brincat seems to approach the review as a chance to expound upon his own vision of the world, rather than as an invitation to engage with the book in question. Thus no one who has not read my book would actually know what it really says by simply reading Brincat's review, which misses most of the book. Instead he focuses on two themes, civil society and the market, but again in a way that seems to have missed or totally misrepresents what my book actually says about these themes. I will first say a few words about the question of the market, which is more straightforward. Next I will address the more complex question of civil society, which involves conceptual, historical and psychological dimensions that are fully distorted in Brincat's essay.

The most glaring error in Brincat's essay is the claim that I am a supporter of market ideology and specifically so-called "anarcho-capitalism," which is a term that appears nowhere in my book. The reason that I do not use "anarcho-capitalism" is because the term is inaccurate and confusing, if not an oxymoron given the attitude of most anarchists, historically and today, toward capitalism. So-called "anarcho-capitalism" is described more accurately (and in a more easily understandable way) by the terms that most people use today, namely "libertarianism"—sometimes also "market fundamentalism" is used. But I do not defend those terms either, in fact, quite the opposite. What I do is call attention to a point that Fernand Braudel had made long ago, a point that got forgotten immediately because apparently we did not have the ideological ear by which to hear it: the free market is *not* capitalism. The fact that the two are confused together, and purposefully so, in current libertarian thought should not mean that we ought to accept that confusion and act according to it. Braudel was in fact surveying a long historical process—three centuries—in which capitalism asserted itself *over* the market. But the two are not the same.

I thought that it would be good if we remembered that distinction, since it does have clear ramifications in terms of how we understand the history of both markets and voluntary associational life. And further, this knowledge may have consequences in terms of how we conceive of the commons or other types of markets today. It is true that my book does not describe the possible structure of such markets, a task which in my opinion deserves a book by itself. In any case, it is not very interesting to criticize a book for not doing what it never claimed to do anyway. More troubling is to jump to conclusions that are clearly the opposite of what I say, namely that I defend "anarcho-capitalism" or market-driven conceptions of human emancipation. My whole book explicitly attempts to describe human emancipation in ways that are *not* beholden to market logic, *nor* to what I consider to be anti-human and limiting logic of materialist analysis.

But first, let me correct one glaring error. I definitely do not, contrary to Brincat's assertion, consider Ayn Rand and Robert Nozick as anarchists. (Strangely, Alex Pritchard made that exact claim in a different review, showing perhaps how dogmatic thought, useful as a handy guide to easy judgment, predisposes one to misread that which otherwise should be obvious.) I thought that my point was clear that Rand and Nozick represented a *departure* from libertarian anarchism and into something else that came to be known simply as "libertarianism." As such, they are definitely *not* part of the anarchist tradition—although "libertarian anarchism" proper is part of that tradition, in my view. It seems that Brincat (like Pritchard) became alarmed with my contention (p. 23) that some libertarian ideas may be considered useful to anarchist thought *if* they involved conceptions of human emancipation that do not see it as merely a function of market fundamentalism. Parts of Hayek's work do indeed fall into that category (as do Stirner and Nietzsche).

The main structure of my argument for anarchy rests on a conception of a civic humanity, which I argue is a long human experience already, and as such verifies the proposition that anarchy appeals in some way because some dimensions of it are *already familiar* to us. Anarchy thus is not simply a theoretical speculation about some hypothetical future, nor does it interest many people if it could be posited purely in abstract, unfelt forms. Thus anarchy has to be latent in some dimension of voluntary human associational life which is already part of our global heritage. "Civil society" is one of the names we give to the organized forms of this experience. The fact that civil society may involve inequalities and "dark forces" is also part of the story. At any given point, civil society can at best reflect who *we* happen to be. Thus, civil society is certainly not utopia, nor is it anarchy, nor, to be sure, is it perfect. But it is what we have right now as a large experience of organizing society outside the state. That makes the concept (and the human experience that comes with it) particularly useful for anarchist possibilities and anarchist learning. And that is true even if participants in civil society do not call themselves "anarchists." *To the extent* that civil society operates as the *alternative* to the state (rather than as a means to lobby the state), civil society could be said to offer a useful apprenticeship on how one may construct or develop further the potentials of voluntary associational life. In principle, when one has placed oneself as the alternative to the state in some area, one is already a step closer to anarchy.

Thus to simply say that civil society is not anarchist does not at all explain why I address it at length in the book as a global (and not simply European or Western) historical experience. I never claimed that civil society was anarchy. But what I did say (which Brincat completely ignores) is that within voluntary associational orders there exist "spaces of anarchy," here and now and always, which are the formations at which we can identify the emergence of self-consciously anarchist practice. This standpoint should bring up an entire range of related discussions to which I have devoted several chapters of the book: on human psychology and "rationality," the different meanings of freedom, the nature of trust, and so on.

None of those chapters show up in this reduction of an argument, although those discussions should have offered some answers to Brincat's complaint that I do not pay much attention to questions of domination, inequality, authority, and so on, in my supposed celebration of civil society. However, for me these are serious issues, so serious, in fact, that they cannot be discussed in a simple way. "Authority," for example, may be a problem, but for whom? Is it an abstract problem that could be described in terms of objective measures, or is it a problem for those who *perceive* it as a problem? The answer is crucial if we are to understand anarchy as a science of life, as I maintain, meaning that our concepts have to resonate with how ordinary notions of authority and freedom from it circulate in our larger reality.

In that sense, "authority" may not be a problem when one who is object to it actually *demands* it, or even consents to it. It is more clearly a problem, however, when it appears to be "out of place," so to speak. We may here be reminded of Mary Douglas's definition of "dirt" as not an absolute condition, but as matter in the wrong place. Thus in histories of civic humanity, we see clearly that voluntary associational life does give rise to what I have called "customary authority," but in a way that is always distinguished from tyrannical or other types of authority that did not arise out of communal demands or that possessed an attribute of non-negotiability (such as the state). The principle here may be generalized as follows: when a student or a child seeks, voluntarily, the authority or guidance of the teacher or parent, should we speak of "domination" here in the same way that we speak of it when we discuss large states and large social or political institutions? This would be infantile leftism, since it is quite obvious that large numbers of people, who may indeed be very interested in the idea of "freedom" in general, also look for guidance and authority *as needed* in practical life. There is therefore always customary authority in civil society, indeed, even in a perfect anarchy. But customary authority is meant for a particular and concrete task, is not meant to be general or permanent, and which we consent to or seek out as free beings.

In this light, I do not think it is very useful to simply say that anarchists should expose "all forms of coercion, domination, and exploitation," with the assumption being that anarchists know *a priori* what these forms look like. Before exposing anything that is social in nature, you do need to talk to other people. In this case, first and foremost you would need to ask the people affected whether they themselves feel "coerced, dominated, exploited" (and if so, how). There is nothing more patronizing than an old leftist position that claims that ordinary people's interpretation of their reality could be dismissed as mere "false consciousness" if it does not adhere to a theoretical script that we already have. How people feel about their reality is always more practically important than how we theoretically presume that they *should* feel about it. That is because if their interpretation differs from what we assumed to be, then that difference should itself serve as an opportunity for us to know something more about reality as well as about how we ought to conceive of it. After all, someone's consciousness of their reality is also *part* of that reality. It is not simply a reflection of it. (And it is in that sense that I endorse the proposition that "the idea [*not* 'ideal', as Brincat misquotes it] is the real").

It is true that civil society habituates power imbalances, and one can safely say that spaces of anarchy are not free from such imbalances either. But if we acknowledge customary authority as consistent with anarchy, and if we have learned anything from Foucault, the question would not be how to abolish "power" in general. The question is rather one of how to assure that power remains rationally and effectively *contestable*. From this standpoint, we can see that even if both state and civil society involve power imbalances, it is easier to contest the power of someone in civil society than that of the state. After all, the state is meant to be permanent, does not cease to impose its laws when you object to them, does not allow an exit from its overall authority over society, and possesses significant coercive muscle to insure all of the above. This could scarcely be compared to civil society, which, while it may house inequalities of various sorts, is not a state and does not have the properties of the state: its institutions do not claim to represent all of society; they may be exited from; they may split; and new organizations may emerge within it.

Obviously, civil society is not perfect, since at most it stands in for what we happen to be at any given moment. And one could always denounce what *we* may be as social beings, as society, as partners to institutions, since our partial knowledge of others and our myopias insure the occurrence of error, even in a perfect anarchy. The point is not to banish error; it is to construct, one step at a time, common social and political theater in which error occurs on a human rather than gargantuan scale; is more easily rectifiable and negotiable; and serves as opportunity from which to learn—and not necessarily in standard ways. Indeterminacy of outcome is indeed a logical consequence of such a theater, since indeterminacy can only be banished by authoritarian rule. But the consequences of this indeterminacy should not trouble us much, since as I say in the book (p. 138), the danger of error is a danger of scale: an individual error always destroys less of the world than a governmental error. So the question is not how to banish error, but how to insure that, (1) that its consequences remain relatively small, and (2) that we are able to rectify it as directly as possible.

The theater in which such learning may happen most effectively is what we call civil society, in which a socially common interest in autonomy cohabits a communicative space with a less common but verdant enough (or so should it appear to be) anarchist science and philosophy of life. Out of these experiences, the civic features of humanity come to the fore. But such a society cannot be perfect, to the extent that we ourselves, the makers of such a society, are not perfect.

Mohammed A. Bamyeh is Professor of Sociology at the University of Pittsburgh and the editor of *International Sociology Reviews.* His books include *Anarchy as Order: The Future and History of Civic Humanity* (Rowman & Littlefield, 2009), *Of Death and Dominion* (Northwestern, 2007), *The Ends of Globalization* (Minnesota, 2000), and *The Origins of Islam: Mind, Economy, Discourse* (Minnesota, 1999). He has also edited *Intellectuals and Civil Society in the Middle East* (Duke, 2012); *Palestine America* (Duke, 2003), and he co-edited *Drugs in Motion*, a special issue of *Cultural Critique* (no. 71, Winter 2009).

Anarchist Developments in Cultural Studies
ISSN: 1923-5615
2013.2: Ontological Anarché: Beyond Materialism and Idealism

Book Review

Christian Anarchism

Anthony T. Fiscella

Christoyannopoulos, Alexandre (2011). *Christian Anarchism: A Political Commentary on the Gospel (Abridged Edition)*. Exeter: Imprint Academic.

This book is a revised version of the doctoral thesis of Alexandre Christoyannopoulos at what may be the world's only university-level anarchist studies program in Loughborough, England. The stated goal is to present, for the first time ever, a general outline of Christian anarchist thought. That goal (and the degree to which it largely succeeds) is what makes this book stand out.

For many people (even—or especially—those who self-identify as Christian or anarchist), the idea of Christian anarchism may sound like a contradiction in terms. A common thread running throughout the book is however the idea that Christian anarchism simply consists of the contention that the teachings and example of Jesus logically imply anarchism. The author writes:

> Ciaron O'Reilly [a writer associated with the Catholic Worker Movement] warns . . . that Christian anarchism "is not an attempt to synthesize two systems of thought" that are hopelessly incompatible, but rather "a realization that the premise of anarchism is inherent in Christianity and the message of the Gospels." For Christian anarchists, Jesus' teaching implies a critique of the state, and an honest and consistent application of Christianity would lead to a stateless society. From this perspective, it is actually the notion of a "Christian state" that, just like "hot ice," is a contradiction in terms, an oxymoron. Christian anarchism is not about forcing together two very different systems of thought—it is about pursuing the radical political implica-

tions of Christianity to the fullest extent. (1)

Now, this contention (as this book makes clear) is hardly new. What is new here is the presentation of a great number of Christian anarchist theorists in a single book. To the best of my knowledge, there is no other book where one can find a similarly comprehensive survey of Christian anarchist theorists. It is a formidable task to say the least. After all, the disparate range of individuals and groups who could fall under the umbrella of "Christian anarchism" stretch far and wide over the last two thousand years. Subsequently, pains are made to clarify the research limitations: coverage is restricted to explicitly Christian *anarchist* thought and therefore does not spend much time on related topics such as liberation theology and Christian pacifism. This stipulation also restricts the focus largely (but not exclusively) to thinkers from the 19th century onward.

The book begins by introducing the reader to key Christian anarchist thinkers (presented presumably in order of importance): Leo Tolstoy, Jacques Ellul, Vernard Eller, Michel C. Elliott, Dave Andrews, Catholic Workers Movement writers (such as Ammon Hennacy), "writers behind other Christian anarchist publications" (such as Stephen Hancock and Kenneth C. Hone), William Lloyd Garrison, Hugh O. Pentecost, Nicolas Berdyaev, William T. Cavanaugh, Jonathan Bartley, George Tarleton, Christian anarcho-capitalists (such as James Redford and Kevin Craig), and "supportive thinkers" (the author's term to describe those who presented arguments that have lent support to Christian anarchist interpretations but who did not themselves "reach the anarchist conclusions"), namely, Peter Chelčický, Adin Ballou, Ched Myers, Walter Wink, John Howard Yoder, and Archie Penner (21, 26).

Then the book continues to delve into exegetical analyses of biblical scripture: Anarchism was inherent in the Jewish culture in which Jesus was raised. The "Israelites had no king, no central government" and major decisions were made either by popular assemblies or temporary "judges" who "possessed only a limited form of authority" (68–69). So, for the early formative part of Jewish history, there was no state, no king, no prisons, no taxes, and no executive or legislative institution. God alone was regarded as the ruling power. The turning point came in I Samuel 8 when the Israelites demanded a king. Samuel is instructed to warn the Israelites of the dire consequences that result from political power and the desire to be like other nations. God essentially regards their choice to submit to human dictatorship to be heretical yet, "even though God does not approve of human government, he accepts or tolerates it" (71). Then with the rise of Jesus the Christ, the rejection of state power became most clearly manifest: Satan attempts to tempt Jesus with political authority and, in doing so, makes clear that the "state derives its power and authority from Satan" (75). Jesus is unambiguous in his devotion to God and shows no desire to accept Satan's offer to rule society from above. The type of society that Jesus advocates organizing is based not on police, courts, and coercion but on forgiveness (Matthew 18: 21–22), refusal to judge (John 8: 1–11), bottom-up organization and voluntary service (Matthew 20: 20–28; Matthew 23: 11; Mark 10: 35–45), direct action (Mark 11: 15–18: Luke 19: 45–48), and non-violence (Luke 22: 35–53). The core of Jesus' anarchist message is traced to the Sermon on the Mount wherein the principles of non-violence are explicitly laid out. The state, based upon the monopoly on violence, is therefore necessarily an heretical institution as it is "founded upon the very thing that Jesus prohibits" (44).

As examples of how Christians throughout the ages have implemented these anarchist teachings, Christoyannopoulos briefly touches on a number of groups: the early Christian communities who refused to worship the state, rejected oaths of allegiance, and refused military service at the same time as they lived in community service of the poor; the Waldenses, Albigenses, and Franciscans of the Middle Ages, and more recent forms of communal living such as the Tolstoyan colonies, the Hopedale Community, and the Catholic Worker Movement.

The book also presents the attempts of Christian anarchists to deal with the "difficult" passages of the Bible such as Matthew 10: 34–39 wherein Jesus says that "I came not to send peace, but a sword" (which Ellul interprets metaphorically and the others ignore) and Romans 13 wherein Paul decrees obedience to the government writing that the state "powers that be are ordained by God" and "rulers are not a terror to good works, but to evil". Romans 13 marks a dividing point in Christian anarchist thought and approach to the state. While Christian anarchists tend to note that this passage clearly contradicts Paul's own practice of disobedience to the state and all agree that Paul's teaching is secondary to that of Jesus, they are still left with the challenge of interpreting the passage. Some (i.e., Hennacy and Tolstoy) dismiss Paul altogether for having begun the historical deviation from Christ's teaching (culminating in the cooptation and corruption of institutional Christianity under the Roman emperor Constan-

tine in the fourth century). Others (i.e., Day) grant Paul legitimacy especially in light of his comment in Galatians 5 that "there is
no law" (150). Redford and Crawford interpret Paul as somewhat
ironic and writing in coded language so that Christians can deal
with the government pragmatically and not stir more trouble
than absolutely necessary. Yet for others such as Yoder, Ellul,
Penner, and Chelčický, there are other implications: the state is a
regrettable institution sent as punishment for human sins but
Christians ought to respect it and turn the other cheek as they
would a fellow human being who assaults them. For them, Paul is
"reminding Christians of the reasons for the state's existence, but
he is also calling them to patiently endure and forgive this pagan
rejection of God" (154). Taking it to an extreme, Eller goes so far
as to argue against civil disobedience altogether.

The common ground is the explicit rejection of violent revolutionary politics while acknowledging that obedience to the state
does not allow for the breaking of God's commandments (should
a conflict arise between the two sets of authority). A similar approach is given to the "Render unto Caesar" passage in that the
state is granted by God a limited domain of control to which the
Christian ought to submit but that the vast majority of life falls
under God's exclusive domain.

It is interesting to note that, of those thinkers who self-
identity as Christian anarchist, none of them seem to interpret
Jesus as legitimizing violent resistance to the state. In fact, according to Christoyannopoulos, the principled commitment to
non-violence is at the center of what Christian anarchism is all
about and also what most distinguishes it from liberation theology where, according to the author, there tends to be an allowance
for the state and the use of violence to pursue the cause of justice,
gain control of the state, and steer human history. For Christian
anarchists, on the other hand, such a strategy would betray the
very message and example of Jesus. The real revolution of sacri-
fice for our fellow humans was demonstrated when he died on
the cross and therefore "what for Christian anarchists remains
clearly contradictory to Jesus' commandments is *violent* resistance" (164). Only through a commitment to non-violence can
the cycle of violence be broken.

The real challenge then for Christian anarchists is to build "a
new society within the shell of the old" as the Catholic Workers
say in borrowing from the Industrial Workers of the World
(IWW). In addition to the principles of forgiveness, non-violence,
and so on, it also entails that "wealth should indeed always be

shared freely within and by the Christian community: every-thing—food, clothes, shelter, property—should be shared" for, as Maurin is quoted, "All the land belongs to God" (178).

In a stylistic sense, this book is a normative study in open advocacy of the idea of Christian anarchism and therefore reads a bit like a combination between an academic study and a lengthy sermon with exegetical commentary on biblical scripture. At the same time, the text is generally accessible and, for the most part, free from overly academic language.

Yet the sermon here is not based on the author's own interpretations of scripture but on his presentation of various Christian anarchists whose interpretations are woven together in an attempt to provide an outline for single Christian anarchist theory. This intent is made clear for, as the author notes, the book presents "fairly different lines of argument as one, as part of one general and generic thesis" (240). This means that confusion may arise as to what is the author's personal stance and what is the actual consensus amongst Christian anarchist thinkers. For example, due to the author's own commitment to the non-violent wing of Christian anarchism, it is difficult to determine to what degree this is representative. After all, the Christian anarchist Taborites and some early Anabaptists clearly advocated violent resistance to the ruling powers. This presents a question for all revolutionaries: Is it possible to advocate violence and coercion to overthrow but not to rule? Hence, this question and the case of non-violence present a challenge for non-Christians as well in terms of what sort of post-state society is being advocated and which methods are realistic for bringing it about.

As it is, such questions are dealt with in the book, but it is not always clear exactly what each thinker believes and even less clear what they actually practice. An alternative structure could have been to present each thinker individually and note the contrasts and similarities between their theories. Instead, the book organizes the text along thematic lines. As there is no attempt to use internal differences to organize the variations of Christian anarchism into sub-categories according to certain criteria (i.e., praxis, stance on violence, denominational origins, etc.), both the challenges and distinctions between these variations become obscured and less apparent to the reader.

Hence, what this book does not necessarily do is provide an overview of Christian anarchism *as such*. While the focus here is admittedly designed to cover no more than theorists (as opposed to activists) and anti-statists (as opposed to pre-state theorists), this has also entailed that the resulting study presents all the main theorists as white males and some, such as the most cited theorist in the book, Leo Tolstoy, furthermore came from the upper class. Only two women are presented, Dorothy Day and Nekeisha Alexis-Baker, as part of broader categories (the Catholic Worker Movement and "Writers Behind Christian Anarchist Publications" respectively). Alexis-Baker seems to be the only person of color presented. Jesus himself, as a non-writer, pre-state person of color who seemed to have done more bumming around than theorizing, would seem out of place here if it weren't for the fact that the entire book is based on what are believed to be his teachings.

In my ideal vision of a book on Christian anarchism, it would include older generations of non-white activism such as the revolutionary perspective of Emiliano Zapata as well as the nonviolent resistance expressed by Sojourner Truth. It would question the relationship between theory and praxis (as was done so well recently in an article on the homepage of the Jesus Radicals which asks how one might approach John Howard Yoder's theory of pacifism in light of his informal position of power and the accusations that he repeatedly crossed sexual boundaries with women[1]). It would include the newer generation of thinkers and activists from Shane Claiborne (author of *Jesus for President*) to the inspirational Philadelphia-based crust-folk band The Psalters.[2] It would also include a discussion on the role of education via Ivan Illich (who called Jesus an "anarchist savior" in 1988[3]). An ideal book on Christian anarchism would address the particular relationship of people and privileges in the wealthier parts of the world to those who endure less power, security, and privilege elsewhere in the world due in part to U.S. and European military domination (thinking here in general of the Plowshare Movement and specifically one of its founders, Phil Berrigan, who spent about 16 of the last 30 years of his life in jail for civil disobedience against the state institutions of war). It would ponder the anarchistic implications of Meister Eckhart's (c. 1260–c. 1327) radical mysticism and St. Basil the Blessed's (c. 1468–c. 1552) Robin Hood

---

[1] Andy Alexis-Baker, "John Howard Yoder and Sex: Wrestling with the Contradictions," *Jesus Radicals*, May 24, 2012: http://www.jesusradicals.com/john-howard-yoder-and-sex-wrestling-with-the-contradictions/.
[2] The manifesto of the Psalters can be accessed here: http://psalters.org.
[3] Ivan Illich, "The Educational Enterprise in the Light of the Gospel," *David Tinapple*, November 15, 1988: http://www.davidtinapple.com/illich/1988_Educational.html.

tactics of stealing goods and distributing to the needy. It would also include an exploration of the difficulties and challenges of espousing Christian anarchism on one hand (such as what the minister Greg Boyd does[4]) while on the other hand succumbing to traditional prejudices toward homosexuals (such as the mega-church that Boyd founded which holds the belief that "God's ideal for human sexuality is that it be expressed only within the bounds of a monogamous, heterosexual marriage covenant."[5] It would examine the teachings of Gerrard Winstanley (1609–c. 1676) and review Raoul Vaneigem's treatment of Christian heretics in *The Movement of the Free Spirit* (1986). It would address issues of vegetarianism (as espoused by Tolstoy and Hennacy) along with the environmental issues (as approached by Jacques Ellul and the Jesus Radicals). It would investigate the structural practices of groups like the anti-state Doukhobors and the horizontally organized Quakers. It would discuss the historical connections between Christians such as Dorothy Day, Ammon Hennacy, and Thomas J. Hagerty (the priest who co-founded the IWW and drafted its original preamble[6]) and secular syndicalism. It would explore the challenges and lessons gained from decades of living, organizing, and struggling within the confines of Catholic Worker collectives. And, ultimately, in those areas that it covered and did not cover, an ideal book on Christian anarchism would, for me, acknowledge its own social location and how that vision may be skewed coming from that perspective.

Yet despite the fact that this book does not do these things (which, of course, are unrealistic expectations for any book), it ought not to detract from its notable accomplishment of coherently presenting a systematic challenge to dominant (mis)readings of scripture. As such, it can be regarded as both a development of research in Christian anarchism as well as an essential introduction to the topic. Along the way, the path is scattered with little gems such as Dorothy Day's comment that "we love God as much as we love the person we love the least" and the suggestion that prison can be a form of "new monastery" where Christians can "abide with honor" (177, 163). The vision that

[4] See, for example, Greg Boyd, "A Call to Christian Anarchy," Random Reflections—Greg Boyd, January 11, 2008: http://gregboyd.blogspot.com/2008/01/call-to-christian-anarchy.html.
[5] See Woodland Hills Church stances here: http://whchurch.org/about/beliefs/controversial-issues.
[6] See IWW Preamble here: http://www.iww.org/en/culture/official/preamble.shtml.

seems to arise here is of an ecumenical theology of various types of Christians who all agree that the institutionalized Church departed from Christ's teachings long ago and the way to bring it back is to follow Christ's example by challenging the authorities, sharing amongst one another, and committing oneself to non-violent resistance.

In this way, *Christian Anarchism* succeeds as a general outline of Christian anarchist thought and simultaneously opens up a discussion for both activists and academics about the contents, implications, challenges, and boundaries of this school of thought (and praxis). Regarding the first aspect, its bibliography alone of more than 450 entries provides plenty of resources for future researchers (more than a quarter of the 76 references in the Wikipedia entry on Christian anarchism make reference to this book). Regarding the latter aspect, the limitations of this work may prove just as fruitful as its contents in that they can provoke debate and dialogue as to what really lies at the core of Christian anarchism and indeed, Christianity itself.

Anthony T. Fiscella is working on his doctorate at Lund University in the history of religion where he also received his Master's degree. He has written about Islam and anarchism, the MOVE Organization, taqwacore, and the anarcho-primitivist religiosity of Lynyrd Skynyrd.

Anarchist Developments in Cultural Studies
ISSN: 1923-5615
2013.2: Ontological Anarché: Beyond Materialism and Idealism

An Interview with Levi Bryant

Christos Stergiou

CS: How would you describe the differences between your ontology and other object-oriented ontologies?

LB: As we use the term, object-oriented ontology (OOO) refers to any ontological position that affirms the mind-independent existence of substances, entities, or objects. In this regard, ontologies as diverse as Aristotle's, Gottfried Wilhelm von Leibniz's, Alfred North Whitehead's, Jane Bennett's, Bruno Latour's, etc., are object-oriented ontologies. Among these ontologies, of course, you have differences and disagreements. Whitehead, for example, holds that actual occasions (his name for substance) are constituted by their relations to other actual occasions and eternal objects. Additionally, he argues that actual occasions are processes. Graham Harman's object-oriented philosophy (OOP), by contrast, argues that objects are withdrawn from their relations and possess abiding essences. There is thus a debate here in object-oriented ontology as to what a substance is.

In the past I referred to my ontology as "onticology," while these days I refer to it as machine-oriented ontology (MOO). I argue that every entity or substance is a machine. Machines are defined by their operations or powers (capacities). Following Ian Bogost, I define an operation as an activity that takes one or more inputs and performs a transformation on it, producing an output. For example, in photosynthesis a tree takes sunlight, water, and carbon dioxide, performs operations on these materials, and produces outputs in the form of cells, energy, oxygen, etc. Similarly, a corporation takes flows of matter and, through operations of labor and signs, produces commodities as outputs. When we approach beings in a machine-oriented framework we investigate entities in terms of the operations of which they are capable, their powers or capacities, rather than in terms of the qualities or properties they possess.

With Harman's OOP, I argue that machines are independent of their relations. Machines can always be severed from their inputs (relations) produced by other machines, and can enter into new relations with other inputs. This, of course, can lead to the destruction of a machine (as in the case of a frog being severed from the input of oxygen). However, with Whitehead I argue that all machines are processes. Not only are machines processes in the sense that they transform inputs producing outputs, but they are processes also in the sense that they must perpetually engage in operations to continue existing across time. My body, for example, must engage in all sorts of metabolic processes to replenish the cells that compose it and that die from moment to moment to continue existing. Likewise, as Marx taught us, capitalism only exists as a process. As Marx showed, value is not a *property* of money and commodities, but is an effect of operations of production and exchange. If those operations or processes cease, value ceases to exist. This is why the Bush administration encouraged everyone to go shopping following 9/11. They understood that if consumption or exchange ceased following the terrorist attacks, capitalism would also cease to exist. Capitalism can only exist as a machine if it engages in these operations of production, distribution, and consumption.

Insofar as machines are processes, we can also call them events. They are events in the sense that they are happenings or occurrences that have a duration or that continue for a certain period of time. A capybara's body will only exist for as long as it is able to continue its operations. Likewise, the feudalist-machine was only able to exist so long as it continued its operations. The being of a machine is not a static substance, brute unchanging matter like Lucretius's atoms, but rather only exists in its activities or processes. Where those processes or operations cease, the machine ceases and falls apart.

CS: Bruno Latour claims that there is no information, only transformation. How would you comment on this?

LB: With Latour and the autopoietic systems theorists—especially the autopoietic system theory of Niklas Luhmann—I reject the thesis that information is something that is "out there" in the world waiting to be found. Information is always information for a machine or system ("machine," "system," "object," "substance," and "process" are all synonyms for me). For example, the sound-waves that constitute a linguistic message do not have information as a *property* of their being. Sound-waves, of course, are real material entities, it's just that the information is nowhere to be found in the sound-wave. Proof of this is found in the fact that no matter how much I talk to a rock, the rock remains unaffected by my speech. It is only when a perturbation like a sound-wave interacts with a particular machine that it takes on informational value. It is thus the machine that constitutes the perturbation (in this case, sound-waves) as information, not the perturbation itself.

In passing through a machine as an input, perturbations undergo transformations determined by the internal structure of the machine carrying out the operations on the perturbation. Let's take the example of communication with an insurance-company. In the United States, insurance-companies are private, for-profit, businesses, rather than government services. This has important consequences for healthcare. When a U.S. citizen fills out a form requesting medical care, the intention animating their utterance is one pertaining to health. When an insurance-machine, by contrast, receives this message, it is transformed and takes on very different informational value, remote from issues of life and death, health and sickness. The form is evaluated by the insurance-machine as a business proposition or investment. The insurance-machine asks itself whether providing care in this case will generate profit or loss, whether it is a good investment, whether it will enhance the value of its stock, etc. As a consequence, it makes its decisions not based on the health or sickness of the person submitting the request, but in terms of economic profit. The message here has become something entirely different.

Information is always a transformation of inputs. Flowers translate sunlight into something else. Crystals transform minerals into something else. People translate utterances from others into something else. But this isn't all. Machines are only selectively open to inputs. They don't have access to all inputs in the world. Bees, for example, can see ultra-violate electro-magnetic waves or light, whereas humans cannot. For this reason, bees are able to see patterns in flowers and give them informational value, whereas we are not; without the assistance of technologies, anyway. The case is the same with insurance-machines. Insurance-machines structure the world about them in terms of a set of categories that can appear on an insurance form. Suppose you're suffering from an unknown disease. You are, in reality, sick. But since this disease is unknown, since it is not a category that appears on these forms, you are invisible to the insurance-machine in the same way that the ultra-violet patterns of flowers are invisible to us.

These features of information have important implications for political engagement. To engage a machine effectively at the political level, we need to know the "language" that the machine is capable of "speaking" and "hearing." This is not for the sake of persuading the machine. Rather, if we are to have real effects on machines, we need to know what sort of inputs they are open to. This is why, for example, strikes have historically been successful in combating corporate machines, whereas protests that speak the language of justice and rights have little effect on corporate machines. A strike understands that a corporate machine is organized around profit and loss. In shutting down productive operations of, say, a factory, it halts the capacity for the factory to produce profit and thereby forces the factory to make concessions. By contrast, talk of justice and rights is a language that a factory can't even hear and that it merely counts as noise.

CS: The object's virtual potentiality exceeds its local manifestation. Therefore, an object is capable of more than what it manifests. Do the powers of an object change over time? Does this affect its manifestation?

LB: The virtual proper being of a machine refers to its powers or those things of which it is capable; its potentials. These powers are "virtual" for two reasons. First, they are virtual because they can exist in a machine without being exercised. A match, for example, has the power to burn, even when it isn't lit. Second, they are virtual in the sense that they can always be exercised in more ways than they happen to be exercised in any particular circumstance. Right now the skin on my arm is prickled because the room I'm writing in is cold. Under different circumstances it would be swollen, such as when it's very hot. The local manifestations, by contrast, refer to the outputs of an operation under particular circumstances. The prickling of my skin is a local manifestation. The red and yellow leaves of a tree in the fall are a local manifestation.

The powers or virtual proper being of an entity can indeed change as a result of operations that take place within an entity, as well as encounters with other entities. Take the example of a change in diet. Changes in diet can affect us in a variety of ways, ranging from how our skin and hair cells are produced, to how efficiently we metabolize food, to the nature of our moods and cognition. Similarly, if a tree contracts a disease, its ability to produce leaves and bark will change. Learning is yet another example of a change in powers. When a person undergoes psychoanalytic training, for example, they hear and witness differently. A bundled action no longer registers as being merely an unfortunate incident, but rather as a manifestation and satisfaction of a repressed desire. Likewise, if a rubber band is stretched repeatedly it gradually loses its elasticity.

Consequently, the powers or virtual proper being of an entity are variable over the life or existence of that entity. Entities can gain and lose powers, and the ability to exercise a power can wax and wane. For example, our power to engage in cognition wanes when we are fatigued or tired. With every gain or loss of powers, and every waxing or waning of powers, there is a change in the local manifestations of which a being is capable. If I learn to play piano, for example, I have gained a new power that can locally manifest itself in the form of the songs that I can play. If I am freezing and therefore shivering, this power of playing piano wanes and I am not able to locally manifest songs on the piano as effectively as when I play under optimal conditions.

CS: Can objects exhibit infinite manifestations? Is every manifestation unique?

LB: I leave open the question of whether every object is capable of infinitely diverse local manifestations, while nonetheless holding that all machines are capable of a wide variety of local manifestations. The first important point is that machines cannot locally manifest themselves in all possible ways. Stones cannot locally manifest themselves in the way that wood is. Water cannot locally manifest itself in the way that hydrogen can. With that said, stones, wood, H_2O, and hydrogen can locally manifest themselves in a variety of ways. Take the example of an emerald. That emerald will locally manifest color in a variety of ways depending on the sort of light it encounters. It will now be brilliant green, now the color of dark moss, now black, now dancing with a variety of different shades of green. All of this is a function of the way in which the emerald enters into couplings or relations with other machines—here photons of light or electro-magnetic waves—that function as inputs for its operations producing outputs in the form of local manifestations.

I think that some local manifestations are "generic," while others are unique. An operation is generic when it can be repeated in the same way under similar circumstances at different times. The emerald will produce a particular shade of green on multiple occasions so long as it is exposed to the same wavelength of light. Here the local manifestations are repeatable and the inputs do not appear to change the powers of the emerald. A local manifestation is unique when it occurs only under a singular set of circumstances, is irreversible, and cannot be repeated. The way a tree grows, is of the order of uniqueness. The nutrients and light that it encounters, the other plants growing in the region, as well as the weather conditions in which it grows produce an absolutely unique set of local manifestations at the level of its shape, the configuration of its bark, the robustness of its leaves and fruit, etc., that cannot be repeated. Were a tree with identical genetic stock grown in the same location, that tree would nonetheless have different characteristics or local manifestations as the circumstances of its development would be different.

CS: If local manifestations aren't identical how we can speak for common properties?

LB: The powers of a machine can be largely identical, while the local manifestations can be different. For example, two emeralds can have the same powers or virtual proper being, while they locally manifest themselves in different ways as a consequence of the different lighting conditions in which they exist. It always depends on what kind of machine we're talking about. An incorporeal machine like the Pythagorean Theorem will always be identical and will produce identical local manifestations given identical inputs. Living entities, by contrast, will only have similarity without identity because even where their genomes are the same, the environment modifies how these machines develop or unfold.

CS: How would you react to the following statement: We fight for a society where there is no identity, but what we are is what we do.

LB: This is a difficult question. In a sense, any social-machine is an identity forming machine. A culture, for example, is a machine that functions to form human minds and bodies with shared characteristics in the form of beliefs, patterns of activity, commitments, etc. Similarly, an educational-machine aims to structure human dispositions of thought along the lines of a shared episteme. I think the absolute absence of similarity would lead to a pretty intolerable life. Imagine, for example, what it would be like to drive on a busy highway without any shared dispositions of movement, where turn signals could just as easily signify that one was turning or not turning and where people could drive in lanes however they like. We need collective habits. The ability to anticipate certain regularities in the behavior of other people allows us to navigate the world about us and also frees up our cognitive powers for other things. Habits are as much liberating as constraining.

The important thing, I think, is to recognize that no machine is ever able to completely integrate another machine. When a social-machine strives to form human bodies and minds, there's nonetheless always a remainder of these bodies and minds that escapes integration. This is the excess of *objet a* that Lacan talked about with respect to the relationship between our bodies and the signifier. Something always slips away. This is why totalitarianisms and party politics always generate such sad passions. These systems dream of complete subordination to the party or the totalitarian regime without remainder. Yet the remainder always persists and reappears. The dream of total control always fails. As a consequence, these machines become paranoid. Because they refuse to recognize that total control is impossible, they instead conclude that they're beset by enemies within and without. They then set about demanding purity pledges, engaging in purges, persecuting what they perceive as double agents, and seeking to eradicate enemies from the outside that they see as a threat to their machine. What is needed is political-machines that are plastic enough not to fall into this sort of paranoia and the persecution it generates.

www.ingramcontent.com/pod-product-compliance
Lightning Source LLC
Chambersburg PA
CBHW050646270326
41927CB00012B/2890